AF556353

ENV BOOKS SERIES

AGRICULTURE DEVELOPMENT AND SUSTAINABLE ENVIRONMENT

Editors

Jaswant Ray

Department of Toxicology
Institute for Industrial Research & Toxicology
Ghaziabad, (U.P.) (India)

&

Dr. Pawan Kumar 'Bharti'

Vice President (Executive)
Society for Environment, Health, Awareness of
Nutrition & Toxicology (SEHAT)
1775, Sohan Ganj, Near Clock Tower, Delhi-7 (India)
E-mail: *gurupawanbharti@rediffmail.com*

DISCOVERY PUBLISHING HOUSE PVT. LTD.
NEW DELHI-110 002

Published by:
Tilak Wasan

DISCOVERY PUBLISHING HOUSE PVT. LTD.
4383/4B, Ansari Road, Darya Ganj
New Delhi-110 002 (India)
Phone : +91-11-23279245, 43596064-65
Fax : +91-11-23253475
E-mail : discoverypublishinghouse@gmail.com
sales@discoverypublishinggroup.com

web : www.discoverypublishinggroup.com

***First Edition:* 2015**

ISBN: 978-93-5056-759-3

Agriculture Development and Sustainable Environment

Printed at:
Infinity Imaging Systems
Delhi

ENV Books Series, India

Calls lengthy and error free chapters for further volumes of books on various environmental issues. (Send your manuscripts to envbooks@gmail.com)

Founding Editor (Editor-in-Chief)

Dr. Pawan Kumar 'Bharti'
Society for Environment, Health, Awareness of Nutrition & Toxicology (SEHAT-India)
1775, Sohanganj, Near Clock Tower, Delhi-7, India
E-mail:*gurupawanbharti@rediffmail.com*

Other Titles by Editor-in-Chief:

1. **Advances in Biotechnology and Ecological Sciences (2013)**
   Bharti, P.K., Chauhan, A. and Ray, J. (eds.)
   (ISBN: 978-93-5056-358-8).
2. **Advances in Agriculture and Ecology (2013)**
   Bharti, P.K.; Chauhan, A. and Ezeaku Peter Ikemefuna (eds.)
   (ISBN: 978-93-5056-362-5).
3. **Agriculture and Environmental Biotechnology (2014)**
   Bharti, P.K. and Chauhan, A. (eds.)
   (ISBN: 978-93-5056-479-0).
4. **Agriculture Ecology and Environment (2014)**
   Bharti, P.K. and Olubukola O. Babalola (eds.)
   (ISBN: 978-93-5056-480-6).
5. **Agro-forestry and Climate Change (2014)**
   Bharti, Pawan K. and Singh, Narayan (eds.)
   (ISBN: 978-93-5056-514-8).
6. **Aquaculture and Fisheries Environment (2014)**
   Gupta, S.K. and Pawan K. Bharti (eds.)
   (ISBN: 978-93-5056-408-0).
7. **Aquatic Biodiversity and Pollution (2013)**
   Bharti, P.K.; Chauhan, A. and Kaoud, H.A.H. (eds.)
   (ISBN: 978-93-5056-359-5).

8. **Aquatic Ecology and Biotechnology (2014)**
   Bharti, P.K. and Zaki, M.S.A. (eds.)
   (ISBN: 978-93-5056-451-6).
9. **Aquatic Environment and Toxicology (2013)**
   Bharti, Pawan K. (ed.)
   (ISBN: 978-93-5056-236-9).
10. **Biodiversity, Biotechnology and Environmental Conservation (2015)**
    Bharti, P.K. and Bhandari, G. (eds.)
    (ISBN: 978-93-5056-750-0).
11. **Biodiversity of Aquatic Ecosystem: *Significance, Threat and Conservation* (2013)**
    Bharti, P.K. and Kaoud, H.A.H. (eds.)
    (ISBN: 978-93-5056-297-0).
12. **Biotechnology, Agro-ecology and Environment (2015)**
    Chauhan, Avnish and Bharti, P.K. (eds.)
    (ISBN: 978-93-5056-757-9).
13. **Clean Technologies and Environmental Protection (2015)**
    Chauhan, A.; Sharma, S. and Bharti, P.K. (eds.)
    (ISBN: 978-93-5056-731-9).
14. **Climate Change and Agriculture (2012)**
    Bharti, P.K. and Chauhan, Avnish (eds.)
    (ISBN: 978-93-5056-148-5).
15. **Climate Change and Biodiversity (2013)**
    Bharti, P.K. and Chauhan, Avnish (eds.)
    (ISBN: 978-93-5056-360-1).
16. **Conservation and Cultivation of Medicinal Plants (2015)**
    Bharti, P.K. and Singh Narayan (eds.)
    (ISBN: 978-93-5056-740-1).
17. **Eco-toxicology and Eco-technology (2013)**
    Bharti, P.K. and Zaki, M. (eds.)
    (ISBN: 978-93-5056-313-7).
18. **Environmental Biotechnology and Application (2013)**
    Bharti, P.K. and Chauhan, Avnish (eds.)
    (ISBN: 978-93-5056-262-8).
19. **Environmental Conservation and Biotechnology (2014)**
    Chauhan, A. and P.K. Bharti (eds.)
    (ISBN: 978-93-5056-512-4).
20. **Environmental Health and Problems (2013)**
    Bharti, P.K. and Gajananda, Kh. (eds.)
    (ISBN: 978-93-5056-263-5).

21. **Environmental Pollution and Biodiversity (2012)**
Bharti, P.K.; Chauhan, Avnish and Kumar, P. (eds.)
(ISBN: 978-93-5056-149-2).

22. **Fisheries and Toxicology (2014)**
Zaki, M.S.A.; Bharti, P.K. and Chauhan, A. (eds.)
(ISBN: 978-93-5056-452-3).

23. **Fish Habitat and Aquaculture (2015)**
Bharti, P.K.; Gupta Kr. Sanjay (eds.)
(ISBN: 978-93-5056-744-9).

24. **Freshwater Ecosystem and Xenobiotics (2013)**
Bharti, P.K.; Zaki, M. and Chauhan, A. (eds.)
(ISBN: 978-93-5056-299-4).

25. **Limnology and Aquatic Science (2015)**
Sharma, S. and Bharti, P.K. (eds.)
(ISBN: 978-93-5056-735-7).

26. **Medicinal Plants: *Distribution, Utilization and Significance* (2015)**
Sharma, P.; Bharti, P.K. and Narayan Singh (eds.)
(ISBN: 978-93-5056-734-0).

27. **Microbial Applications and Environment (2014)**
Bharti, Pawan K. (ed.)
(ISBN: 978-93-5056-515-5).

28. **Microbial Ecology and Habitat (2014)**
Bharti, Pawan K. (ed.)
(ISBN: 978-93-5056-514-8).

29. **Natural Ecosystem and Climate Change (2015)**
Bharti, P.K., and Kh. Gajananda (ed.)
(ISBN: 978-93-5056-745-6).

30. **Prakriti me Aushadhi (*in Hindi*) (2012)**
Singh, J.R.; Bharti, P.K. and Bharti, B.
(ISBN: 978-93-5056-200-0).

31. **Seed Technology, Plant Growth and Cropping System (2015)**
Tyagi, P.K. and Bharti, P.K. (eds.)
(ISBN: 978-93-5056-738-8).

32. **Soil Characteristics and Agro-ecology**
Chauhan, Avnish and Bharti, P.K. (eds.)
(ISBN: 978-93-5056-758-6).

33. **Soil Contamination and Conservation (2015)**
Ezeaku, P.I. and Bharti, P.K. (eds.)
(ISBN: 978-93-5056-737-1).

34. **Soil Quality and Contamination (2013)**
Bharti, P.K. and Chauhan, Avnish (eds.)
(ISBN: 978-93-5056-361-8).

35. **Waste Disposal and Management (2015)**
Bharti, P.K.; Tabassum, B. and Bajaj, P. (eds.)
(ISBN: 978-93-5056-729-6).

36. **Water Resources and Agriculture (2014)**
Bharti, P.K. and Ezeaku Peter Ikemefuna (eds.)
(ISBN: 978-93-5056-481-3).

Preface

In the end of year 2011, the world population reached the seven billion mark. This historic event took place 12 years after the six billion mark. It took 123 years to double from one to two billion but only 33 years to cross the three-billion threshold. Although, the demographic growth is slowing down in the entire world, the fact that it has taken the ever shortest time to add one extra billion signals a major shift in both the pace and scale of global demographics. An important facet of this shift is the historic milestone achieved in 2007 when more than half of the global population was living in cities and towns, thus making urban centres the dominant habitat for humankind. This seemingly geographical shift has tremendous consequences for the current and future dynamics of human development.

The change in the predominant habitat of world population makes the process of urbanization to be among the most significant global trends of the twenty-first century. Cities and urban places in general now occupy the centre stage in global development. They no longer function as mere spaces for settlement, production and services. They now profoundly shape and influence social and political relations at every level; determining advances and setbacks in modes of production; and providing new content to norms, culture and aesthetics. Cities have become a major locus of power and politics consequently influencing vision achievement and dictating policy outcomes. They are also a major factor in environmental trends and sustainability processes. Urbanization is thus providing the setting, the underlying base, and also the momentum for global change.

Indeed, rapid urban change is likely to occur in the world's poorest countries, those least equipped with the means to invest in basic urban infrastructure – water, sanitation, tenured housing – and least able to provide vital economic opportunities for urban residents to live in conditions above the poverty line. In this context, the urban poor face great exposure to biological and physical threats and also more restrictions in their access to protective services and infrastructures. Thus, the contemporary process of urbanization in the developing world is characterized not just by a shift in the locus of poverty from rural to urban, but more significantly compounded with the 'urbanization of poverty and social exclusion' that derive from socio-economic, gender and ethnic inequalities.

The present book provides comprehensive coverage of the fundamental principles and current practices and trends in the relevant fields. This book updates the subject matter, illustrations and problems to incorporate new concepts and issues related to environmental pollution, industrial development, natural resources, earth ecosystem, biodiversity, ecology, environmental degradation and sustainable development.

Thanks are due to contributors from different institutions and publisher for their interest in this book. We hope this book will provide a multi-disciplinary forum to explore emerging areas in the field of environmental pollution, industrial development, natural resources, earth ecosystem, biodiversity, ecology, environmental degradation and sustainable development.

–Editors

(envbooks@gmail.com)

Contents

Preface

Chapter 1: Sustainable Development and Environmental Protection — 1-18
Deeksha Dave

Chapter 2: An Overview of Nigeria's Agriculture and Environment: *Problems and Prospects* — 19-31
Odeleye Taiwo Grace

Chapter 3: Optimization of Growth and Antimicrobial Metabolite Production by Marine *Aspergillus* Strain — 32-39
Ariole C.N. and **Ezeah O.I.**

Chapter 4: Effects of Social Capital in Agricultural Productivity of Selected Food Crops: *A Case Study of Imo State, Nigeria* — 40-60
Chukwukere Ndubuisi Steve, Jeribe Chigoziru Ugochi Okafor, Okafor Akudo Juliet

Chapter 5: Inhibition Effect of Clindamycin on the Corrosion of Zinc in tetraoxosulphate (vi) Acid Medium — 61-72
E.C. Ogoko, Osu Charles I., A.O. Ogunsipe

Chapter 6: Diversity of Vertebrates in the Campus of Institute for Social and Economic Change: *A Conservation Case Study* — 73-94
Mahalakshmi, B.R., Imran Khan, Y.D and **Sunil Nautiyal**

Chapter 7: Effects of Pesticides on Aquatic and Aerial Oxygen Consumption in an Air Breathing Murrel Fish, *Channa gachua* — 95-104
Qaisur Rahman and **D.N. Sadhu**

Chapter 8: Biotechnological Production of Poly Lactic Acid (PLA) Biopolymer and its Applications 105-116
Amit Kumar

Chapter 9: Safe Use of Chlorine with Special Reference to Production, Storage, Handling and Emergency Preparedness in Case of Leakage/Accident 117-133
G.C. Kisku

Chapter 10: Biodiesel Production from Microalgae 134-158
Farouk K. El-BAZ, Amal A. Mohamed and **Sami I. ALI**

Chapter 11: Water Pollution: *Effects and Control Measures* 159-168
Rupali Salunkhe and **Resham Bhalla**

Index 169-173

Pages: 1-18

AGRICULTURE DEVELOPMENT AND SUSTAINABLE ENVIRONMENT

Edited by: **Jaswant Ray; Dr. Pawan Kumar 'Bharti'**

ISBN: 978-93-5056-759-3

Edition: **2015**

Published by: **Discovery Publishing House Pvt. Ltd., New Delhi (India)**

1 Sustainable Development and Environmental Protection

Deeksha Dave

INTRODUCTION

The needs of the primitive men were limited and earth's resources were sufficient to satisfy those needs. Different components of environment were in a balanced state and the condition of the planet was hospitable for the survival of living organisms. As time passed, man curiously got to know about the gifts of nature and devised tools to make his life more comfortable. It was the beginning of an era where human living significantly changed by utilizing earth's resources. There is a complex relationship between *Homo sapiens* and nature and it is equally important to understand that human beings are a large part of biological living systems. Like any other organism, there is mutual interdependence between human beings and other components of ecosystems. Before industrialisation, the nature was efficient enough to deal with the growth and consequent aftermaths of waste and there was no question raised on the survival of living beings. Development brought about by economic growth was considered to be the panacea of all the distress and poverty existing in the

Assistant Professor, Department of Environmental Studies, School of Agriculture, Indira Gandhi National Open University, New Delhi - 110 068, (India).

society. Even today, we recognize that the development of the society is dependent upon the resources available. Natural resources like forests, fresh water, minerals, energy resource and the diverse plants and animals are valuable nature's assets. These resources particularly forests, water, minerals, etc have been exploited much above their replenishing capacity. The consequence of ignoring nature and following haphazard development models by over exploiting natural resources can have disastrous consequences. It reminds an age old story of old greedy woman who had killed a golden egg lying hen to get all the golden eggs in one stretch. Present model of development adopted does not seem to fulfil the needs, requirements and aspirations of all the billion people residing on Earth.

There are a number of examples to clearly demonstrate that nature has lost its intrinsic value. The forests have been cleared, cities are polluted, fresh water has become a precious resource and many more dreadful consequences of unplanned development are on the way. In the state of environmental degradation it is clear that to adopt a steady and stable development, a clear understanding of the intricacies between nature, society and economy is required.

Therefore, adoption of sustainable development model is a prerequisite to maintain steady flow of resources and to provide equal opportunities to fellow human beings and promote inter-generational and intra-generational equity. It is a philosophy based on human goals and seeks to achieve holistic well being of individuals. Sustainable Development calls for a clear cut understanding of inter-relatedness between various actions and their consequences in order to have sustainable and inclusive growth.

Most actions today are aimed at eliminating some unsustainable trends like rapidly-growing population, the dwindling forests, and exploitation of natural resources or steady increase in levels of pollution. Sustainability is a dynamic balance in constantly mobile society owing to continuing succession of generations. Such sustainability or balance is thus relative in time and space. The major goal of sustainable development is thus ensuring sustainability by conservation of natural resources including living things. This not only centers on using such resources in a wise manner that will prevent their depletion, but also on using them in a manner that will not degrade their quality for future generations. Although roots of sustainable development arise from the environmental concerns, the concept calls for a convergence between economic development, social equity and environmental protection. Merely focussing on green agenda without taking societal needs in consideration, the model of sustainable development will collapse.

Against this backdrop, the current paper aims to highlight that sustainable development is not just environment protection. Today, sustainable development has become the key subject of debate under development and environment. (Jennifer Elliott, 2012). Instead of Green Vs. Growth debate, we need to ensure, it is Green plus Growth. Moreover, the importance of human development concerns cannot be overlooked and appropriate measures are needed to strengthen the social and economic aspect of sustainable development as well. Issues like human health, provision of education, equality of women and sustainable livelihoods are also very crucial and need to be addressed to meet the goals of sustainable development. No development is economically feasible unless and until it make provisions for human development and environment conservations. One of the key issues pertaining to sustainable development is over-consumption by a portion of the world's population. Only a segment of the world's population lives in relative comfort and is able to afford luxuries of modern living. Therefore it is very important to recognise that the model of development adopted should bring equality in the society. Sustainable development has three pillars: economic development, environment conservation and social equality. All the three components must be given equal importance in order to achieve desirable situation. The time has come to incorporate sustainable development thinking and to find sensible and simple solutions to the growing challenges.

Meaning and Concept of Sustainable Development

The theoretical framework for sustainable development evolved between 1972 and 1992 through a series of international conferences and initiatives. The definition of the term sustainable development is the result of a mix of debates and deliberations. Realising the deterioration of the state of the environment by human activities UN General Assembly set up Brundtland Commission in 1983. The commission dissolved after releasing its report "Our Common Future". The classic definition of sustainable development: "development which meets the needs of the present without compromising the ability of future generations to meet their own needs" emerged from the same report also known as Brundtland Report published in 1987.

Thereafter, United Nations set up UN Commission on Sustainable Development in 1992 to ensure effective follow-up of United Nations Conference on Environment and Development (UNCED), also known as the Earth Summit. The character of the conference was motivated by the slogan "Harmony with Nature", brought into the fore with the first principle of the Rio Declaration: "Human beings are at the centre of concerns for sustainable development. They are entitled to a healthy and productive life in harmony with nature".

In 2002, ten years after the Rio Declaration, a follow-up conference, the World Summit on Sustainable Development (WSSD) was convened in Johannesburg to renew the global commitment to sustainable development. The Summit marked a further expansion of the standard definition with the widely used three pillars of sustainable development: economic, social, and environmental. The Johannesburg Declaration created "a collective responsibility to advance and strengthen the interdependent and mutually reinforcing pillars of sustainable development-economic development, social development and environmental protection-at local, national, regional and global levels". In doing so, the World Summit addressed a running concern over the limits of the framework of environment and development, wherein development was widely viewed solely as economic development.

Most recently, the UNDP's *Human Development Report 2011* suggested a new concept of "sustainable *human* development". This new concept is intended to address some of the criticisms of the concept of sustainable development, taking out reference to needs, and bringing in the concept of freedom. The report defines sustainable human development as: "the expansion of the substantive freedoms of people today while making reasonable efforts to avoid seriously compromising those of future generations". (UNDP, 2011, p. 18)

Sustainable development has recorded widespread following in the last several decades. A number of non government organizations and voluntary groups have taken up for the cause of sustainable development. Many of these have contributed towards increased awareness and improved performance. Inspite of being an over-used and confusing term, sustainable development addresses a number of inter-related global issues such as poverty, inequality, hunger and environmental degradation.

One Term and Various Interpretations

While the concept is widely accepted and sustainable development has been adopted as a desirable goal by many institutions, governments, businesses, and NGOs; the term sustainable development suffers from definitional ambiguity or vagueness Majority of the governments and businesses believe that sustainable development is taking care of environment while carrying out business operations. Others argue that sustainable development is a means to promote economic growth and improve the standard of living of the masses. Economic growth is seen as a tool to mitigate environmental impacts of development activities.

In view of all this, it is generally observed that sustainable development remains fundamentally concerned with environmental issues. In its early manifestations, sustainable development was largely a green agenda, or bringing environmental considerations in economic development. The perception of sustainable development as an environment issue is reflected in the fact that in various important meetings and forms of CSD, mainly environment ministries are involved and environmental sectors are given priority.

To many sustainable development is anti-growth. However, the truth is that sustainable development never demoralizes the importance of economic development rather it calls for steady and sustainable economic growth by also ensuring social and ecological well being of individuals. It tries to fulfill the demand for economic growth along with ensuring the sustainability of that growth. Sustainable development is both an end and means. As an end it implies equitable development for present and future generations. However, as means it implies setting policies in such a way that not only economic factors but environmental and social factors are also taken into consideration. Thus when asked "what is to be sustained," it implies nature, life support systems, and community along with their culture.

Similarly, there are several contrasting views on what is to be developed. Early works point towards economic development which will create employment opportunities and wealth generation. More recently, attention has been shifted to human development, including an emphasis on values and goals, such as increased life expectancy, education and equality.

Developed countries have envisioned development only in terms of economic growth. This course is still blindly followed by the developing countries. The result is over exploitation of natural resources and degradation of environment.

Clearly, sustainable development rests on three pillars-economic, environment and social pillar. The key elements of sustainable development are shown in Figure 1.1. Focusing solely on economic gains will put ecosystem health in peril and social fabric disrupted. Many a times, sustainable development is assumed to be acronym for environment protection. However, the real picture is that it calls for balanced set of actions promoting economic growth along with maintaining ecological and social balance.

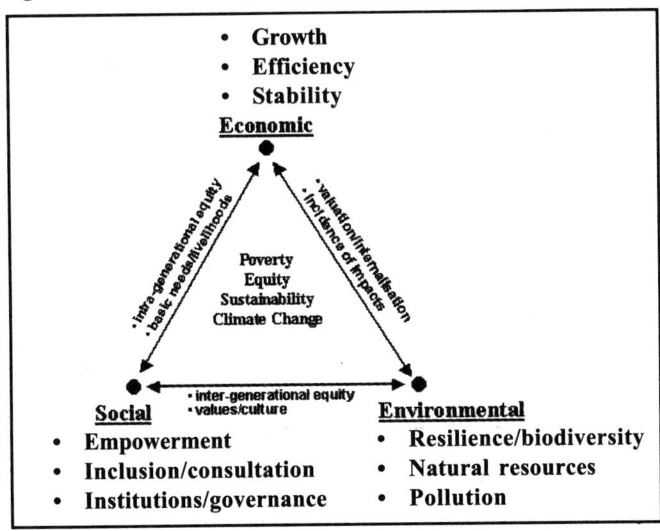

Fig. 1.1: Key Elements of Sustainable Development and Interconnections
Source: Munasinghe (2001)

Our long term economic growth depends on conservation of natural resources and protection of environment that underline it along with promoting social equality. As we move on to ensure well being of masses, it is important to not just to focus our attention to economic growth but also to human well being. The quality of life of individuals must improve by safeguarding human rights.

The Green Philosophy on Sustainable Development

The concept of sustainable development supports strong economic and social development, in particular for people with a low standard of living. At the same time it underlines the importance of protecting the natural resource base and the environment. Economic and social well-being cannot be improved with measures that destroy the environment. Along with this, intergenerational solidarity is also crucial. It means that current development should also take into account its impact on the growth prospects for future generations. The green philosophy on sustainable development revolves around three main concerns: present degraded state of the environment, uncertainties with regards to climate change and deterioration in the quality and quantity of natural resources.

State of Earth's Environment

Increasing consumption, combined with population growth, mean that humanity's demands on the planet have more than doubled over the past 45 years (WWF, 2008, p. 2). These impacts are revealed in a number of disturbing trends. Global biodiversity continues to decline, and species in all groups with known trends are, on average, being driven closer to extinction. For example, fishery stocks are at the point of collapse, with around 80 per cent of the world marine fish stocks for which data is available are fully exploited or overexploited (Secretariat of the CBD, 2010, p. 48). The Millennium Ecosystem Assessment reveals that the provision of many critical ecosystem. Services—such as water, biodiversity, fibre, and food—are being compromised due to the impact of human development (Hassan et al., 2005). Scarcity of and competition over freshwater is a growing concern for many regions in the world, with around 50 countries currently facing moderate to severe water stress (WWF, 2008). Climate change will exacerbate water stress and other problems. Current predictions, summarized in the IPCC's 2007 assessment report, indicate that the carrying capacity of large parts of the world will be affected by climate change. Significant political divisions threaten international progress on climate change, yet the skylight for action to ward off the most dangerous effects of global warming is shrinking by the day.

There is no denying that the Earth's environment is changing on all degrees from local to global due to human activities. The climate is warming at a rate faster than that at any time during the last 10,000 years, biodiversity is being lost at a record rate, aquatic resources are in peril in most of the world's water bodies, air pollution has crossed all limits and extensive areas of land is being degraded. Majority, if not all, of the environment problems today are attributed to the unsustainable production and use of energy, water, food, and other natural resources. Worse still, the projected changes in the environment are likely to bring more challenges for sustainable development. Climate change, loss of natural resources and increasing population are already posing threat and need attention on priority. The Earth's climate is projected to warm by between 1.4 and 5.8 °C over the next 100 years. The higher temperatures will bring changes in precipitation patterns leading to extreme weather events caused by increase in sea level. It will adversely affect the distribution of water resources, thereby causing undesirable effects on water resources, human health, agriculture, forestry, fisheries, and ecological systems. Apart from this, fragmentation of habitats and ecological degradation is leading to imbalances in ecosystem functions. Ecological degradation adversely affects the provisioning (providing food, fibre, etc.), regulatory (maintain the natural cycles) and cultural (quality of life of human beings) services of ecosystems.

Climate Change and the Uncertainties Thereof

As the climate has warmed, some types of extreme weather have become more frequent and severe in recent decades, with increases in extreme heat, intense precipitation, and drought. Heat waves are longer and hotter. Heavy rains and flooding are more frequent. In a wide swing between extremes, drought, too, is more intense and more widespread.

All weather events are now influenced by climate change because weather now develops in a different environment than before. While natural variability continues to play a key role in extreme weather, climate change has shifted the odds and changed the natural limits, making certain types of extreme weather more frequent and more intense. The extreme weather events including floods, cyclones, storms, etc. that are expected to occur more often in a warming world are indeed increasing.

The IPCC third assessment report confirms that global mean temperatures will rise 1.5-6 degrees Celsius during the next century. Furthermore, climate change will significantly affect the economic, social, and environmental dimensions of sustainable development, as well as key issues like poverty and equity. (Munasinghe, M. 2001.)

There is a dual relationship between sustainable development and climate change. On one hand, climate change influences human living conditions and thereby also the basis for social and economic development, while on the other hand, society's move towards sustainable development influences emission of green houses gases thereby influencing climate change and vulnerability of the planet towards the consequences if it gets unchecked.

For developing countries, climate change issue is a development issue. If even the modest projections of climate change become apparent, the development process would be upturned. Until now climate change topics were dealt separately by a group of climate scientists. There was no contribution from the experts from other disciplines such as social sciences and economists to present an overview on the impact of climate change on global issues. The literature on climate change and sustainable development is fragmented and thus sustainable development process remains a backdrop in the evolving climate change debate.

Policy makers all over the world are pressed with the challenges towards sustainable development. While it is certain that the climate will change, there is great uncertainty as to what the local or regional impacts will be and what will be the impacts on societies and economies. Coupled with this is often great disagreement among policy makers about underlying assumptions and priorities for action. Many decisions to be made today have long-term consequences and are sensitive to climate conditions – water, energy, agriculture, fisheries and forests, and disasters risk management. Therefore, sound decision making is required to address the coming climate change related challenges.

Scarcity of Natural Resources

Natural resources are defined as the materials or substances occurring in nature which can be exploited for economic gain. Minerals, forests and fossil fuels are examples of *natural resources*. Not all the resources are available in unlimited amounts and the earth at present suffers from the scarcity of non renewable natural resources like coal, oil, minerals, etc. Similarly renewable natural resources like fresh water and fertile soil have lost their character and often found in degraded state. There is also a growing scarcity of these natural resources. It is referred to as Environmental scarcity. There are three basic ways in which such scarcity can arise:

Demand-induced scarcity: Due to increasing population growth, there is demand of more natural resources and over exploitation of these leads to their scarcity. The population of sub-Saharan Africa, for example, has increased from 177 million in 1950 to 657 million in 2000, shrinking the amount of land and freshwater available to the average person. Similarly scarcity of oil due to increased demand in last several years.

Supply-induced scarcity: Due to environmental degradation and loss of natural resources, the amount available to each individual decreases. In western China, due to overgrazing in portions of the Qinghai-Tibet Plateau, herders and farmers find it increasingly difficult to earn a living in the area.

Structural scarcity: Inspite of decreased availability of natural resources, the elite section of the society deprives the access of these resources to the lower segments of population. It therefore becomes a kind of structural scarcity where few are denied access to the resources. In South Africa, the whites are provided with 87 per cent of the land, while blacks (almost 75% of the country's population) lived within restricted areas having just 13 per cent of the land. (Bingham Kennedy, Jr, 2001) Resources were also inequitably distributed within the restricted areas, as local elites controlled access to productive agriculture and grazing land. In many cases, it has been revealed that different kinds of environmental scarcity interact with each other and aggravate the problem.

Resource capture: When a resource becomes relatively scarce says, because of population growth it often becomes more valuable. This increase in value may motivate powerful groups within society to take greater control of the resource, making it scarcer still. In this way, the demand-induced scarcity that accompanies an increase in population may lead to an increase in structural scarcity following efforts to monopolize the resource.

Ecological marginalization: Ecological marginalization entails the take-over of local natural resources by powerful private and/or state interests, and the gradual or immediate disorganization of the ecosystem via withdrawals and additions. (Koulis, 1998). When vital resources such as fertile land become scarce due to population growth and unequal access, poor people often move into ecologically-sensitive areas such as hillsides, tropical rain forests, and areas at risk of desertification. The rising population in these areas, combined with unsustainable land use practices, leads to environmental degradation and further scarcity. Due to diversion of the waters from Ganga and Brahmaputra to low lying areas, the Bangladeshi communities suffer from the devastating effects and become environmental refugees.

Similarly, Philippines is one of many countries in which ecological marginalization have taken place. High population growth rate (over 2% per year) have made cropland relatively scarce in the fertile lowlands, forcing many farmers to move into the less productive uplands. This migration was also encouraged by the fact that the land ownership in the lowlands was concentrated in the hands of a few elite landholders. As the lowland-to-upland migration proceeded, rising cultivation in the ecologically fragile uplands has led to erosion and ecological degradation, further shrinking the supply of available cropland.

Environment Conservation and Sustainable Development

Environment conservation today holds priority for healthy human survival than it was 20 years ago, and serious efforts are taken to integrate environmental considerations more effectively into economic decision-making. The increasing popularity of the concept of sustainable development has put environment protection in the frontline. The thrust is on the preservation of the natural state of the environment by curbing pollution and conservation of nature's assets.

Examples include legislative efforts in various developed countries to place a price on carbon, a growing of the value of eco system services to business and society, and efforts to measure progress toward sustainable development. The environment and climate change in particular continues to be rated a top concern for citizens in many countries (Pew Research Centre, 2010), despite the recent economic down turn and the hubris of the Copenhagen Climate Change Conference. Concerns over environmental degradation and increasing pollution have led to increased investment in Green Technologies. The Montreal Protocol has been successful in phasing out ozone- depleting substances, and atmospheric concentrations of these substances have either levelled off or decreased since the protocol came into effect in 1989.

Climate change and other global environmental issues such as loss of biodiversity, desertification, and ozone depletion are inseparably linked with each other. Recognition of these key linkages and their close relationship to basic human needs provides policy makers the motivation to address global environmental issues at the local, national, and regional levels.

It is clear from the interventions made so far that to incorporate sustainable development strategies, environment conservation holds prime importance. The roots of the term sustainable development have originated from the environment agenda and present day actions are aimed mostly at promoting ecofriendly products and services. Inspite of increasing emphasis on other pillars of sustainable development, environment conservation continues to be major thrust area in the field of promoting sustainable development programmes and policies.

Top of Form

Demographic Trends and Sustainable Development

World population is increasing and so are our worries to meet the demands of this increasing number of individuals. Not just the number of individuals living on this planet is increasing but the characteristic of population is also witnessing a change. Population distribution, population structure and the composition of population are changing. Policies that do not address population issues will not be able to address sustainable development issue. This has been put forward by various demographers. Sustainable development is as much about health, education, and jobs, as it is about ecosystems. Sustainable development aims to transform impoverished peoples, communities, and countries into informed, educated, healthy and productive societies. It can be achieved only when there is tolerance and respect for human rights in individuals.

Decreasing sex ratio, increasing maternal mortality rates and increasing child mortality puts a big question mark on future demographics if current trends continue. The quality and dignity of human life need to be maintained and equal opportunities of health, education and livelihood should be made available to all without any distinction.

Current efforts towards population control have to be shifted to population stabilisation. Instead of top-down approach there is a need to adopt bottom-up approach and consider human population as a vital resource. The importance of population trends on sustainable development can be put under following points:

- Population dynamics have a significant influence on sustainable development; For example population growth, population distribution by age and sex, household size and urban and rural – All affect people's health and education, and can influence their participation in economic, social and political life, their earnings and their living standards.
- Efforts to promote sustainable development that do not address population dynamics have, and will continue to, fail; and, For example Success in eliminating food insecurity and hunger; ensuring a sustainable use of land, or reducing natural and man-made disasters are strongly and inseparably linked to population dynamics. Efforts to promote sustainable development cannot succeed as long as these remain disassociated from the knowledge and policy options linked to population dynamics.
- Population dynamics are not destiny. Change is possible through a set of policies which respect human rights and freedoms and contribute to a reduction in fertility, notably access to sexual and reproductive health care, education beyond the primary level, and most importantly empowerment of women.

According to the UN Millennium Development Goals Report 2014, India is home to the largest number of poor with one-third of the world's 1.2 billion extreme poor living here. The divide line between the rich and the poor is continuously growing. With growing disparities, it is very difficult to bring all in one roof for sustainable development goals. By allowing foreign investments in India and creating markets, we are adding fuel to the fire. Unplanned development not only results in ecological catastrophes but also creates social and economical disparities. The fruits of development hardly reach the under privileged. In case of any calamity whether natural or artificial it is the poor who suffer the most.

Food, shelter and clothing are the basic human right and every person living on the planet is entitled to healthy and nutritious food, decent clothing and a roof above head. No growth is possible if a section of the population is deprived of this basic human right. Provision of fundamental human rights to all without any distinction is the tagline of sustainable development. This can be achieved by equal distribution and allocation of resources. For e.g., food production is proposed to be increased by improvements in the technology and advances in agriculture. However, again one can cite the unsustainable trend continuing here also. Modern agriculture has increased the agricultural yield but has also led to ecological imbalances by following unsustainable methods of agriculture and social imbalances by leaving farmers under debts. In view of this, there is a striking evidence of increasing social and economic disparities.

Urbanization/Migration

Sustainable development aims at improving the quality of human settlements, including the living and working conditions of both urban and rural dwellers in the context of eliminating poverty and setting sanitation measures. All people should have access to basic services including proper housing and nutrition. With the growth of urbanization, the challenge to ensure healthy living and safe means of livelihood is becoming inevitable. Urbanization has created manifold environmental problems and disrupted the socio-economic fabric of the society. Increase in employment avenues and rise in economy is compensated by decline in social values. Managing our cities and urban places is essential to ensure social equality and solidarity. Urbanization has also increased the extent of damage caused by natural disasters. In view of this, no development can be made sustainable if issues related to urban areas and future trajectory of the growth of urbanization is ignored. Therefore, for example, disaster prone regions should be designed in such a way so that the risk is considerably reduced and urban planning should be in accordance to the demographic needs. There is a need to consider the changing population trends and population projections made so far. Through forward looking approach, we can seize the opportunities and address the challenges associated with demographic change, including migration and urbanization.

We accentuate the rising number of metropolitan regions, cities and towns that are implementing policies for sustainable urban planning and design in order to effectively address the estimated increase in urban population in coming decades. To make sustainable planning procedures, involvement of multiple stakeholders and adequate information about the demographic trends plays an important role. Along with internal, international migration too has recorded highest levels in last several years. It is stated that one person out of seven in the world is in a migratory state in some form or the other. Migration has become a global mega trend of the 21st century. Number of women migrants is also increasing. Migrants bring cultural and traditional diversity and increase social mobility.

In recent years, international and internal migration has increasingly been recognized as a positive force for development, as migrants transfer knowledge and skills to both receiving and origin locations, promote investments, and encourage economic linkages and business opportunities between countries and regions. Sustainably managed migration can promote economic growth and reduce poverty. (United Nations Population Division, 2012) In certain situations, migration can counterbalance labour surpluses in sending them across countries. If managed with forward looking policies and strategies, both international and internal migration can contribute significantly to sustainable development: it can build social and political networks, encourage skill development and provide sources of capital, investment and transfer of knowledge.

However, if poorly managed and in the absence of skills and expertise, and due to barriers in capital flow – migration can potentially contribute to chronic labour market imbalances, chronic fiscal imbalances and severe income disparity – all of which are risks to the global economy.(World Economic Forum, 2012). Mainstreaming migration and development issues into country level planning frameworks is the most systematic and appropriate way to harness migration's benefits and to mitigate its potentially negative consequences. Migration benefits include cultivating the path for sustainable development.

Gender Equality and Sustainable Development

As a group, women – and their potential contributions to economic advances, social progress and environmental protection – have been marginalised. (OECD, 2008). A serious shift towards sustainable development requires gender equality and putting an end to persistent discrimination against women. We have learnt so far that the sustainable development depends on an equitable distribution of resources for today and for the future. This cannot be achieved without gender equality. Gender equality and equity are not only a question of fundamental human rights and social justice, but are also instrumental, for environmental conservation, sustainable development and human security.

Sustainable development encapsulates satisfying the needs of both men and women. (Lisa Warth Malinka Koparanova, 2012). Therefore, it is pertinent to involve women in every decision making concerning matters related to them. Chapter 24 of Agenda 21 states that Women should be fully involved in decision-making and in the implementation of sustainable development activities (and in) research, data collection and dissemination of information.

The community has recognised the status of the women and their contribution in not only managing their families, but also in social development of the entire community. Women have shown their capacity to play a major role in community development. Today, women are participating in Gram Sabhas, many are active in the Self Help Groups, co-operative bodies and other village level organisations. The leadership of women has been recognised by the society. They are now able to influence the Panchyati Raj

Institutions to work for the benefit of the communities. The dark days when they had to struggle for their rights and status in the society, are vanishing. Women are also the care takers of nature and its surroundings. Women are more likely to recycle, buy organic food and eco-labelled products and place a higher value on energy-efficient transport (OECD, 2008a)

Their proximity to nature also makes them more susceptible to environmental catastrophes than their male counterparts. In a sustainable development framework, the economy has to fulfil social progress taking into account environmental limits. Women's livelihoods depend on a healthy planet and access to natural resources. The dominant monetary economy is linked to and depends on a healthy planet, and on both women's visible and women's invisible economic contributions. Investing in women and girls – in their education, health, and access to assets and jobs – has a multiplier effect on productivity, efficiency and sustained economic growth in developing countries (World Bank, 2006).

While women are guaranteed equality under the constitution, legal protection has little effect in the face of prevailing patriarchal traditions. Women lack power and the legal loopholes deny women certain rights. Owing to all this, women have many poor representations in decision making. Beyond that, in both developed and developing countries, women often lack basic understanding of governmental processes. Capacity-building and creative policy-literacy programmes are among the urgent measures that need to be undertaken by governmental and non-governmental organizations to better integrate women in policy planning and implementation.

Female economic empowerment creates additional resources. As consumers and producers, caretakers of their families and educators, women play an important role in promoting sustainable development through their concern for the quality and sustainability of life for present and future generations. As a step ahead in the direction, it is pertinent to recognize women's role in sustainable development. The nutritional requirements of women change at every stage viz. childhood, adolescence and elderly. Therefore, proper attention should be given to women right from the childhood to make them live a healthy life. Similarly, provision of education, equal opportunities for livelihood must be provided to them to ensure their active participation in sustainable development.

The Forthcoming Challenges

It is widely accepted that sustainable development calls for a convergence between economic development, social equity, and environmental protection. Sustainable development is a farsighted development model; and over last few years for governments, businesses, and civil society sustainable development is a guiding principle to stride towards progress. It is evident that business has improved and NGO participation has increased in the sustainable development process. To quote an example, climate change has become the de facto proxy for implementation of the sustainable development agenda. Yet the concept remains elusive and implementation has proven difficult. Unsustainable trends continue and sustainable development has not been able to make real progress.

While sustainable development is intended to include three pillars, over the past 20 years it has often been categorized as an environmental issue. These days, environment sells like a political hot potato. Issues like energy security, infrastructure development, land acquisition, water, mining, land and forest rights all have links with environment.

Added to this, and potentially more limiting for the sustainable development agenda, is the popular orientation of development as purely economic growth. This has been the framework used by developed countries in attaining their unprecedented levels of wealth, and major and rapidly developing countries are following the same course. The problem with such an approach is that natural resources are in looming threat of being exhausted or their quality is degraded to such an extent that biodiversity and natural environments are at stake.

Environment catastrophes continue to lure mankind and raise a question mark against the past models of development. Taking the case of India, this is a home to 18% of world population, 15% livestock population, 7-8% of recorded species but only 2-4% of land area in the world. This puts an immense pressure on all natural features: air, land, water, animals and vegetation.

Population growth combined with higher income levels has further worsened the situation in urban areas. It has given rise to consumerism and created resource intensive society. It has also led to degradation of drinking water and contaminated fruits and vegetables production. Especially in developing countries this increasing population and expanding cities pose great challenges with respect to access to clean drinking water, sanitation, waste water treatment and protection against floods. 59.4 per cent and 8.8 per cent households in rural India and urban India, respectively, had no latrine facilities, says this 69th round NSSO survey report on drinking water, sanitation, hygiene and housing condition in India. The survey also shows that 62.3 per cent and 16.7 per cent of households in rural India and urban India respectively did not have any bathroom facility.

By 2050, around 70% of the world's population of 9.2 billion people is expected to live in an urban environment. Accommodating this huge number will be a total nightmare if sound policy measures and effective steps towards sustainable urban management are not taken. The key to provision of basic services lies in concretisation of planned programmes and strategies. Without major policy changes, substantial improvements in water management and techniques as well as 'smart' spatial development, this trend is likely to affect quality of life; for example, through increasing impacts on human health. However, higher sanitation coverage rates could have a direct positive effect on human health, but may also have adverse effects on the environment if these improved sanitation connections are not combined with waste-water treatment.

Towards Equity and Equality

Sustainable development prima facie aims to bring equality at all levels from top to bottom segments of society and also across generations. This calls for equality in the allocation of resources and making fruits of economic development available to all. Addressing the challenge of sustainable development requires changes at the production and consumer level in developed countries. Living standards that go much beyond the basic minimum are sustainable only when the sustainable production and consumption is possible. Developed countries have the wealth and technical capacity to implement more sustainable policies and measures, yet the required level of political leadership and citizen engagement is still a long way off. Developing countries are restricted by slow economic growth and blindly follow resource intensive model of developing countries. Without change and real action to address levels of consumerism and resource use in developed countries, one can hardly expect a receptive audience among developing countries when attempts are made to direct attention to their economic development practices. More sustainable development pathways are needed in both developed and developing countries; which require a level of dialogue, cooperation and, most importantly, commitment that simply is not reflected in today's multilateral institutions or regime.

There are many stakeholders like men and women, children and youth, tribal communities, the under privileged group, workers and farmers, leaders, businessmen and scientists. Such a wide range of stakeholders with their distinct priorities never agree upon common goal of sustainable development. There is always an uncertainty and difference of opinion about various environmental issues and their impact on human lives. There is a marked variation in the consumption patterns and lifestyles of people. Developing countries are following the lifestyle of the developed countries.

However, it is submitted that any rise in the standard of living in developing countries should be balanced by the lowering of ecological footprint of the developed countries. For example, sea level rise is seen as the result of global warming, a problem attributed to the wealthy developed nations of the west. The victims are inhabitants of low-lying coastal areas and islands. Wealthy nations can afford to build coastal defences, whereas poorer countries cannot cope with the situation because of limited means and resources. Despite the prevalence of the term sustainable development, different groups of people all around the world are still struggling to understand what it means for them and how they can make it possible. When all people and government share sustainability as a common concern and work towards it, the vision of sustainable development in fact is realized.

Sustainable development is not an end but means to continuously work to improve the quality of life of individuals living on the planet. There is a huge gap between the promises that we make for our planet and results that we provide. Actions towards sustainable development which are directed with their broad goals and policies when implemented reflect domestic political and economic realities. Achieving equity and equality among populations across diverse regions is a matter of prime concern.

CONCLUSION

Sustainable development involves more than growth. It requires a change in the content of growth, to make it less Material- and energy-intensive and more equitable in its impact. (Our Common Future, 1987). There is lot of discussions and deliberations on sustainable development round the globe but no firm line of action seems to be there for its proper implementation. A lot of mismatch is seen between the perception and objectives with regards to the character of sustainable development. Significant measures need to be taken to manage economic, social and environmental affairs of the state to bring out desired outcomes.

The need is to take out the idea of sustainable development out of the environment "box" and think over wider social, economic and political agenda (Drexhage and Murphy 2010). Issues outside the environment domain are equally critical and growth of a country must be perceived taking a holistic approach. Greater emphasis should be placed on taking pertinent measures rather than framing policies and action plan on papers. The idea is that we need to go beyond the present view of sustainable development as a framework or concept, to concrete action that includes bottom-up measurable activities. This includes a shift from framing agreements and plans to implementation of those plans.

It is also important to take a stock of the impact of the activities undertaken in the name of sustainable development. An improved sustainable development system must be performance-based. Public-private partnership can be utilized to leverage sustainable private investments. In this regard, strong political leadership is required to address the difficult challenges such as population control, reducing per capita demand of natural resources, etc.

The idea of sustainable development is simple, much more than what it is made to appear. The basic idea is that by all means the earth should remain a safe and healthier place for the survival and enjoyment of benefits by the future generations. "We have not inherited but borrowed earth from our ancestors", this idea should be remembered while explaining sustainable development. It is a process which makes us realize that every individual is an element in a larger entity. A holistic approach considering the well being and equality of mankind is a first step towards sustainable development.

REFERENCES

Bingham Kennedy, Jr (2001) Population and Social Dynamics in the Twenty-first Century, Environmental Scarcity and the Outbreak of Conflict, Population Reference Bureau.

Hassan, Rashid, Robert Scholes and Neville Ash (eds.), 2005. Ecosystems and Human Well-being: Current State and Trends, Vol. 1, Washington, D.C.: Island Press.

Jennifer Elliott, (2012) An Introduction to Sustainable Development: Vol. 7, Routledge Perspectives on Development.

John Blewitt, (2008) Understanding Sustainable Development, Routledge Publishers.

John Drexhage and Deborah Murphy (2010) "Sustainable Development: From Brundtland to Rio 2012" Background Paper International Institute for Sustainable Development (IISD).

Kousis, M. (1998), Ecological Marginalization in Rural Areas: Actors, Impacts, and Responses. Sociologia Ruralis, 38: 86-108.

Lisa Warth and Malinka Koparanova (2012) Empowering Women for Sustainable Development UNECE., Discussion Paper Series.

Munasinghe, M. 1993. *Environmental Economics and Sustainable Development.* World Bank, Washington, D.C., USA.

Munasinghe, M. (2001) Exploring the Linkages Between Climate Change and Sustainable Development: A Challenge for Transdisciplinary Research. Conservation Ecology 5(1): 14. [online] URL: http://www.consecol.org/vol5/iss1/art14/.

OECD (2008), Gender and Sustainable Development: Maximising the Economic, Social and Environmental Role of Women.

OECD (2008a), Environmental Policy and Household Behaviour: Review of Evidence in the Areas of Energy, Food, Transport, Waste and Water.

Our Common Future Report (1987) Chapter 2: Towards Sustainable Development World Commission on Environment and Development.

Pew Research Centre, 2010. "Environmental Issues." 22- Nation Pew Global Attitudes Survey. Washington, D.C.: Pew Research Center. Chapter 8, pp. 69- 72.

Secretariat of the Convention on Biological Diversity, 2010. Global Biodiversity Outlook 3. Montreal: Secretariat of the Convention on Biological Diversity. Accessed athttp://www.cbd.int/doc/publications/gbo/gbo3-final-en.pdf

United Nations Population Fund, Website, "Linking Population, Poverty and Development: Migration: A World on the Move.

Val Percival & Thomas Homer-Dixon (1998) Environmental Scarcity and Violent Conflict: The Case of South Africa Journal of Peace Research Vol. 35 No. 3, pp. 278-298.

World Bank (2006), Gender Equality as Smart Economics, World Bank.

World Economic Forum, Global Risks Seventh Edition 2012. http://www3.weforum.org/docs/EF_GlobalRisks_Report_2012.pdf

World Wide Fund for Nature, 2008. Living Planet Report. Gland, Switzerland.: WWF International.

Pages: 19-31

AGRICULTURE DEVELOPMENT AND SUSTAINABLE ENVIRONMENT

Edited by: Jaswant Ray; Dr. Pawan Kumar 'Bharti'

ISBN: 978-93-5056-759-3

Edition: 2015

Published by: Discovery Publishing House Pvt. Ltd., New Delhi (India)

2

An Overview of Nigeria's Agriculture and Environment
Problems and Prospects

Odeleye Taiwo Grace[1,2]

ABSTRACT

This chapter explores the negative environmental impacts of agricultural on human, animal and vegetation. It focuses on agricultural activities and the potential health hazards associated with various agricultural practices. Personal observation and secondary data revealed the effects of environmental pollution in Nigeria. It was discovered that environmental pollution in Nigeria generally is diverse in nature and are caused by man's interaction with nature particularly in rural areas where agriculture thrives. The study further reveals that pollution impede the socioeconomic development of Nigeria as a nation. Hence, this paper recommends creating environmental awareness among the rural based population with low literacy levels, this was viewed as the best option to curbing the problems of environmental pollution. And it will be achieved by organizing workshops, seminars, and training to educate on how to manage and improve on the relationship between human society and the environment in an integrated and sustainable manner that will effect changes in attitude for good environmental management strategies.

1 Department of Agricultural Extension and Rural Development, University of Ibadan, Nigeria.

2 5213 Goldmar Drive Irondale, Alabama, USA.

INTRODUCTION

Environmental pollution is a challenge in most developed societies of the world and developing countries of Africa. Nigeria, in particular, is facing this menace in recent times. According to CNBC (2012), Nigeria was ranked as the 9th most polluted nation in the world. The agricultural activities of farmers have far reaching effects on the environment and human health. The farmers do this by altering the lithospheric and atmospheric pathways of hydrologic cycles, thus impacting negatively on the air, soil and water substances mostly used by man. Hence, pollution is closely related to the productive activities of people including agriculture. Empirical evidence has shown that primitive farmers use fire to clear parcels of farmlands, modify the soil by ploughing, alter the drainage by irrigation and introduce or breed new animals and crops. These activities no doubt alter the natural vegetation of the environment. This major trend in agriculture can be expected to affect the environment over the next 30 years.

The social and economic implication of yield losses from pollution in Nigeria is potentially much greater and there is the need to increase crop productivity to meet the need of a growing population. While the research institutions provide farmers with new high yielding and disease resistant seedlings at subsidized rate, agricultural extension workers on the other hand must disseminate the relevant information.

Farmers need up to date information on production activities such as land clearing, pest management, weed management, fertilizer application, harvesting, storage and marketing. The role of information in technology transfer is to help farmers acquire new techniques to change their practices and become better informed (Adejare, 2014). Due to the great importance of agriculture in the national economy, and consequently the effect output and yield might have on farmers' economic well being.

HISTORICAL ANALYSIS OF AGRICULTURAL DEVELOPMENT IN NIGERIA

Agriculture was the main occupation of the Nigerian population before the colonial era. Most especially the economically active labour force engaged in agricultural production. During the colonial era, the British government became actively involved in agricultural development in Nigeria after the Second World War. In 1945-1955, government instituted, designed and launched research stations. After 1945, the major priorities of the colonial government for agricultural development included among others; increase in production of crops, introduction of modern agricultural methods and the provision of loans. The colonial government was determined to increase the production of crops, especially export crops, through better seed distribution and modern methods of cultivation. The colonial government also aimed at introducing modern agricultural method through farm settlements, plantations, improved farm implement and greatly expanded agricultural services (Afolabi, 1997).

By 1951, there was an establishment of a federal department of agriculture apart from the provision for research and extension for eastern and northern region. The Federal Government of Nigeria established the Agricultural Technical Committee (ATC) in 1955. The primary issues in the administration of research in Nigeria. The ATC was an advisory body to guide agricultural research at the national level. It formulated and coordinated federal and regional research (Afolabi, 1997).

However, the advent of oil in the sixties as a major foreign exchange earner caused a drastic reduction in the contribution of agricultural production to the national economy. Nigeria an essentially agrarian economy veered off agriculture as its main foreign exchange earnings to become a mono product economy entirely dependent on petroleum. The oil boom gave Nigeria a false sense of hope; it makes the country complacent while earnings from oil was not judiciously utilized to improve the nation's infrastructural facilities particularly in rural areas. Investments in urban centers were overlapping and there were conflicts in strategies and operations in most cases. The most perplexing thing is that despite these investments, food production crises started in this era. This era was also marked by greatest withdrawal of human labour from the agricultural sector (Iyegba, 1988).

Besides, the government misplaced its priorities on agricultural production strategies by embarking fully on direct food production through agencies they established. Some of the agencies and institution are River Basin Development, operation feed the nation, agricultural credit banks, integrated agricultural development projects, green revolution just to mention a few. All aimed at tackling specific problems of agricultural development. These agencies have specific roles to play ranging from direct food production, credit availability, adaptive research and extension services. It involved a combination of private, small farms and government direct food production. It is in this era that large plantation agriculture was developed. (Adesina, 1989). Up till this time, little is known about the effect of environmental pollution on agricultural production. It has been just recently that environmental issues occupy a central theme.

But with recent changes in governance, agriculture accounted for 34.5 per cent of the nation's GDP in 2004 (CBN, 2004) and 42 per cent in 2006 (CBN, 2006). Besides, it engaged 43 per cent of the economically active population (CBN, 2004). The estimated output of some major crops showed an average growth rate of 3.0 to 5.7 per cent. But the value of food import and live animals, grow at the rate of 130.7 per cent annually over a period of eight years from 1990 to 1997 (Idachaba, 2000). In addition, CBN (2004) reported an increase in the output of cassava, yam, maize, oil palm and cocoa by 3.0, 6.5, 10.0, 8.1 and 9.2 per cent, respectively.

This improved performance notwithstanding, the agricultural sector is still confronted with numerous production problems preventing it from providing adequate and affordable food for the nation. The nation is witnessing an increment in prices of food stuffs which is not attributed to inflationary tendencies alone, but also production related problems. The government has identified agriculture as their main priority sector by devoting a proportion of their budgetary allocation to it. However, marginal success so far been recorded since the output is not sufficient to meet the ever increasing demand and enhance foreign exchange earning capacity of the sector. Thus, successive governments have programmes aimed at revamping the agricultural production.

AGRICULTURE AND ITS ENVIRONMENT IN NIGERIA

FEPA (1990) defined the environment as water, air, land and all plants and human beings and or animals living therein, and the interrelationships which exist among any of them. Apart from being the physical surroundings for natural habitats, the environment provides the basis for human exploits and agricultural development. It has been observed that man through agricultural activities tend to directly and or indirectly pollute the environment. Crop and livestock production have a profound effect on the wider environment. Modern agricultural practices have started the process of agricultural pollution. This process causes the degradation of the ecosystem, land and animal due to the modern day by products of agriculture. According to the United States National Research Council (1965), pollution is an undesirable change in physical, chemical, biological characteristics of our air, land and water that may or will harmfully affect human life or that of other desirable species, our industrial processes, living conditions cultural assets that may or will waste or deteriorate our raw material resources.

Unrestricted use of pesticides, insecticides, herbicides and indiscriminate dumping of refuse, excreta and animal dung as well as spillage from refineries, large scale bush burning and so on are perceived as some of the leading factors of environmental pollution in Nigeria. (Aja, 2005; Gbehe, 2004). Substances introduced into the environment that has undesired effect tend to constitute pollutants. It may adversely affect the usefulness of a resource. A pollutant may cause long or short term damage by changing the growth rate of plant or animal species or by interfering with its comfort, health or property values. Some pollutants are biodegradable and therefore cannot persist in the environment in the long term.

Pollution is a disorder within an environment and is a by-product of energy conversion and use of resources. Undesirable change in the environment through harmful substances, waste materials and resources, caused by man's activity or natural disaster which also results in degradation of the environment with its attendant consequences on biodiversity. As the population increases, individual member of the society exert pressure on the scarce available resources such as land and other natural resources for survival. As they carry out their activities, they directly or indirectly pollute the environment. Pollutants also interact with other components to form acid. These acids have significant consequences on agricultural output. Major categories of pollutants include nutrient fertilizer, sewage, sludge, slur, acids, heavy metals, radioactive element and organic chemical (herbicides) insecticides, fungicides and pesticides.

Major Forms of Pollution:

- Air pollution
- Water and soil pollution
- Housing and improper sewage disposal

AIR

Air pollution directly influences every human activity and agriculture. Besides, gases like carbon dioxide, methane, nitrous oxide and so on causes greenhouse effect. Vegetation is affected when sulphur dioxide enters the plants through stomata pores leading to the destruction of chlorophyll and disruption of photosynthesis in plants. Air pollution must be seen as a constraint to agricultural production and It could have significant impact on agricultural production in the future.

WATER POLLUTION

Pollution of ground water by agricultural chemicals and wastes is the major issue in increasingly many developing countries. Use of pesticides has increased considerably over the past years. Pesticides, insecticides, fertilizers and herbicides are chemicals and they don't just stay on the field, particularly, if they are applied wrongly. Due to inappropriate water management and irrigation technology, fertilizer, pesticides are also commonly run off from field to adjacent plants thus polluting the

HOUSING AND IMPROPER SEWAGE DISPOSAL

In many instances, unplanned housing with inadequate sewage system constitute a major source of pollution in Nigeria. In some places, sewage and waste products are discharged into water bodies. Some people delight in defecating on the ground surface, sometimes directly into nearby streams.

AGRICULTURE AS SOURCES OF POLLUTION

Agrochemical

Agrochemical is a generic term for various chemical products used in agriculture. In most countries, exposure to agrochemical (pesticides, insecticides, herbicides, fungicides and nematicides) may pose significant environmental health risk particularly in events of accidental spills. It can also accumulate in animals that feed or eat contaminated pest and soil organism. It can be harmful to beneficial insects such as pollutants.

Direct visible Injury	Direct effect on growth and yield	Indirect effect
• Injury to the leaves • It affects crop yield and lower its value	• Reduce yield with increasing exposure to pollutants • Poor output	• It causes a range of unpleasant physiological, chemical and anatomical changes

Fig. 2.1: Schematic Representations of the Three Major Ways Pollutants may Cause Damage to Crops

On farms, agrochemicals are applied to improve yield and control pests and diseases. However, improper storage, handling, and disposal may be hazardous to human, animal and the environment. Indiscriminate use of pesticides by farmers has also caused serious problems. Many pesticides are toxic and move through the air, water and soil and accumulate or concentrate in food chains leading to serious ecological and human health problems. Pesticide leaching occurs when pesticides are mixed with water and move through the soil, ultimately contaminating ground water.

Pesticide drift often occurs and it is as a result of the unintended diffusion of pesticides. Besides, potential negative effects of pesticide application, including but not limited to: off-target contamination due to spray drift as well as run-off from plants. This can lead to damage in human health, environmental contamination and property damage. Animal health may also be in danger when they feed on plants covered with toxic particles from pesticides. Toxic pesticides – pesticides often don't just kill the target pest. Beneficial insects in and around the field can be poisoned or killed as can other animals eating poisoned insects. Pesticides can also kill soil microorganisms.

Sims (1994) listed health problems of women in pesticide exposure with adverse effect on pregnancy outcome. Pesticides are absorbed into the body through three routes inhalation (lungs), ingestion (stomach), dermal absorption (through the skin, eyes and mucous membrane of the respiratory tracts). The symptoms vary from headaches to cancer. Other notable symptoms of pesticide poisoning are abdominal pain, vomiting, headache, dizziness, mucous spasm, delirium, watery or bloody diarrhea and sometimes convulsion which reflects direct injury to the central nervous system plus extra cellular electrolyte disturbances and shock showing chemical poisoning. As a result of heavy reliance on chemical pesticides, large quantities of toxic materials remaining in the environment cause irreparable human health hazards. Pesticide poisoning is toxic in small absorbed doses while others have harmful effects only when very large amount are consumed or absorbed. Yet, farmers resort to injudicious and excessive use of pesticides due to illiteracy.

FERTILIZERS

This includes synthetic fertilizers, hormones, chemicals, growth agents and raw animal manure. Mineral fertilizers occur when fertilizers are applied more heavily than crops can absorb or when they are washed or blown off the soil surface before they are incorporated. Excess nitrogen and phosphorus can leach into ground water or run off into waterways. Besides, excess nitrogen in the atmosphere can produce pollutants such as ammonia and ozone, which can impair ability to breathe, limit visibility and alter plant growth. This causes major damage as well as serious health problems. Nutrient overload cause eutrophication of lakes, reservoirs and ponds leading to an explosion of algae, which suppress other aquatic plants and animal environment through a range of activities and the air and water can become polluted. Organic matter used as organic fertilizers in agriculture generates heat as it decomposes, and it is possible for manure to ignite spontaneously if stored in a very large pile and may require considerable effort to extinguish it. Besides, when such a large pile of manure is buried, it will foul the air over a whole area

Asides, fertilizers contain not only major elements necessary for plant nutrient and growth, but also trace metal impurities such as Cadmium (Cd), lead (Pb), mercury (Hg), Arsenic (As) or Nickel (Ni). The uptake of these heavy metals by plants, especially leafy vegetables is an avenue of their entry into the human food chain with harmful effects on health. The uptake of some heavy metal pollutants is usually through waste water, marshy ground "akuro", since these heavy metals are soluble and mobile in ground water. It is a common practice by farmers in southwestern Nigeria to plant vegetables close to water, river (flowing or non flowing).

To enhance the yield of food crops, fertilizers and manures are occasionally added to the soil. There are, therefore, the possibilities of over application of these fertilizers and manure. Rural farmers sometimes out of ignorance over fertilize their farms because they are not aware of the nutrient content of the soil upon which they farm. This practice also damages the soil tops and result to poor yields.

BURNING

Kelvin and Lewis (1994) believed that human beings have destroyed enormous tracts of natural vegetation, excavated large areas of land, greatly modified the landscape in recent times. The economic importance of vegetation to mankind cannot be underestimated. It serves as a primary source of food to man and it also provide shelter.

According to Aiya (2009), the use of fire to clear farmlands which sometimes could be used to help improve the quality of the soil in arid regions through adding fresh organic materials, generally causes a reduction in natural vegetation.

Preparation of land for cultivation by burning produces secondary problem associated with the clearance of vegetation, such as erosions by wind and water are flooding. Continuous and frequent burning often reduces the capability of an area to regenerate and replenish its natural vegetation, inflict the atmosphere with severe pollution, thus endangering life and property as well as threatening the very survival of the environment. The simple fact is that whatever reason one may adduce for indulging in the act of bush burning and or farming activities, this practice is most unacceptable in contemporary times and must be discouraged. More so, its consequences far outweighs its advantages. This practice is mostly common among the rural farmers in Nigeria.

As plants are destroyed the ecosystem is generally upset. More than half of the agricultural pollution is due to slashing and burning of farm lands. Burning of forests releases carbon dioxide to the atmosphere and so contribute to the air pollution. The burning of plant biomass is a major source of air pollution, including carbon dioxide, nitrous oxide and smoke particles. The deliberate burning of the vegetation causes deforestation and reduces pasture and crop residue though it promote re-growth and destroy pest habitats.

OVERGRAZING

Livestock farming commonly practiced in the northern and north central regions of Nigeria has a major polluting impact on the land surface. Heavy grazing of cattle leads to trampling and compaction of the soil, thus reducing its capacity to hold water and alters its structure at the same time. This lead to soil erosion by wind and water. Although, grazing may have positive effects on the land because the animal provides feaces, a natural fertilizer rich in nitrates and several other nutrients. These feaces are sometimes washed into the streams and rivers during rainy seasons, which serve as a source of drinking water for most farmers in the rural areas and thus, constituting health hazards.

In addition, the rate of depletion of forest resources is alarming. The deliberate deforestation to create new land for other purposes than agriculture deprives the wealth of diversity and the potential use of many of the unique biological compounds often of great medicinal value. This act also upsets the nutrient cycles, especially the oxygen and carbon dioxide cycles, of which trees form an important component. This practice also leads to an increase in the magnitude and frequency of flooding, soil erosion and increase sediments in rivers, causes slopes instability and degradation of adjacent lands. Examples include forest clearing in southern, western and eastern Nigeria. Forest clearing leads to vegetation removal which increases in fertility of land and subsequently desertification.

HEAVY METALS

In Nigeria, the use of polluted water in the immediate surroundings of big cities for growing of vegetables is a common practice. Although this water is considered to be a rich source of organic matter and plant nutrients, It also contains sufficient amount of soluble salts and heavy metals like iron (Fe), manganese (Mn), copper (Cu), Zinc (Zn), lead (Pb), nickel (NI), mercury (Hg), chromium (Cr), and Aluminum (Al). When such water is used for cultivation of crops for a long period, these heavy metals may accumulate in soil and may be toxic to plants and cause deterioration of soil. Heavy metals like Fe, Cu, Zn and Ni are important for proper functioning of biological system and their deficiency or excess could lead to a number of disorders. However, studies reveal that the presence of toxic heavy metals like Fe, Pb and Hg reduce soil fertility and agricultural output.

These heavy metals (pollutants) may have direct or indirect phytotoxic impacts on plants themselves, leading to a decline in crop yields and threatening our food supply. On the other hand, the plant may act as a vehicle for transferring pollutants into the food chain. For example, cadmium (cd) is readily accumulated by plants and may get to levels which are adverse to the plants themselves, consequently posing a significant threat to animals and humans that consume plants. Heavy metals and pesticides are major pollutants in this respect (Radojevic and Bashkin, 1999). Heavy metals concentration in soil is associated with biological and geochemical cycles and is influenced by anthropogenic activities such as agricultural practices and waste disposal methods (Eja, Ogri and Arikpo, 2003; Zauyah, Juliana, Noorhafizah, Fauzah, Rosenami, 2004). Due to their cumulative behavior and toxicity, however, they have a potential hazardous effect not only on crop plants but also on human health.

SOLUTION/RECOMMENDATION

Tackling agricultural production problems, including negative impact of environment on agricultural activities is a prerequisite for increasing per capita food production of farmers. Adebowale (2000) opined that agricultural development programmers in recent years must give attention to solving world food problems. Oyemakinde (2000) also recommended that a nation's objective should remain as one of striving for self-sufficiency in agricultural production, promoting generation of agricultural surpluses for export and improving the socioeconomic welfare of farmers and rural people in general. More attention should be paid to the production problems of farmers and effort made to alleviate them. Food crises currently experienced in the country are as a result of rapid population growth and decrease in per capita food production.

However, communication strategies are of great import as they are used to influence changes in farming practices and enhance agricultural development. One of the interesting aspects of extension is development communication that was intended to link agricultural research to farmers. Since research should be based on actual farmers' activities so that findings can be relevant, easy to adopt, focus on real problems and constraints faced by farmers, hence, the technology transfer group should be aware of the technology available to farmers and as well disseminate needed ones to them appropriately (Adejare, 2014).

Agricultural extension services will play pivotal role in meeting the information needs of farmers. For any meaningful and successful technology transfer, particularly those related to use, handling and storage of agrochemicals, the role and activities of extension services are inevitable. Farmers make systematic use of information gained from extension agents to effect positive changes in their production. It is generally believed that different tools can be used successfully as a means of communication to farmers, however, this can only be efficient when complemented by a field organization like an extension service.

Numerous recommendations to combat agricultural and environmental related problems among others include:

1. Use of biological pest control agents such as predators, parasitoids, parasites, pathogen to control agricultural pests. It has potential to reduce agricultural pollution associated with the other pest control technique. Avoid indiscriminate use of pesticides, no use of toxic pesticides.
2. Judicious use of farmyard manure – farmyard manure is the mixture of animal manure, comprising beddings and feaces of animals. Different animals have different qualities of manure and agricultural land usually require different amount of animal manure. For example, chicken litter is very concentrated in nitrogen and phosphorus.
3. Use compost moderately– compost comprises decomposed remnant of organic material. It is usually of plant origin, but often include some animal dung or bedding.
4. Avoid excessive use of green manure- green manure are plant grown for the purpose of plowing them in, thus increasing fertility through the incorporation of nutrients and organic matter into the soil.
5. Planting of the cover crops.
6. Buffer planting of trees, shrubs and grass around the field. It helps plants absorb or filter out nutrient before they reach water body.
7. Practice agroforestry, plant grass, construct swells and contour ridging to protect the fields and to prevent erosion by terracing, contouring etc.
8. Practice crop rotation. Mono cropping aggravates pests and diseases that thrive on the new intensive crops.

8. Drastic land use changes from converting land into cultivated land.
9. Avoid flooding of farmland with excess water.
10. Encourage conservation tillage- reduce how often field are tilled. This will reduce erosion and soil compacting and build soil organic matter.
11. Nutrient management – applying fertilizers in the proper amount, at the right time of the year and with the right method can significantly reduce the potential for pollution. Also ensure deep placement of fertilizer.
12. Exploring potential changes in agricultural practices to reduce negative environmental impacts.
13. Bush burning laws should be reinforced to apprehend and prosecute offenders.
14. Pesticides should be subjected to more rigorous testing, and residue build up must be closely monitored.
15. Through radio, television and electronic media, the public should be informed on why it is so important to keep the environment safe for man, animals and plants. Emphasis should be laid on why we need to sustain the environment.

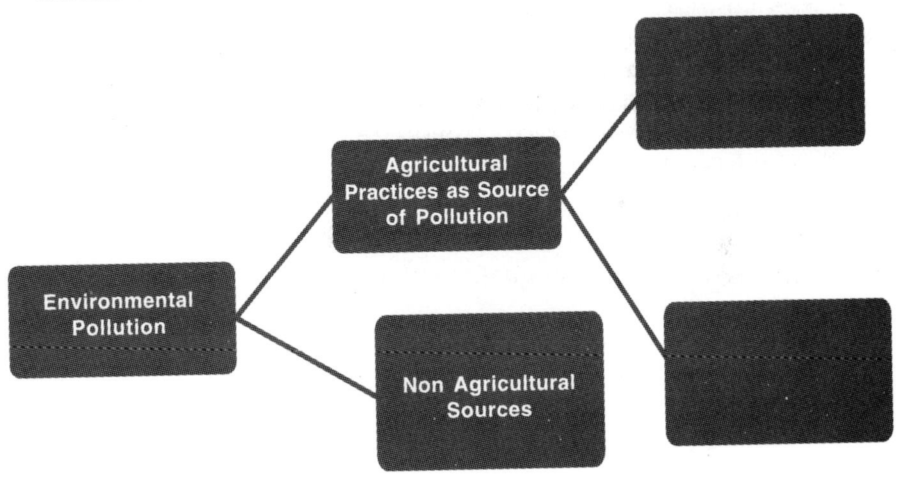

Fig. 2.2: Schematic Representations of the Agriculture Pollution

CONCLUSION

Although, in general, Nigeria has developed a number of important policies, laws and regulations applicable to the environment which may serve as effective instrument for environmental protection, planning, pollution, prevention and control. Environmental programmes through extensive methods will give way to safe environment and increased agricultural production. In order to mitigate the potential negative effects of environmental pollution on agricultural production, government must take necessary measures. Identification of well targeted intervention is equally necessary to reduce its impact. Its impacts on agriculture must be widely disseminated and properly incorporated into agricultural and environmental policy development. Besides, implementation of successful pollution control policies

Agricultural extension still plays a pivotal role in meeting the information needs of peasant farmers.

Access to reliable information is an integral part in any farmers' ability to raise productivity.

REFERENCES

Adebowale, E.A. 2000. Eradicating Hunger in the New Millennium. *A Research Development Perspective Paper Presented at the 2000 World Food Day* Symposium at NUC Maitama, Abuja. 1-4.

Adejare, G.T.F. 2001. Health Problems of Women Cassava Processors in Oluyole Local Government Area. Unpublished M.sc., Thesis. Department of Agricultural Extension and Rural Department. University of Ibadan.

Adejare, G.T.F. 2014. Determinants of Labour Availability and Utilization Among Food and Tree Crop Farmers in Southwestern Nigeria. Ph.D., Thesis. Department of Agricultural Extension and Rural Development, University of Ibadan.

Adesina, O.C. 1989. A Historical Evaluation of the Western Nigerian Government Agricultural Policy. 1955-1966. M.A Thesis. Department of History, Obafemi Awolowo, University, Ile Ife.

Afolabi, A.B. 1997. A Historical Analysis of Agricultural Research Agencies in Nigeria, 1945-1980. Ph.D. Thesis. Department of History, University of Ilorin, Kwara State.

Aja, J.O. (2005). Environmental Education as a Panacea for a Sustainable Development in Nigeria: Schools Environment in Focus.

Ayia, O.N. (2009). An Assessment of the Bush Burning Prohibiting Laws of Benue 2004. pp. 69-80, in M.O. Odey, N.T. Gbehe and Ter Rumun Avav (ed) Agricultural and Environmental Issues in Nigeria: Essays in Honour of Rt. Hon. Austion Igoji. Awodi, Markurdi, Oracle Business Ltd.

Central Bank of Nigeria (CBN) 2004. Central Bank of Nigeria Annual Report and Statement of Account for the Year Ended 31st December, 2004. Abuja. 33, 64-66.

Central Bank of Nigeria (CBN) 2006. Central bank of Nigeria Annual Report and Statement of Account for the Year Ended 31st December, 2006. Abuja.

CNBC 2012. World most Polluted Countries Accessed Jan. 25, 2012.

Das, P. Samantarary, S. and Rout, G.R. 1997. Studies on Cadmium Toxicity in Plant. A Review, Environmental Pollution, 98: 29-36.

Eja, M.E., Ogri, O.R. and Arikpo, O.E. 2003. Bio Concentration of Heavy Metals in Surface Sediment from the Great Kwa River Estuary, Calabar SEN. J. Nigerian Environmental Society, 1: 247-256.

FEPA (1990) Federal Protection Agency Acts of 1990 Under Section 38.

Gbehe, N.T. (2004). Land Development in Nigeria: An Examination of Environmental Degradation Associated with Land Use Types. Conference Paper at the Department of Geography, Benue State University, Markurdi.

Idachaba, F.S 2000. Topical Issues in Nigerian Agriculture; Desirable and Workable Agricultural Policies for Nigeria in the First Decade of 21st Century. Department of Agricultural Economics, University of Ibadan.

Iyegha, D.A. 1988. Agricultural Crisis In Africa. The Nigerian Experience, New York.

Kelvin, T.P. and Lewis, A.O. (1994). An Introduction to Global Environment Issues, London.

Oyemakinde, W. 2000. Strategies for Revamping the Nigerian Economy. Ibadan: Sunlight Syndicate Ventures. 38-40.

Radojevic, M. and Bashkin, N.V. 1999. Practical Environmental Analysis Royal society of Chemistry and Thomas Graham House, Cambridge 180-430.

Sims, J. 1994. Women Health and Environment Anthropology. Geneva: WHO.

Zauyah, S., Juhana, B., Novrhafizah, R., Fauzah, C.I. and Resenami, A.B. 2004. Concentration and Speciation of Heavy Metals in Some Cultivated and Uncultivated Utisols in Penisula Malaysia, Super Soil 3rd Australian New Zealand Soil Conference, University of Sydney, Austria.

Pages: 32-39

AGRICULTURE DEVELOPMENT AND SUSTAINABLE ENVIRONMENT

Edited by: Jaswant Ray; Dr. Pawan Kumar 'Bharti'

ISBN: 978-93-5056-759-3

Edition: 2015

Published by: Discovery Publishing House Pvt. Ltd., New Delhi (India)

3

Optimization of Growth and Antimicrobial Metabolite Production by Marine *Aspergillus* Strain

Ariole* **C.N.** and **Ezeah O.I.**

ABSTRACT

The influence of pH, temperature and salinity on growth and antimicrobial metabolite production by *Aspergillus* strain previously isolated from a marine alga (*Cladophora* sp.) and found to be antagonistic to fish pathogenic *Aeromonas* sp. was studied. The optimal conditions were assessed by growing the isolates at various pH (3, 4, 5, 6, 7, 8 and 9), temperatures (25, 28, 30, 37 and 45°C) and salinities (0.5, 1.0, 1.5, 2.0, 2.5, 3.0 and 3.5% NaCl) in 25ml potato dextrose broth for a period of 7 days. Incubation was at 28°C for pH and salinity levels. Fungal growth was expressed as dry weight of mycelia (mg/25ml). The production of antimicrobial metabolite was determined by measuring the diameter of the inhibition zone against fish pathogenic *Aeromonas* strain using agar well diffusion assay. The maximum growth (47.6 mg/25ml) as well as antimicrobial metabolite production (21mm) was obtained at pH 5. The optimum temperature for maximum mycelial growth (45.0 mg/25ml) as well as antimicrobial metabolite production (22mm) was obtained at 28°C. Salinity of 3.0% NaCl was recorded as optimal for maximum mycelial growth (50.0mg/25ml) and antimicrobial metabolite production (19mm

Department of Microbiology, University of Port Harcourt, P.M.B. 5323, Port Harcourt, Rivers State, Nigeria.

zone of inhibition against fish pathogenic *Aeromonas* strain). These optimal physical factors (pH 5, 28°C and salinity of 3.0% NaCl) may be employed for industrial production of antimicrobial metabolite from this marine *Aspergillus* strain.

Key words: Marine *Aspergillus*, growth optimization, bioactive metabolite, process parameters.

INTRODUCTION

In aquaculture, the usage of live cultures of antagonistic microbes as probiotics is developing to prevent outbreaks of diseases in aquatic organisms (Chandrika, 1996; Prado *et al.*, 2009). There is also an increasing need of alternative novel drugs to control the dominant infectious diseases and multidrug resistant microorganisms. The problem of antibiotic resistance and its epidemiological consequences led to the exploration of several alternate approaches for disease management in aquaculture systems. The range of probiotics examined for use in aquaculture encompasses both Gram-negative and Gram-positive bacteria, bacteriophages, yeasts and unicellular algae (Irianto and Austin, 2002). Searching for unknown microbial strains is an effective approach to obtain new biologically active substances.

Marine microbes are producers of unique substances which have never been found in terrestrial organisms (Fenical and Jensen, 1993; Wagner-Dobler *et al.*, 2002). Marine fungi are known to originate from a wide variety of habitats within the marine environment. The marine environment is ultimately a unique habitat presenting marine fungi with a number of physical challenges such as salinity and pH of the water, low water potential, high sodium-ion concentration, low temperatures and high hydrostatic pressure (Monton *et al.*, 2012). These unusual circumstances inevitably lead to organisms with novel genes and unique properties (Jones, 2000; Raghukumar, 2008).

The natural products are chemical compounds derived from primary and secondary metabolites of the organisms (Berdy, 2005) and they play an important role in pharmaceutical and agricultural research (Fitton, 2006). The natural chemistry of endophytes from algae is an area where few studies have been undertaken (Jones *et al.*, 2008).

It has been reported that physical and chemical factors can greatly influence antibiotic biosynthesis (Thakur *et al.*, 2009). Therefore, optimization and maintenance of proper culture conditions are necessary criteria to achieve maximum production of bioactive metabolites by an antagonistic microbial strain. There are no investigations as regards to optimization of cultural conditions for better growth and production of bioactive metabolite by antagonistic fungal strain associated with a marine alga (*Cladophora* sp.) from the Niger Delta coastal region.

Therefore, in the present study, we report the influence of the physical conditions for the growth and production of the antimicrobial metabolite by a marine fungus (*Aspergillus* sp.) previously isolated from a marine alga (*Cladophora* sp.) and found to be antagonistic to fish pathogenic *Aeromonas* sp. (Ariole *et al.*, 2014).

MATERIALS AND METHODS

Effect of pH on Growth and Antimicrobial Metabolite Production by *Aspergillus* sp.

The effect of pH on the growth and antimicrobial metabolite production by fungal isolate was assayed in 25ml potato dextrose broth at various pH levels (3, 4, 5, 6, 7, 8 and 9). The medium was adjusted to the desired pH by adding 0.1N NaOH or 0.1N HCl. Flasks were sterilized at 121°C at 15psi for 15 minutes. Each flask was aseptically inoculated with 5mm diameter mycelial disc of a 7 day old culture of *Aspergillus* sp. and incubated at 28°C for 7 days.

Estimation of Growth and Antimicrobial Activity Assay

The mycelia were harvested by filtration using cheesecloth and were allowed to dry to a constant weight at 80°C in an oven. Growth was determined as dry weight in 25ml of culture medium. The filtrate was bioassayed against fish pathogenic *Aeromonas* sp. by agar well diffusion assay. Wells were punched with a cork borer (6mm, diameter) in plates of nutrient agar freshly seeded with 0.1ml of 24 hour old broth culture of *Aeromonas* sp. Then, 0.1ml of each filtrate and the control (uninoculated potato dextrose broth) were separately put into the wells. The plates were incubated for 24 hours at 37°C. The diameter of clear zones surrounding the wells were measured and recorded expressing the antimicrobial activity.

Effect of Temperature on Growth and Antimicrobial Metabolite Production by *Aspergillus* sp.

The fungal isolate was subjected to different temperature ranges (25, 28, 30, 37 and 45°C) to study the optimum temperature required for growth and antimicrobial metabolite yield. Twenty five millilitres of potato dextrose broth was prepared and sterilized at 121°C at 15psi for 15minutes. Each flask was aseptically inoculated with 5mm diameter mycelial disc of a 7 day old culture of *Aspergillus* sp. and incubated at 28°C for 7days. Estimation of growth and antimicrobial activity assay were carried out using the methods described above.

Effect of Salinity on Growth and Antimicrobial Metabolite Production by *Aspergillus* sp.

The optimal conditions for growth and production of antagonistic principle by *Aspergillus* sp. was assessed by growing on potato dextrose broth supplemented with different sodium chloride concentrations (0.5, 1.0, 1.5,

2.0, 2.5, 3.0 and 3.5%). Flasks were sterilized at 121°C at 15psi for 15 minutes. Each flask was aseptically inoculated with 5mm diameter mycelial disc of a 7 day old culture of *Aspergillus* sp. and incubated at 28°C for 7 days. The methods used for growth estimation and antimicrobial activity assay were the same as described previously.

Statistical Analysis: Standard deviations for each of the experimental results were calculated using Excel Spreadsheets, with Microsoft excel software. Differences between treatments were examined for significance by one-way ANOVA and $P = 0.05$ was considered to be statistically significant.

RESULTS AND DISCUSSION

The effect of pH on growth and production of antimicrobial metabolite by *Aspergillus* sp. in culture broth (bioassayed against fish pathogenic *Aeromonas* sp.) is presented in Fig. 3.1.

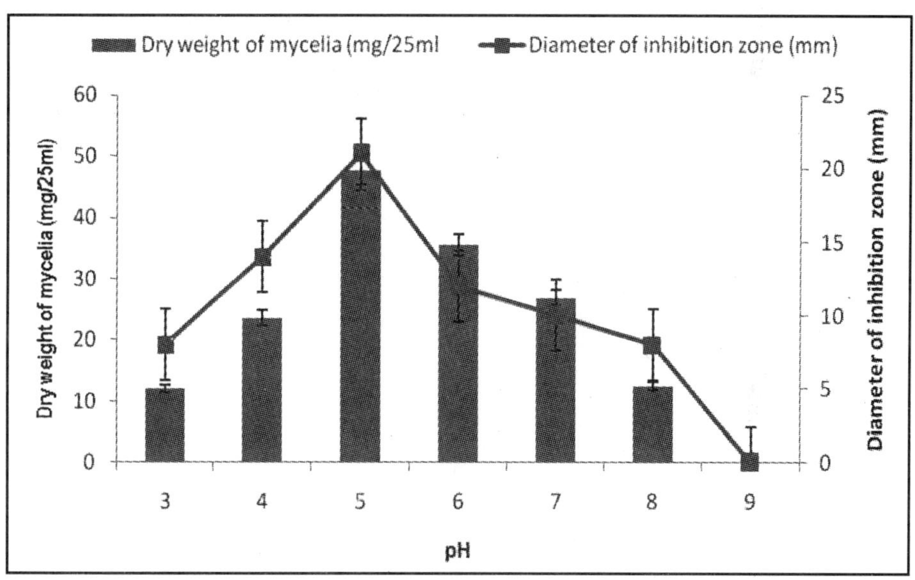

Fig. 3.1: Effect of pH on Growth and Production of Antimicrobial Metabolite by *Aspergillus* sp. in Broth Culture (Bioassayed Against Fish Pathogenic *Aeromonas* sp.)

The maximum growth (47.6mg/25ml) as well as antimicrobial metabolite production (21mm) was obtained at pH 5. This suggests the acidophilic nature of the isolate. Marine derived microbes especially fungi have long been recognized as a potential source of novel and biologically potent metabolites (Saleem *et al.*, 2007).

No growth and antimicrobial metabolite production was observed at pH <3 and >8. Similar observations were also made by Bhattacharyya and Jha, 2011. They pointed out that no growth and antagonistic activity was observed at pH < 3.5 and > 7.5 when they studied the growth and antibacterial activity of *Aspergillus* strain TSF 146 in broth culture (bioassayed against *Bacillus subtilis*). The authors reported that optimum antimicrobial metabolite production (zone of inhibition 25mm) as well as mycelial growth (68mg/25ml medium) was recorded at pH 5.5. Furthermore, Digrak and Eluk, 2001 reported that maximum production of biomass by *Fusarium equiseta* was at pH 8 while maximum toxic metabolite was produced at pH 5. The medium with initial pH 6 was found to be optimal for growth (3.5mg/ml) and bioactive metabolite production (14.72μg/ml) by *Fusarium solani* (Merlin *et al.*, 2013). Mathan *et al.* (2013) reported that *Aspergillus terrus* had a maximum mycelial growth (53mg/25ml) and antibacterial activity (21mm zone of inhibition against *Klebsiella oxytoca*) at pH 5.5. These reports indicate that pH of culture medium is one of the determining factors for the metabolism and biosynthesis of secondary metabolites (Merlin *et al.*, 2013).

The influence of temperature on the growth and antimicrobial metabolite production of the fungal isolate bioassayed against fish pathogenic *Aeromonas* sp. is presented in Fig. 3.2.

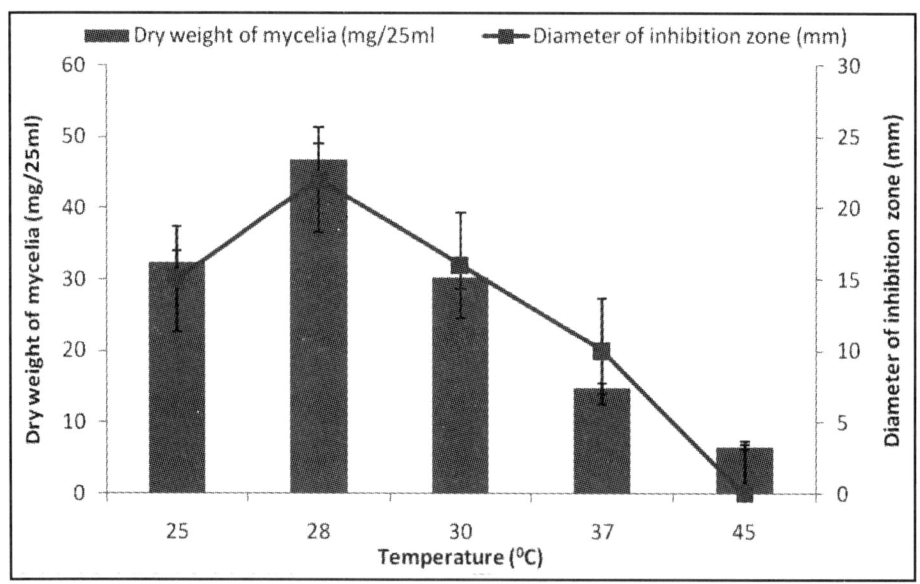

Fig. 3.2: Effect of Temperature on Growth and Production of Antimicrobial Metabolite by *Aspergillus* sp. in Broth Culture (Bioassayed Against Fish Pathogenic *Aeromonas* sp.)

The highest growth (45.0mg/25ml) as well as antimicrobial metabolite production (22mm) was obtained at 28°C. There was a decrease in growth and antimicrobial metabolite production when the temperature was increased from 28°C to 45°C. The increase in the incubation temperature from 25°C to 28°C enhanced the growth of the cells and production of antimicrobial metabolite. These results showed that temperature plays active role in the fungus metabolism and biosynthesis of antimicrobial metabolite. Maximum growth (2.45mg/ml) and bioactive metabolite production (13.06µg/ml) by *Fusarium solani* LCPANCF01 was record at 25°C (Merlin et al., 2013). Mathan *et al.* (2013) also reported that the highest growth (72mg/ml) as well as bioactive metabolite production (20mm) of *Aspergillus terrus* assayed against *Vibrio parahaemolyticus* was at 25°C. Ritchie *et al.* (2009) reported that incubation temperature ranging from 20°C to 25°C was optimum for the mycelial growth of the fungus *Rhizoctonia solani*. It has been reported that physical factors such as temperature and pH can greatly influence antibiotic biosynthesis (Thakur *et al.*, 2009).

The influence of salinity on the growth and antimicrobial metabolite production is presented in Fig. 3.3. Supplemented sodium chloride concentration of 3.0% was recorded as optimal for the maximum mycelial growth (50.0mg/25ml) and antimicrobial metabolite production (19mm zone of inhibition against fish pathogenic *Aeromonas* sp.) Sodium chloride concentration of 2.5-3.0% was found to be optimum for maximum growth (4.3mg/ml, 3.8mg/ml) and production of bioactive metabolite (10.61g/ml, 10.11g/ml) by an antagonist fungus *Fusarium* sp. (Gogoi *et al.*, 2008). Furthermore, sodium chloride concentration of 3.0% was found to be optimum for growth (4.9mg/l) and production of the antibacterial agent (11.90µg/ml) while the concentration above 6% reduced the growth as well as the metabolite. The decrease in growth and antimicrobial metabolite production with increase in NaCl concentration beyond 3.0% observed in this study showed that salinity has a major impact on the growth of microbes and the production of microbial products.

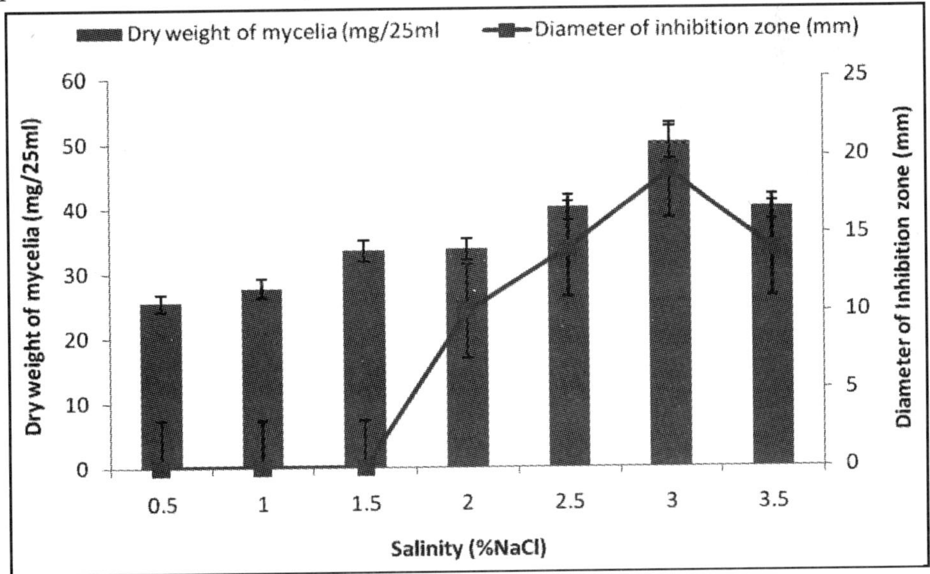

Fig. 3.3: Effect of Salinity on Growth and Production of Antimicrobial Metabolite by *Aspergillus* sp. in Broth Culture (Bioassayed Against Fish Pathogenic *Aeromonas* sp.)

CONCLUSION

The present study has revealed that physical factors such as pH, temperature and salinity have impact on the growth as well as antimicrobial metabolite production by *Aspergillus* strain previously isolated from a marine alga (*Cladophora* sp.) and found to be antagonistic to fish pathogenic *Aeromonas* sp. (Ariole *et al.*, 2014). The maximum growth and antimicrobial metabolite production by this antagonistic marine *Aspergillus* sp. could be achieved at pH 5, 28°C and salinity of 3.0% NaCl.

REFERENCES

Ariole, C.N., Nwogu, H.A. and Chuku, P.W. (2014): Enzymatic Activities of Intestinal Bacteria Isolated from Farmed *Clarias gariepinus. International Journal of Aquaculture*, 4(18): 108-112.

Berdy. J. (2005): Bioactive Microbial Metabolites. *Journal of Antibiotics* (Tokyo). 58 (1):1-26.

Bhattacharyya, P.N. and Jha, D.K. (2011): Optimization of Cultural Conditions Affecting Growth and Improved Bioactive Metabolite Production by a Subsurface *Aspergillus* Strain TSF 146. *Int. J. Appl. Biol. Pharm. Technol.* 2(4): 133-143.

Chandrika, V. (1996): Incidence of Antagonistic *Bacillus* spp. An Eco-friendly Aquatic Probiotic from Aquaculture Pond. *The Fourth Indian Fisheries Forum.* 147-150.

Digrak, M. and Eluk, S.Z. (2001): Determination of Some Fungal Metabolite as Influenced by Temperature, Time, pH and Sugars by Bioassay Method. *T J Biol.* 25:197-203.

Fenical, W. and Jensen, P. (1993): *Marine Biotechnology.* New York, Plenum Press. 419-457.

Fitton, J.H. (2006): Antiviral Properties of Marine Algae. Section 9. Advances in Applied Phycology Utilization. In: Crichley AT, Ohno M, Largo DB, eds. *World Seaweed Resources, an Authoritative Reference System.* Amsterdam, ETI Bioinformatics.

Gogoi, D.K., Deka, B.H.P., Saikia, R. and Bora, T.C. (2008): Optimization of Process Parameters for Improved Production of Bioactive Metabolite by a Novel Endophytic Fungus *Fusarium* sp. DF2 Isolated from *Taxus wallichiana* of North East India. *World J. Microbiol Biotecnol.* 24: 79-87.

Irianto, A. and Austin, B. (2002): Probiotics in Aquaculture. *Journal of Fish Diseases.* 25: 633-642.

Jones, E.B.G. (2000): Marine Fungi: Some Factors Influencing Biodiversity. *Fungal Divers.* 4: 53-73.

Jones, E.B.G., Stanley, S.J. and Pinruan, U. (2008): Marine Endophyte Sources of New Chemical Natural Products: A Review. *Bot Mar.* 51(3): 163-170.

Mathan, S., Subramanian, V. and Nagamony, S. (2013): Optimization and Antimicrobial Metabolite Production from Endophytic Fungi *Aspergillus terreus* KC 582297. *Euro. J. Exp. Bio.* 3(4): 138-144.

Merlin, J.N., Christhudas, I.V.S.N., Kumar, P.P. and Agastian, P. (2013): Optimization of Growth and Bioactive Metabolite Production: *Fusarium solani. Asian J. Pharm Clin Res.* 6(3): 98-103.

Mouton, M., Postma, F., Wilsenach, J. and Botha, A. (2012): Diversity and Characterization of Culturable Fungi from Marine Sediment Collected from St. Helena Bay, South Africa. *Microb Ecol.* 64: 311-319.

Prado, S., Montes, J., Romalde, J.L. and Barja, J.L. (2009): Inhibitory Activity of *Phaeobacter* Strains Against Aquaculture Pathogenic Bacteria. *Int Microbiol.* 12(2):107-14.

Raghukumar, C. (2008): Marine Fungal Biotechnology: An Ecological Perspective. *Reviews Crit.* New Technol *Fungal Divers.* 31: 19-35.

Ritchie, F., Bain, R.A. and McQuilken, M.P. (2009): Effects of Nutrient Status, Temperature and pH on Mycelial Growth, Sclerotial Production and Germination of *Rhizoctonia solani* from Potato *J. Plant Pathol.* 91: 589-596.

Saleem, M., Ali, M.S., Hussain, S., Jabbar, A., Ashraf, M. and Lee, Y.S. (2007): Marine Natural Products of Fungal Origin, *Nat. Prod. Rep.* 24: 1142-1152.

Thakur, D., Bora, T.C., Bordoloi, G.N. and Mazumdar, S. (2009): Influence of Nutrition and Culturing Conditions for Optimum Growth and Antimicrobial Metabolite Production by *Streptomyces* sp. 201. *J. Med. Mycol.* 19: 161-167.

Wagner-Dobler, I., Beil, W., Lang, S., Meiners, M. and Laatsch, H. (2002): Integrated Approach to Explore the Potential of Marine Microorganisms for the Production of Bioactive Metabolites. *Adv Biochem Eng Biotechnol.* 74: 207-238.

Pages: 40-60

AGRICULTURE DEVELOPMENT AND SUSTAINABLE ENVIRONMENT

Edited by: Jaswant Ray; Dr. Pawan Kumar 'Bharti'

ISBN: 978-93-5056-759-3

Edition: 2015

Published by: Discovery Publishing House Pvt. Ltd., New Delhi (India)

4

Effects of Social Capital in Agricultural Productivity of Selected Food Crops

A Case Study of Imo State, Nigeria

Chukwukere Ndubuisi Steve[1*], Jeribe Chigoziru Ugochi Okafor[2]
Okafor Akudo Juliet[3]

ABSTRACT

The work is on effects of social capital in agricultural productivity of selected food crops in Imo State. Primary data were used gotten through structured questionnaire. Multiple stage statistical analysis involving descriptive statistics, regression and trend analysis were used to analyze the data. Result showed that the respondents have favourable socioeconomic features such as age, marital status, household size, major occupations and years of farming experience. Cassava is revealed to be the major crop; farm size, cost of labour and output were not favourable; revenue is reported low while cost of fertilizer, seeds and pesticides were high. A lesser percentage of the farmers are not in partnership with family/ friends. A greater percentage of the respondents are members of co-operatives with the purpose of accessing loan and a high percentage have actually accessed loan from co-operative society.Quantity of seed used significantly influence

1 Department of Agricultural Economic, Extension and Rural Development, Imo State University, Owerri, Imo State, Nigeria.

2 Department of Social Sciences, Federal Polytechnic Nekede, Owerri, Imo State, Nigeria.

3 School of Crop Science, Federal University of Technology, Owerri, Imo State, Nigeria.

income from sale. Lack of trust is significant for not partnering. The need to buy fertilizer and to reduce cost of production is significant in influencing membership of cooperative society. It is recommended that trust among friends/relatives, availability of fertilizer and seeds and soft loan to farmers be emphasized.

Key words: Social capital, agricultural productivity, trust, partnership, co-operative society.

INTRODUCTION

Agricultural productivity refers to "the ratio of the value of total farm outputs to the value of total inputs used in farm production" (Olayide and Heady, 1982; Fulginiti and Perrin, 1998). It is measured as the ratio of final output, in appropriate units, to some measure of inputs. Agriculture plays a major role in the economy of many developing countries, as it is a significant source of nourishment for citizens and a means of livelihood for the most vulnerable members of these countries (Lenis *et al.*, 2011). Consequently, raising agricultural productivity is an important policy goal for concerned governments and development agencies. Increasing agricultural productivity requires one or more of the following: an increase in output and input with output increasing proportionately more than inputs; an increase in output while inputs remain the same; a decrease in both output and input with input decreasing more; or decreasing input while output remains the same (Adewuyi, 2006; Oni *et al.*, 2009).

Social capital however does not have clear, undisputed meaning, for substantive and ideological reasons (Dolfsma and Danreuther, 2003; Foley and Edwards, 1997). Although it has gained interest among both academic and policy decision makers, but there is no generally accepted definition of it (Tompe, 2008). The definition adopted by a study will depend on the disciple and level of investigation (Robison *et al.*, 2002). Astone and Mclanahan (1991) refer social capital as the relationship between different family members that determines how individual members can take advantage of whatever financial and human capital other family members possess. For the purpose of this work, we'll adopt Putman's definition; which seems to be the most cited in related literature (Baranyai *et al.*, 2011). He defined social capital "as those features of social organization, such as trust, norms and networks, which can improve the efficiency of society by facilitating coordinated actions" (Putnam *et al.*, 1993). It is believed to be an economic idea that refers to the connections between individuals and entities that can be economically valuable. In times of financial hardship, food shortages, or severe illnesses, various studies in Africa have shown that the social capital that families have access to make a big difference in their abilities to surmount these adverse events (Mtika, 2001; Kaschula, 2008; Muga and Onyango-Ouma, 2009). Review of definition and history of social capital is presented by Adlerand Kwon (2002), Claridge (2004), Keskin (2011) and more recently Bylok (2010).

Social capital is used as a tool for supporting the implementation of rural and agricultural policies in many countries or regions of the world – and it also plays an important role in explaining both efficiency of political institutions and related economic outcomes (Baranyai *et al.*, 2011). This shows that social networks that include people who trust and assist each other can be a powerful asset. Thus, these relationships between individuals and firms can lead to a state in which each will think of the other when something needs to be done. Along with economic capital, social capital is a valuable mechanism in economic growth. Like other forms of capital, social capital can be understood as an asset that has the potential to yield streams of benefit that make future productive processes more efficient, effective, innovative, or simply expanded, just like physical and natural capital (Lenis *et al.*, 2011). Increasing inputs in order to expand output involves raising both the quality and quantity of inputs (Lenis *et al.*, 2011); examples of which would include the mechanization of agricultural processes, use of high yield varieties, use of fertilizers, irrigation in areas where rainfall is inadequate, and the use of agrochemicals such as herbicides and pesticides. Though all of the aforementioned activities have the potential for productivity enhancement, smallholder farmers, who account for the vast majority of farmers in Imo State, often cannot afford these investments due to their limited resources and restricted access to credit (Anisude, 2010), and thus emphasizes the need for them to utilize their social capitals to improve productivity. Unlike physical or human capital, however, social capital is not embodied in one person; rather it is in the relations a person has with other individuals and with the socioeconomic institutions within which that individual operates (Coleman, 1988).

CONCEPTUAL FRAMEWORK

Social capital has been recently held up as a conceptual framework to build a bridge between the diverse disciplines involved in rural development (Thomas *et al.*, 2006). Rural development embraces social, civic, environmental and economic aspects in a broader sense (Wiesinger, 2005). Social capital is a mediator for collective action and can help people build common property resources (Ostrom, 1990). Not only can social capital improve access to natural resources, it can also improve access to physical capital (World Bank, 2011). It is significant because it affects rural people's capacity to organize for development especially in food crop production (World Bank, 2011).

The most contributions of social capital is conceptual because it adds a social dimension to the development equation of capital that has been mostly ignored in economic exploitations of determinants of agricultural productivity and household welfare (Narayan, 1997). Despite the problems that are recognized at the moment, we cannot help denying that the notion of social capital is considered a trump for eradicating poverty and enhancing the well-being of dwellers through increased agricultural productivity in backward areas, particularly in poverty-stricken rural areas of developing countries (Grootaert, 1999; Grootaert and Narayan, 2000). It is, therefore, important to obtain insights into the links between social capital using social capital indicators such as interpersonal trust, civil responsibility, volunteer activity and agricultural productivity, not only to bring us closer to understanding several debatable issues in rural/community development in general, but also to provide a useful practical framework for making rural/community development strategies more effective. Hence, the main objective of this work is to broadly describe the role of social capital in agricultural productivity of the selected food crops.

METHODOLOGY

Study Area

The study was carried out in Imo State. Imo State lies between latitudes 5°45′N and 6°35′N of the equator, and longitude 6°35′E and 7°28′E of the Greenwich Meridian (Chukwukere, 2013). The annual average temperature is 28°C, with an average annual relative humidity of 80% and annual rainfall of between 1800 and 2500mm, and an altitude of about 100 above sea levels (ISMLSUP, 1999). The state is made up of 27 Local Government Areas. Agriculture is a major occupation of the people (Chukwukere, 2013).

DATA SOURCE

The study used primary data derived with the use of structured questionnaire. The state has three agricultural zones; Owerri, Orlu and Okigwe agricultural zones which are mainly for administrative purpose and not because of any distinct agricultural or climatic difference. Two Local Government Areas were purposively selected from each zone. A total of 20 copies of the questionnaire were distributed to contact farmers in Owerri and Orlu zones each while 15 copies were distributed in each of the selected L.G.A's in Okigwe zone. This is because Okigwe zone has a lesser number of L.G.A than Owerri and Orlu zones. The variables considered for the study are number of partnership with relatives, reasons for partnership, that is,either to raise fund, to access credit, to access government support, to buy inputs, to reduce cost and/or to secure land; membership of cooperative society, purpose of such membership, that is, either to raise fund, to access credit, to access government support, to buy seed, to buy fertilizer and to reduce cost; agro production indicators such as farm size, cost of input used in farming, cost of labour, output size and income from sales were studied. A total of 110 copies of questionnaire were distributed and 100 copies retrieved and analyzed.

MODEL SPECIFICATION

The pattern of relationship between social capital and agricultural productivity of selected crops is determined by building an econometric analysis around the social capital indicators. The models are thus used in estimating the effects of these indicators on agricultural productivity of the selected crops in Imo State.

The social capital indicators that were taking into consideration include number of partnership with relatives/friend (%); purpose of partnership (%); membership of any cooperative society (%); purpose of such membership (%) and membership to volunteer activity that support agriculture (%).

The agro production indicators include total farm size per cropping season (ha); farm input used (kg, litres); cost of input (N); cost of labour (N); total farm output per cropping season(kg) and income from sales per cropping season (N).

It is expected that partnership with relatives/friend will lead to increase in total farm size cultivated per season. This is because relatives that own land not in immediate use can lease such land to these farmers for production.

Partnership is expected to increase farm inputs used. This is because when resources are pulled together, they will enjoy bulk purchase as their purchasing power is increased. Also, since it is expected that more farmland will be cultivated the inputs used will consequently increase.

Partnership with relative/friends is expected to result in reduction in cost of input and labour. This is because the farmers will receive some of these items free and the number of family labour available will increase.

All these a priori expectations will have resultanteffects on increase in total farm output and/or income from sales per season.

The model is thus formulated:

Povi = f(soc; cap,:) .... (1)

With soc.cap; = f(Imp.prt, Imp.fu, Imp.crt, Imp.gvst, Le.inp) .... (2)

When equation (2) is substituted into equation (1) it then becomes

Povi = f(Imp.prt, Imp.fu, Imp.crt, Imp.gvst, Le.inp) .... (3)

When transformed into a multiple linear relationship, the model thus become

$$InPov = In\beta_0 + \beta_1 Imp.ha + \beta_2 Imp.frt + \beta_3 Imp.sd + \beta_4 Imp.pst + \beta_5 Le.clb + U \quad (4)$$

Where

InPov = Log of agricultural productivity in Imo State proxied by farm size (ha), quantity of fertilizer used (kg), quantity of seed/seedlings/stem used (kg), pesticides/herbicides used (litre) and cost of labour (#).

Imp.ha = farm size (ha)

Imp.frt = quantity of fertilizer used (kg)

Imp.sd = quantity of seed/seedling/stems used (kg)

Imp.pst = quanitity of pesticides/herbicides used (litres)

Le.clb = cost of labour (#)

$\beta_0, \beta_1, \beta_2, \beta_3, \beta_4, \beta_5$= Estimation parameter associated with the influence of the indicators of the farm inputs on agricultural productivity in Imo State.

$$InPov = In\beta_0 + \beta_1 Imp.prt + \beta_2 Imp.fu + \beta_3 Imp.crt + \beta_4 Imp.gvst + \beta_5 Le.inp + U \quad (5)$$

Where

InPov = Log of partnership with family/friends in Imo State proxied by access to fund, access to credit, access to government support and access to inputs.

Imp.fu = Access to fund (%)

Imp.crt = Access to credit (%)

Imp.gvst = Access to government support (%)

Le.inp = Access to input (kg)

$\beta_0, \beta_1, \beta_2, \beta_3, \beta_4, \beta_5$= Estimation parameter associated with the influence of the indicators of the social capital on agricultural productivity in Imo State.

$$InCop = In\beta_0 + \beta_1 Imp.fu + \beta_2 Imp.crt + \beta_3 Imp.gvst + \beta_4 Le.inp + U \quad (6)$$

Where

InPov = Log of membership of co-operative society in Imo State proxied by access to fund, access to credit, access to government support and access to inputs.

Imp.fu = Access to fund (%)

Imp.crt = Access to credit (%)

Imp.gvst = Access to government support (%)

Le.inp = Access to input (%)

$\beta_0, \beta_1, \beta_2, \beta_3, \beta_4$= Estimation parameter associated with the influence of the indicators of the social capital on agricultural productivity in Imo State.

RESULTS AND DISCUSSION

Socio-economic Characteristics

Analysis of the results in Table 4.1 revealed that majority (63%) of the farmers are male, 65% are between the ages of 41 to 60 years while 55% are married.It can be deduced from this that majority of these farmers have access to land based on land tenure system prevalent in the study area which is by inheritance. Farm holdings across Nigeria are often inherited rather than purchased (Adeyemo, Oke and Akinola, 2010; Adewuyi, 2002; Egwuda, 2001; Ojo, 2005; Ekunwe, Orewa, and Emokaro, 2008). It is noted that based on this land tenure system, adult male inherits and mostly hold family land in trust, thus, giving them access to land which can be used for farming. A high distribution of 29% of the farmers have household of 7-9 people with a mean size of 7. This is in tandem with Onyemuawa *et al.*,(2013) that farmers in Idemili North, Anambra State have a household size of 8.

Table 4.1: Socio-economic Distribution of the Farmers

Sex	Frequency	Age	Frequency	Marital Status	Frequency	Household Size	Frequency	Major Occupation	Frequency	Farming Experience	Frequency
Male	63	30-40	6	Single	8	1-3	10	Civil service	16	1-10	6
		41-50	32	Divorced	15	4-6	28	Farming	28	11-20	22
		51-60	33	Married	55	7-9	29	Trading	31	21-30	41
Female	37	61-70	22	Widow/widower	14	10-12	14	Artisan	24	31-above	22
		Above 70	7	No response	8	13-15	1	No response	1	No response	10
						No response	8				
Total	**100**	**Total**	**100**	**Total**	**100**	**Total**	**100**	**Total**	**100**	**Total**	**100**

Source: Field survey, 2014.

A greater percentage (31%) takes trading as major occupation. This however, is followed by farming (28%) It is reported that many farmers in Nigeria engage in other occupations to supplement their incomes such as hunting, trading, crafts, and fishing (Adewuyi, 2002; Ogunsanya, 2009; Ajani, 2000; Ojo, 2005; Yaro, 1999). The result revealed that 41% of the farmers have farming experience of 21-30 years with mean years of 22 years 7 months 5 days. This implies that they are experienced farmers. This results is in agreement with Onyemauwa *et al.*,(2013) that majority (60%) of farmers in Idemili L.G.A in Anambra State are males, average respondents are 54 years, 78% married with 20 years of farming experience.

AGRO PRODUCTION INDICATORS

Result in Table 4.2 shows the major crops grown by farmers in Imo State. It reveals cassava to be most dominant crop (37%) of the major crops. This is in agreement with Lenis *et al* (2011) that in Nigeria output produced for most crops was stagnant or declining, with the exception of cassava, which saw modest increases in output. This is because cassava is easily planted, the stem is cheaper and readily available than other crops, it can strive even in an erosion prone areas, it can be in the field for all year round, it's a source of garri and fufu, a daily staple in most families in the zone and can be stored for a long time without perishing.

Table 4.2: Distribution of Major Crops Grown in Imo State

Crop	Frequency	Percentage (%)
Cassava	37	37
Cocoyam	13	13
Maize	7	7
Palm fruit	18	18
Rice	4	4
Yam	20	20
No response	1	1
Total	**100**	**100**

Source: Field survey (2014)

Result in Table 4.3 reveals on average that 75% of the farmers cultivates not more than 1ha of land during the period (Table 4.3). Mean hectare of land cultivated is 0.92888ha.Farm holdings across Nigeria are generally small with less than 5 hectares on average (Adeyemo, Oke and Akinola 2010; Akintayo 2011; Oladeebo 2006; Adewuyi 2002; Egwuda 2001; Ojo 2005; Ekunwe, Orewa, and Emokaro 2008; Adejoh 2009; Oviasogie 2005; Haruna *et al*. 2009; David et al. 2009; Yaro 1999). While a study of small scale food crop farmers in the South South (Idumah, 2006) also revealed small land holdings with an average of 1.56 hectares. Lenis *et al* (2011) reported that land cultivated to selected major crops in Nigeria were either stagnant or modestly increasing with the exception of cassava. A distribution of 57% of the farmers spent not more than #100,000 on labour during the period. However, mean cost of labour is #127,177.20. This implies small scale level of production. Most rural residents are engaged in smallholder semi-subsistence agriculture (Oviasogie 2005; Ajibolade 2005). According to Lenis *et al* (2011) in Nigeria, the level of growth in agriculture lagged behind other sectors due to a wide variety of factors including scarcity and high cost of inputs like land and labour. It is expected that these farmers would require external aid especially in the form of partnership with family members and friends in other to access inputs required for their production.

Table 4.3: Distribution of Production Indicators, 2008-2013

Variable	2008	2009	2010	2011	2012	2013
Cultivated Area (ha)						
0.1-1.0	79	72	77	74	74	73
1.1-2.0	17	21	20	17	16	16
2.1-3.0	4	7	1	9	10	10
3.1-4.0	-	-	2	-	-	1
Total	**100**	**100**	**100**	**100**	**100**	**100**
Cost of Labour (#10,000)						
1-10	62	59	58	54	55	54
11-20	27	33	29	33	26	28
21-30	6	2	6	7	13	12
31-40	1	2	2	1	1	1
41-50	2	-	-	2	3	-
51-60	-	3	1	-	1	2
61-70	1	-	3	2	-	-
71-80	-	1	-	-	1	-
81-90	-	-	-	1	-	2
No response	1	-	1	1	1	1
Total	**100**	**100**	**100**	**100**	**100**	**100**
Farm Output (1000kg)						
0.1-1.0	11	11	11	10	11	11
1.1-10.0	43	36	37	41	38	32
10.1-20.0	33	40	37	30	32	35
20.1-30.0	6	7	11	14	12	11
30.1-40.0	2	1	1	2	5	8
No response	5	5	3	3	3	3
Total	**100**	**100**	**100**	**100**	**100**	**100**

(Table Contd...)

Variable	2008	2009	2010	2011	2012	2013
Revenue from sales (#10,000)						
1-20	36	48	37	35	40	37
21-40	39	32	40	46	39	43
41-60	12	13	15	15	14	16
61-80	1	3	2	-	2	-
81-100	1	-	2	-	1	-
No response	11	4	4	4	4	4
Total	**100**	**100**	**100**	**100**	**100**	**100**
Quantity of Fertilizer (25kg)						
1.0-10.0	72	57	62	53	56	59
10.1-20.0	11	34	33	30	27	25
20.1-30.0	14	8	5	14	10	8
30.1-40.0	3	1	-	3	7	8
40.1-50.0	-	-	-	-	-	-
No response	-	-	-	-	-	-
Total	**100**	**100**	**100**	**100**	**100**	**100**
Quantity of Seed/Stem/Seedling (10kg)						
0.1-1.0	11	13	12	11	10	11
1.0-10.0	60	61	59	60	53	49
10.1-20.0	11	8	14	13	22	24
20.1-30.0	14	16	13	14	11	12
30.1-40.0	3	-	1	1	3	2
40.1-50.0	-	1	-	-	-	-
No response	1	1	1	1	1	2
Total	**100**	**100**	**100**	**100**	**100**	**100**
Quantity of Pesticide/herbicide (litre)						
1-3	36	36	37	37	36	37
4-6	6	6	6	6	7	6
7-9	1	1	-	-	-	-
10-12	1	2	-	-	-	-
13-15	1	-	-	2	1	1
15-17	-	1	-	1	1	-
No response	55	54	57	54	55	56
Total	**100**	**100**	**100**	**100**	**100**	**100**
Cost of fertilizer (#10,000)						
0.1-3.0	71	74	71	67	75	71
3.1-6.0	22	20	22	23	14	17
6.1-9.0	4	5	3	5	5	5
9.1-12.0	-	-	1	1	2	3
12.1-15.0	-	-	-	-	-	1
15.1-18.0	2	1	1	-	-	-
18.1-21.0	-	-	-	1	1	1
No response	1	-	2	3	3	2
Total	**100**	**100**	**100**	**100**	**100**	**100**

(Table Contd...)

Variable	2008	2009	2010	2011	2012	2013
Cost of seed/stem/seedling (#1000)						
0.1-1.0	19	17	16	14	13	14
1.1-10.0	42	41	43	41	40	42
10.1-20.0	14	25	25	23	25	23
20.1-30.0	16	11	10	12	10	13
30.1-40.0	1	-	-	1	3	1
40.1-50.0	3	1	-	2	1	-
50.1-60.0	-	-	1	2	2	1
No response	5	5	5	5	6	6
Total	**100**	**100**	**100**	**100**	**100**	**100**
Cost of Pesticide/herbicide (#1000)						
0.1-1.0	11	8	8	7	8	7
1.1-3.0	12	15	16	17	16	16
3.1-6.0	18	18	17	17	17	17
6.1-9.0	3	3	3	3	3	3
No response	56	56	55	57	57	57
Total	**100**	**100**	**100**	**100**	**100**	**100**

Source: Field survey, 2014.

Analysis of farm output revealed that averages of 12.17%, 37.8% and 34.5% of the farmers recorded farm output of not more than 10,000kg, 100,00kg and 200,000kg respectively. Mean output for the period is 12,107.35kg. Adewuyi (2002) reported a decline in output in the agricultural sector. Muhammad-Lawal and Atte (2006) concluded a slow growth in output. Average percentages of 38.83%, 39.83% and 14.17% of the farmers had total revenues of not more than #200,000, #400,000 and #600,000 respectively during the period. Mean revenue is #273,453.20. This is in agreement with Lenis *et* al (2011) when they noted that incomes from farming are generally low in Nigeria.

Results on fertilizer use revealed that average percentages of 59.83% and 26.67% of the farmers used not more than 10 and 20 bags each of fertilizer per cropping season. Average quantity of fertilizer used is 6.475 bags. This implied that the farmers have access to fertilizer for use. Majority (57%) of the farmers used not more than 100kg of seed/seedling/stem in farming per cropping season with average of 101.8501kg.This is viewed to be low and implied a small scale level of production. Majority (55.17%) of the farmers do not use herbicide/pesticides while 36.5% used not more than 3litres per cropping season with average usage of2.453488litres. This low figure can be attributed to negligence by the farmers to its importance and use, high cost and unavailability.

High majority (71.5%) of the farmers spent not more than #30,000.00 on fertilizer in the study area. Average fertilizer cost during the period is #27,622.81. Majority (41.5%) of the farmers spent not more than #10,000.00 on seed/seedling/stem. Average cost is #10,185.01. Result on the average cost of herbicides/pesticide during the period revealed that majority (56.33%) of the farmers did not spend on herbicides/pesticides, while 17.33%, 15.33% and 8.17% spent not more than #60,000.00, #30,000.00 and #10,000.00 respectively. Average cost of herbicides/pesticides is #31,888.62.

Results of the regression analysis showed that quantity of seed/seedling/stem used significantly influence income from sales at 95% level of significance. Result of the regression analysis showed that lack of trust more significantly influence partnership with family/friends at 95% level of significance. Result of the regression showed that need to buy fertilizers and reduce cost of production significantly influence membership of co-operative society at 95% level of significance.

Table 4.4: Average Values of Selected Agro Production Indicators

Year	Cultivated Area (ha)	Cost of Labour (#10,000)	Farm Output (1000kg)	Revenue (#10,000)
2008	0.92778	11.80808	13.59545	27
2009	0.891	11.93378	13.25056	26.57813
2010	0.872	12.95374	13.73844	28.76563
2011	0.9585	12.83657	14.58813	26.21458
2012	0.9545	13.05677	14.63062	27.76042
2013	0.9695	13.71737	15.47179	27.75313
Average	0.92888	12.71772	14.2125	27.34532

Source: Field survey, 2014.

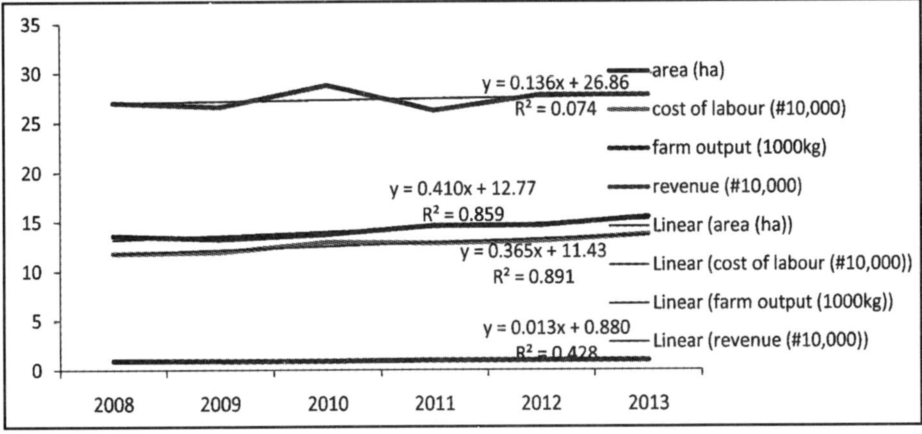

Fig 4.1: Distribution of Average Values of Agro Production Indicators

Result of the trend analysis revealed that cultivated area increases by 0.0139ha for every change in time. The coefficient of determination (R^2) is 0.4288, implying that ourmodel accounted for 42.88% of the relationship. The result revealed that cost of labour increases by #0.3657 for every change in time. The coefficient of determination (R^2) is 0.891 implying that our model accounted for 89.1% of the relationship. The result revealed that farm output increases by 0.4106kg for every change in time. The coefficient of determination (R^2) is 0.8596 implying that our model accounted for 85.96% of the relationship. The result revealed that revenue from sales increases by #0.136 for every change in time. The coefficient of determination (R^2) is 0.0746 implying that the model accounted for 7.46% of the relationship.

Table 4.5: Average Quantities and Costs of Inputs Used: 2008-2013

Year	Quantity of Fertilizer (Bag)	Quantity of Seed (10kg)	Quantity of Pesticide/ Herbicide (Litre)	Cost of Fertilizer (#10,000)	Cost of Seed (#1000)	Cost of Pesticides/ Herbicides (#1000)
2008	6.58	10.33959	2.604651	2.685052	10.71392	3.109432
2009	6.13	9.952092	2.604651	2.604948	8.96484	3.16625
2010	6.13	9.513265	2.372093	2.786082	9.534789	3.157045
2011	6.53	10.24699	2.372093	2.820313	10.79713	3.21625
2012	6.81	10.36842	2.395349	2.776042	11.19878	3.204773
2013	6.67	10.42887	2.372093	2.90125	9.900585	3.279419
Average	6.475	10.14154	2.453488	2.762281	10.18501	3.188862

Source: Field survey, 2014.

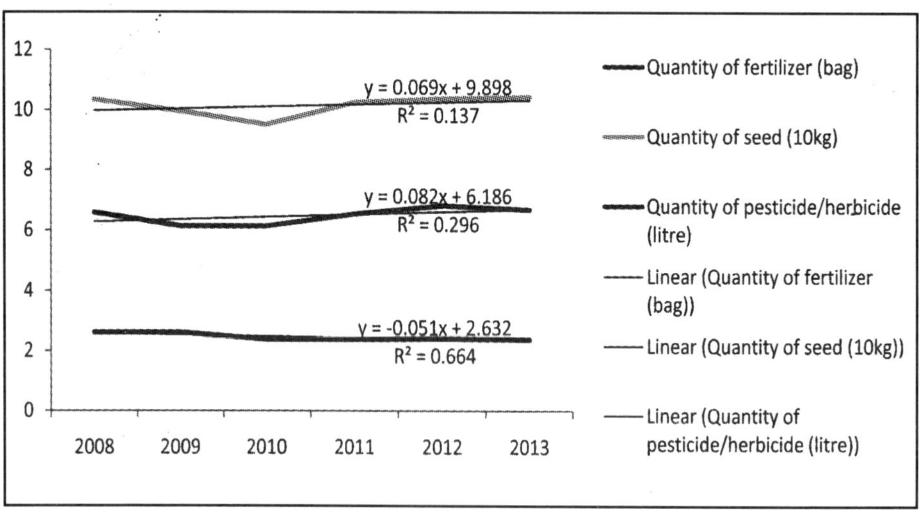

Fig. 4.2: Average Quantity of Inputs Used

Result of the trend analysis revealed that quantity of fertilizer used increases by 0.0826 bags for every change in time. The coefficient of determination (R^2) is 0.2965 implying that our model accounted for 29.65% of the relationship. The quantity of seed/seedling/stem increases by 0.0694kg for every change in time. The coefficient of determination (R^2) is 0.1371 implying our model accounted for 13.71% of the relationship. Quantity of pesticide/herbicide used decreases by 0.0512 for every change in time. The coefficient of determination (R^2) is 0.6643 implying our model accounted for 66.43% of the relationship.

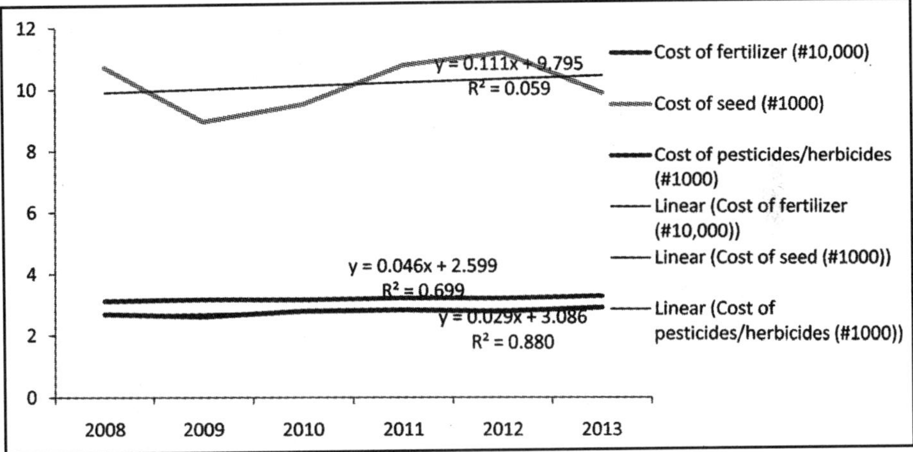

Fig. 4.3: Average Costs of Inputs Used

The result of the trend analysis revealed that cost of fertilizer increases by #0.0293 for every change in time. The coefficient of determination (R^2) is 0.8805 implying our model accounted for 88.05% of the relationship. Cost of seed increases by #0.1114 for every change in time. The coefficient of determination (R^2) is 0.0591 implying that our model accounted for 5.91%. Cost of pesticides/herbicides increases by #0.0465 for every change in time. The coefficient of determination (R^2) is 0.6996 implying that our model accounted for 69.96% of the relationship.

SOCIAL CAPITAL INDICATORS

Result in Table 4.6 shows that 47% of the farmers are in partnership with family and friends. The implication of this is increased accessibility to agricultural inputs which is expected to result in increased production by these farmers. Such inputs may include land, fertilizer, labour, seed and credit/ agricultural loan and government support.

Top of the reason for partnership include access to credit/loan (27.66%) and access to land (21.28%). This is expected as these farmers receive remittances from family members and friends which they used in their farming activity. It can be noted that farmers in Imo State have access to extended family land which they use for farming. Such lands are given free and on trust until the right owner chooses to develop the land.

Table 4.6: Social Capital Indicators

Parameter	Frequency	Percentage (%)
Partnership		
Yes	47	47
No	53	53
Total	**100**	**100**
Reason for partnership		
To raise fund	5	10.64
To access credit/loan	13	27.66
To access government support	7	14.89
To buy input	6	12.77
To reduce cost	6	12.77
To secure land	10	21.28
Total	**47**	**100**
Reason for no partnership		
Don't have a relation to partner	7	13.21
Don't have trust	13	24.53
No need to	33	62.26
Total	**53**	**100**
Membership of Co-operative Society		
Yes	54	54
No	46	46
Total	**100**	**100**
Reason for Co-operative		
To raise fund	13	24.07
To access credit/loan	22	40.74
To access government support	13	24.07
To buy seed	0	0
To buy fertilizer	4	7.41
To reduce cost	2	3.71
Total	**54**	**100**
Involvement in Volunteer Activity		
Yes	56	56
No	44	44
Total	**100**	**100**

(Table Contd...)

Parameter	Frequency	Percentage (%)
Receive financial assistance		
Yes	31	55.36
No	25	44.64
Total	**56**	**100**
Year		
2008	4	12.90
2009	8	25.81
2010	8	25.81
2011	4	12.90
2012	3	9.68
2013	4	12.90
Total	**31**	**100**

Source: Field survey, 2014.

However, 53% of the farmers did not partner with their family member and friends. About 62% of these farmers did not see any need for partnership while 24.53% did not partner for lack of trust. Putnam (2000) argues that social capital has "forceful, even quantifiable effects on different aspects of our lives such as enhanced economic achievement through increased trust and lower transaction costs (Fukuyama, 1995) and improved welfare (Cote and Healy, 2001). The implication of this result is that these farmers will continue production at a subsistent level.

Table 4.6 revealed that 54% of the respondents are members of agricultural co-operative society. About 41% of these farmers join these co-operatives for loan/credit accessibility. About 56% of these farmers have received credit/loan from co-operative society. It is reported that membership of cooperative societies (Shehu *et al*. 2010; Idiong *et al*. 2009), and access to credit (Ogundari, 2006; Oluwatosin, 2011) have an unambiguous impact on the efficiency of agricultural productivity.

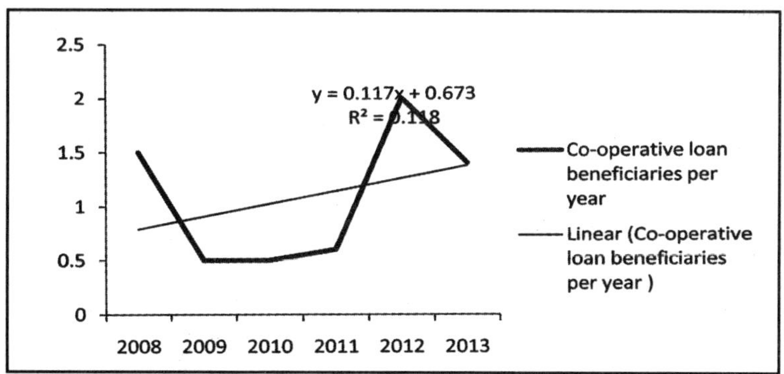

Fig. 4.4: Beneficiaries of Co-operative society loan per year: 2008 to 2013

Result of the trend analysis revealed that the number of farmers accessing these loans increases by 0.117 per unit change in time (Fig. 4.4). This implies that cooperative society is a source of finance to the farmers in the study area. The co-efficient of determination (R^2) is 0.1184 showing that the model accounted for 11.84% of the relationship.

Table 4.7: Distribution of Agricultural Co-operative Loan by Farmer: 2008-2013

Year	Frequency (#10,000)	Percentage (%)
2008	67	12.41
2009	154	28.52
2010	156	28.89
2011	64	11.85
2012	37	6.85
2013	62	11.48
Total	**540**	**100**

Source: Field survey, 2014.

Result in Table 4.7 reveals that majority (57.41%) of the loan were given between 2009 to 2010 years. Average of #900,000 per year was received as loan by these farmers from co-operative society. This indicates non-reliability of farmers on co-operatives as source of loan/credit to finance their agricultural activities.

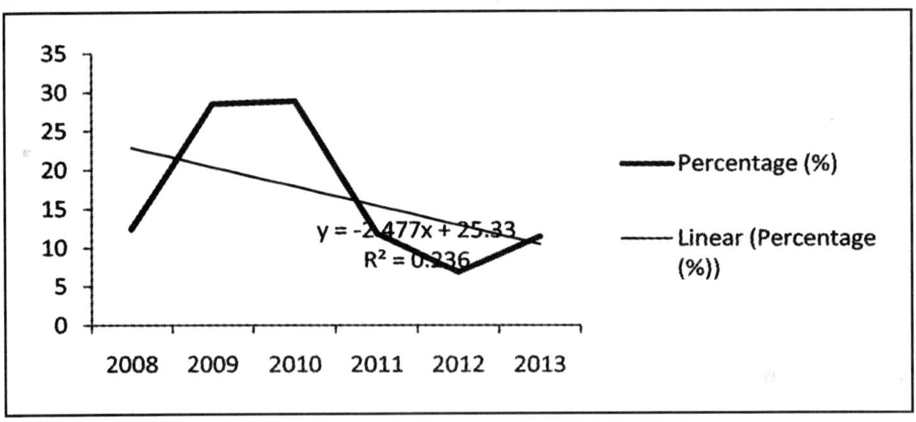

Fig. 4.5: Co-operative Loan to Farmers in Imo State: 2008-2013

Result of the trend analysis revealed that the rate of loan received from co-operatives decreases by #2.48 per unit of time. The coefficient of determination (R^2) is 0.2363, implying that the model accounted for 23.63% of the relationship.

CONCLUSION

Majority of the farmers are adult males, experienced with household size of 7, trading and farming as their major occupations. Cassava is the most dominant crop grown in the area. Mean hectare of land, cost of labour and output are 0.92888ha, #127,177.20 and 12,107.35kg respectively. Mean revenue from sales is #273,453.20; average quantity of fertilizer used is 6.475bags, seed/seedling/stem is 101.8501kg and pesticides/herbicides is 2.453488litres. Average cost of fertilizer, seed/seedlings/stem and pesticides/ herbicides are #27,622.81, #10,185.01 and #31,888.62 respectively. Results revealed that 47% of the respondents are in partnership with family/friends with access to credit/loan (27.66%) and access to land (21.28%) as their major reasons. A total of 53% did not partner with family/friends with 62% of them not having reason to do so and 24.53% for lack of trust. A total of 54% are members of co-operative societies with 41% having to join for the purpose of accessing agricultural loan/credit while 56% have actually received loan from co-operatives. The study recommends efforts to boost trust amongst friends and relative to be emphasized with the aim of increasing access to land and farm inputs; co-operative societies in the area to intensify effort to source fertilizer and seed/seedlings/stem in other to boast production and measures for more favourable loan/credits from government agencies and financial institutions to farmers in the area.

REFERENCES

Adejoh, S.D. (2009). "Analysis of Production Efficiency and Profitability of Yam-Based Production Systems in Ijunmu LGA Of Kogi State." Msc Thesis Department of Agricultural Economics and Extension, Ahmadu-Bello University, Zaria.

Adewuyi, S.A. (2006). "Resource Use Productivity of Rural Farmers in Kwara State, Nigeria." *International Journal of Agricultural Sciences, Sciences, Environment and Technology* 1(1).

Adewuyi, S.A. (2002). "Resource Use Productivity in Food Crop Production in Kwara State, Nigeria." Ph.D. Thesis Department of Agricultural Economics University of Ibadan, Ibadan.

Adler, P. and Kwon, W.S. (2002): Social Capital: Prospects for a New Concept. *Academy of Management Review*, 27(1): 17-40.

Ajani, O.I.Y. (2000). "Resource Productivity in Food Crop Farming in the Northern Area of Oyo State, Nigeria." Phd Thesis, Department of Agricultural Economics University of Ibadan, Ibadan.

Ajibolade, E.O. (2005). "Effects of Land Acquisition for Large Scale Farming on the Productivity of Small Scale Farming in Okitipupa, LGA, Ondo State." Master's Thesis, Department of Agricultural Economics And Extension, FUTA, Akure.

Akintayo, O.I. (2011). "Output Differentials, Total Factor Productivity and Factor Use Intensity in Rain-Fed Rice Production Systems in Ekiti and Niger States." Ph.D., 2nd Seminar Presentation, Department of Agricultural Economics University of Ibadan, Ibadan.

Anisude, G. (2010). "Access and Utilization of Social Capital in Anaocha LGA Of Anambra State, Nigeria." Bsc Thesis, Department of Agricultural Economics, EBSU, Abakaliki.

Astone, N.M., and McLanahan, S.S. (1991). Family Structure, Parental Practices, and High School Completion. *American Sociological Review*. 56: 309-320.

Baranyai Zs. -Béres D. -Szabó G. G. -Vásáry M. -Takács I. (2011): Factors of Trust in Machinery Sharing Arrangements. ANNALS of the Polish Association of Agricultural and Agribusiness Economists. Vol. XIII. No. 6. 18-22 pp. (Angol és lengyel nyelvû összefoglalóval.) ISSN 1508-3535.

Baranyai Zsolt, Náar Zsuzsanna Toth and Farkas Maria Fekete (2011). Role of Trust in Building Social Capital and Rural Development. *International Journal of Social Sciences and Humanity Studies.* Vol. 3, No 2, 2011 ISSN: 1309-8063 (Online)

Bylok F. (2010). Social Capital as a Factor in the Development of a Business Cluster, In: Bylok F. and Cichoblazinski L., *Humanization of Work and Modern Tendencies in Management.* Czestochowa. pp. 184-199.

Chukwukere, N.S. (2013). Major Factors Affecting the Use of Fertilizer by Rice Farmers in Imo State, Nigeria. Vol. 2 No. 2; February 2013. Esxpublishers.

Claridge, T. (2004). 'Social Capital and Natural Resource Managment'. Unpublished Thesis, University of Queensland, Brisbane, Australia. Brisbane, Australia: University of Queensland.

Coleman, J.S. (1988). "Social Capital in the Creation of Human Capital." *The American Journal of Sociology* 94: 95-120.

Cote S. and Healy, T. (2001).The Well Being of Nations. "The Role of Human and Social Capital". Organisation for Economic Cooperation and Development, Paris.

David, H.D., S. Abdurrahman, R.M Sani, S. Kushwaha, and Nasiru, M. (2009). "Resource Use Efficiency in Irrigated Crop Production by Fadama Users in Bauchi State, Nigeria: Implication For Food Security and Poverty Alleviation." In *Sustaining Agricultural Growth toMeet National Economic Development Goal.* Proceedings of the 23rd Annual Conference of the Farm Management Association of Nigeria, FAMAN.

Egwuda, Joseph Ekwute. (2001). Economic Analysis of Lowland Rice Production in Ibaji LGA of Kogi State. Msc thesis, Department of Agricultural Economics and Extension, Ahmadu- Bello University, Zaria.

Ekunwe, P.A., S.I. Orewa, and C.A. Emokaro. (2008). "Resource Use Efficiency In Yam Production in Delta and Kogi States of Nigeria." *Asian Journal of Agricultural Research* 2(2).

Foley, Michael W. and Bob Edwards (1997). Editors' Introduction: Escape from Politics? Social Theory and the Social Capital Debate. *American Behavioural Scientist* 40 (5): 550-561.

Fukuyama, Francis. (1995). *Trust: The Social Virtues and the Creation of Prosperity.* London:Hamish Hamilton.

Fulginiti, LE, Perrin, R.K. (1998). Agricultural Productivity in Developing Countries. Department of Agricultural Economics, University of Nebraska, Lincoln, USA.

Grootaert, C. (1998). Social Capital: The Missing Link? Social Capital Initiative Working Paper 3/1998. Washington DC, USA: The World Bank.

Grootaert, C., D. Narayan, V.N. Jones, and M. Woolcock. (2003). Measuring Social Capital – An Integrated Questionnaire. World Bank Working Paper 18/2003. Washington DC, USA: The World Bank.

Grootaert, C., G.T. OH, and A. Swamy. (2002). Social Capital, Household Welfare and Poverty in Burkina Faso. *Journal of African Economies* 11 (1): 4-38.

Grootaert, Christiaan, and Deepa Narayan. (2000). "Local Institutions, Poverty, and Household Welfare in Bolivia." Local Level Institutions Working Paper 9. World Bank, Social Development Department, Washington D.C

Ha, N.V., S. Kant, and V. Maclaren. (2004). The Contribution of Social Capital to Household Welfare in a Paper-recycling Craft Village in Vietnam. *Journal of Environment and Development* 13 (4): 371-399.

Haruna, B., U.B. Kyiogwam, I.D. Senchi, and A. Singh. (2009). "Resource Use Efficiency in Cotton Production in Selected Local Government Areas of Zamfara State." In *Sustaining Agricultural Growth to Meet National Economic Development Goal.* Proceedings of the 23rd Annual Conference of the Farm Management Association of Nigeria, FAMAN.

Idiong, I.C., D.I. Agom, E.O. Effiong, and S.B. Ohen. (2009). "Analysis of Technical And Economic Efficiencies in Rice Production Systems in The Niger Delta Region of Nigeria." In *Sustaining Agricultural Growth to Meet National Economic Development Goal.* Proceedings of the 23rd Annual Conference of the Farm Management Association of Nigeria, FAMAN.

Idumah, F.O. (2006). "Productivity Differentials Among Food Crop Farmers in the Niger Delta." Ph.D., Thesis, Department of Agricultural Economics, University of Ibadan, Ibadan.

Kaschula, SA (2008) Wild Foods and Household Food Security Responses to AIDS: Evidence from South Africa. *Population and Environment,* 29: 162-185.

Keskin, S. (2011), Social Networks, Innovations and Nations, *International Journal of Business and Management Studies,* Vol. 3., No. 1. ISSN 1309-8047. (online).

Lenis SL, Kuku, O and Ajibola A (2011). A Review of Literature on Agricultural Productivity, Social Capital and Food Security in Nigeria. International Food Policy Research Institution. Nigeria Strategy Support Programme (NSSP) NSSP Working Paper No. 21.

Mtika, M. (2001). The AIDs Epidemic in Malawi and its Threat to Household Food Security. *Human Organization,* 60: 178-188.

Muga, G. and Onyango-Ouma, W.(2009). Changing Household Composition and Food Security Among The Elderly Caretakers in Rural Western Kenya. *Journal of Cross Cultural Genrontology,* 24: 259-272.

Muhammad-Lawal, A. and O.A. Atte. (2006). "An Analysis of Agricultural Production in Nigeria." *African Journal of General Agriculture* 2(1).

NARAYAN, D. (1999). Bonds and Bridges: Social Capital and Poverty. Policy Research Working Paper 2167/1999. Washington DC, USA: The World Bank.

Ogundari, Kolawole. (2006). "Economic Efficiency of Food Crop Production in Ondo State of Nigeria." Msc Thesis, Department of Agricultural Economics and Extension, FUTA, Akure.

Ojo, A. (2005). "Economic Analysis of Irish Potato Production Innovations Among Contact Farmers In Plateau State." M.sc., Thesis, Department of Agricultural Economics and Extension, Ahmadu-Bello University, Zaria.

Oladeebo, J.O. 2006. "Economic Efficiency of Rain-Fed Upland Rice Production in Osun and Oyo States Of Nigeria." Ph.D., Thesis Department of Agricultural Economics and Extension, FUTA, Akure.

Olayide S,O and Heady E,O (1982). *Introduction to Agricultural Production Economics.* University Press, Ibadan.

Oluwatosin, F.M. (2011). "Measuring Technical Efficiency of Yam Farmers in Nigeria: A Stochastic Parametric Approach." *Agricultural Journals* 6(2).

Oni, O., J. Pender, D. Phillips, and E. Kato. (2009). Trends and Drivers of Agricultural Productivity in Nigeria. Nigeria Strategy Support Programme (NSSP) Report 001: IFPRI.

Onyemauwa, C., Eze C., Emenyonu A., Osugiri I, Nnadi N., and Tasie, C. (2013). Resource Use Efficiency and Productivity of Food Cropfarmers in Idemili North of Anambra state Nigeria. *Woodpecker Journal of Agricultural Research.* Vol. 2(2), pp 043-048, February, 2013.

Ostrom, Elinor. (1990). Governing the Commons: The Evolution of Institutions for Collective Action.New York: Cambridge University Press.

Oviasogie, D.I. (2005). "Productivity of Yam-Based Farming System in Edo State, Nigeria."Msc Thesis, Department of Agricultural Economics, FUTA, Akure.

Putnam, R.D. (2000). *Bowling Alone: The Collapse and Revival of American Community.* New York: Simon and Schuster.

Putnam, Robert D (1995): Bowling Alone: America's Declining Social Capital. *Journal of Democracy* Vol. 6 (1995) 1, 64-78.

Putnam, Robert D., Leonardi, Robert and Raffaella Y. Nanetti. (1993). *Making Democracy Work: Civic Traditions in Modern Italy.* Princeton: Princeton University Press.

Robison, Lindon J.,A.Allan Schmid, and Marcelo E. Siles.(2002)."Is Social Capital Really Capital?" *Review of Social Economy* 60: 1-24.

Shehu, J.F., J.T. Iyortyer, S.I. Mshelia, and A.A.U. Jongur. (2010). "Determinants of Yam Productivity and Technical Efficiency Among Yam Farmers in Benue State Nigeria." *Journalof Social Science* 24(2).

Thomas, D., Frankenberg, E. and Smith, J.P. (2001) 'Lost but Not Forgotten: Attrition and Follow-up in the Indonesia Family Life Survey.' *Journal of Human Resources.* 36(3): 556-592.

Tömpe, F. (2008): Assessing the Magnitude of Social Capital in Hungarian Farming Enterprises and its Relations to Some of Their Features. In: I. Szûcs. and M. Farkas Fekete (eds.), *Hatékonysága mezõgazdaságban (Efficiency in agriculture) (Elmélet és gyakorlat [Theory and Practice])*, Budapest: Agroinform Publisher, 95-104.

Wilfred Dolfsma and Charlie Dannreuther (2003). Globalization, Social Capital and Inequality: Contested Concepts, Contested Experiences. In Association with the European Association for Evolutionary Political Economy (EAEPE) 2003 200pp Hardback 9781840645149 ebook isbn 9781781950029.

Yaro, Muhammed Abdu. (1999). "Economic Analysis of Groundnut Production in Dambatta LGA of Kano State". MSc Project at Agricultural-Economics and Extension Department, Ahmadu-Bello University, Zaria.

Pages: 61-72

AGRICULTURE DEVELOPMENT AND SUSTAINABLE ENVIRONMENT

Edited by: Jaswant Ray; Dr. Pawan Kumar 'Bharti'

ISBN: 978-93-5056-759-3

Edition: 2015

Published by: Discovery Publishing House Pvt. Ltd., New Delhi (India)

5

Inhibition Effect of Clindamycin on the Corrosion of Zinc in tetraoxosulphate (vi) Acid Medium

E.C. Ogoko[1*], Osu Charles I.[2], A.O. Ogunsipe[1]

ABSTRACT

The corrosion inhibition of zinc by clindamycin, an antibacterial drug has been investigated using weight loss method. The results obtained indicate that clindamycin is good inhibitor for the corrosion of zinc in 0.001 to 0.04M tetraoxosulphate (vi) acid medium. The inhibition efficiency increased with increase in inhibitors concentration. Thermodynamic and adsorption parameters were determined and discussed. The absorption of clindamycin on Zn surfaceis endothermic, spontaneous, and is best described by Langmuir adsorption isotherm. The calculated values of activation energies and free energies of adsorption indicate that the adsorption process supports the mechanism of physical absorption.

Key words: Corrosion, inhibition, zinc, clindamycin, H_2SO_4

INTRODUCTION

Corrosion is the gradual destruction of materials especially metals by chemical reaction with its environment. Zinc is a metal which is often

1 Department of Chemistry, National Open University of Nigeria, Lagos, Nigeria.

2 Department of Pure and Industrial Chemistry, University of Port Harcourt, Nigeria.

destroyed by contact with aggressive media such as bases, acids and salt solutions. The zinc metal is used in the corrosion protection of steel and the study of corrosion protection of zinc and its inhibition is a subject of practical significant (Ogoko et al., 2009; Odoemelam et al., 2009; Eddy et al., 2010). Treatment of zinc with acidic solutions cannot be completely avoided and is necessary for scale removal and cleaning of zinc surfaces, hence, the use of inhibitors.

Several researchers in the literature studied the corrosion inhibition of Zn in acidic solutions using organic compounds containing hetero atoms (N,O,S, or P) and centers for Π-electron in their aromatic or long carbon chain system.These inhibitors includes, quinoline, epheridrine, brucine, piperazine, caffine, barbitone, aniline, narcotine, azithromycin, clarithromycin, erythromycin, lincomycin and pyridine derivatives. The presence of hetero atom orpi-electron provides electrons which enhances adsorption of inhibitors on the surface of metals.Several eco-friendly inhibitors which are extracts from naturally occurring plants proved very effective as corrosion inhibitors for metals (Abiola et al., 2007; Arora et al., 2007; Chauhara and Gunasekara, 2006; James et al., 2006; Rjappa et. al., 2008).

However, the use of clindamycin as corrosion inhibitor for zinc has not been reported in the literature by researchers. The inhihition potentials of clindamycin for the corrosion of zinc in H_2SO_4 are investigated by this study. Clindamycin is a lincosamide antibiotics usually used to treat infections with anaerobic bacteria and some protozoa diseases, such as malaria (Daum 2007). The IUPAC name of clindamycin is (methyl 7-chloro-6, 7, 8-trideoxy-6-{[(4*R*)-1-methyl-4-propyl-L-prolyl]amino}-1-thio-L-threo-α-D-galacto-octopyranoside).The compound has a molar mass of 424.98g/mol, and molecular formula of $C_{18}H_{33}ClN_2O_5S$,and its structural formula is as shown in Fig. 5.1.

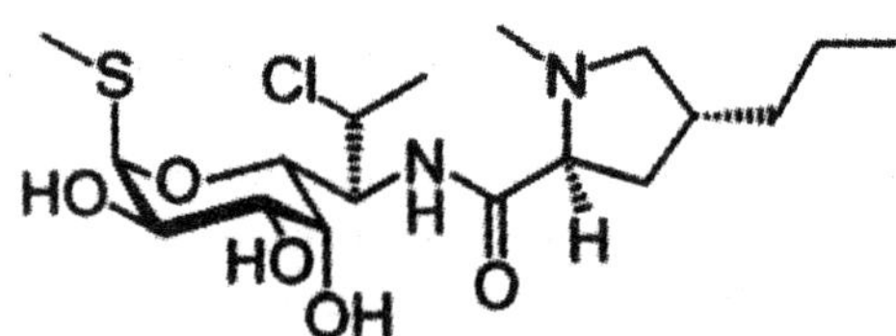

Fig. 5.1: Chemical Structure of Clindamycin

It is apparently clear from the above chemical structure that clindamycin has some functional groups and hetero atoms (O, N, and S) in its structure that may facilitate its adsorption on zinc surface.

EXPERIMENTAL DETAILS

Materials

The material used for this study was zinc sheet of composition (w %); Pb (0.001), Fe (0.002), Cd (0.001), Cu (0.003) and the remaining, zinc. Initially, the sample was mechanically pressed cut into different coupons, each of dimension, 5 × 4 cm. Each coupon was degreased by washing with ethanol, dipped in acetone and allowed to dry in air before it is preserved indesiccators. All reagents used in this study were Analar grade and double distilled water was used for the preparation.

The inhibitor used (clindamycin) was supplied by RUFUS OBI Pharmaceutical Company, Aba, Abia State, Nigeria, and was used without further purification. The concentration range used for the inhibitor (clindamycin) was 0.0001 to 0.0004M.

Gravimetric Method

In the weight loss experiment, the pre-cleaned coupon was dipped in 200mL of the test solution maintained at 303K in a thermostated bath. The weight loss was determined by retrieving the coupons at 24 h intervals progressively for 168 h (7 days). Prior to measurement, each coupon was washed in 5% chromic acid solution (containing 1% silver nitrate) and rinsed in deoxidized water. Thedifferences in weight were taken as the weight loss of zinc. The experiments were also carried out at 313 and 323 K, as described above.

From the weight loss measurements, the inhibition efficiency (%I) of the inhibitor, degree of surface coverage (θ) and the corrosion rate (CR) of zinc were calculated using equations 1, 2and 3, respectively.

$$\%I = (1 - W_1/W_2) \times 100 \quad (1)$$

$$\theta = \%I/100 \quad (2)$$

$$CR = W/At \quad (3)$$

Where,

W_1 and W_2 are the weight losses (in g) for zinc in the presence and absence of inhibitor in H_2SO_4 solution, θ is the degree of surface coverage of the inhibitor, A is the area of the zinc coupon (in cm^2), t is the period of immersion (in hours), W is the weight loss of zinc after time t, and CR is the corrosion rate of zinc in $gh^{-1}cm^{-2}$.

RESULTS AND DISCUSSION

Effect of Concentration of Clindamycin/H_2SO_4 on Zinc Corrosion

Figures 5.2a to 5.2c show the variation of weight loss with time for the corrosion of zinc in 0.01M H_2SO_4 containing various concentrations of clindamycin at 303, 313 and 323K, respectively. The figures revealed that the rate of corrosion of zinc increases with increase in temperature. The weight losses of zinc for the blank solutions were higher than those obtained for solution containing various concentrations of clindamycin. The plots is also indicative that weight loss of zinc decreases with increasing concentration of clindamycin, but increases with increase in temperature. The variation of weight losses of zinc in 0.02, 0.03 and 0.04M H_2SO_4 solution, containing various concentration of clindamycin, were found to follow patterns similar to those obtained for 0.01MH_2SO_4(plots not shown).

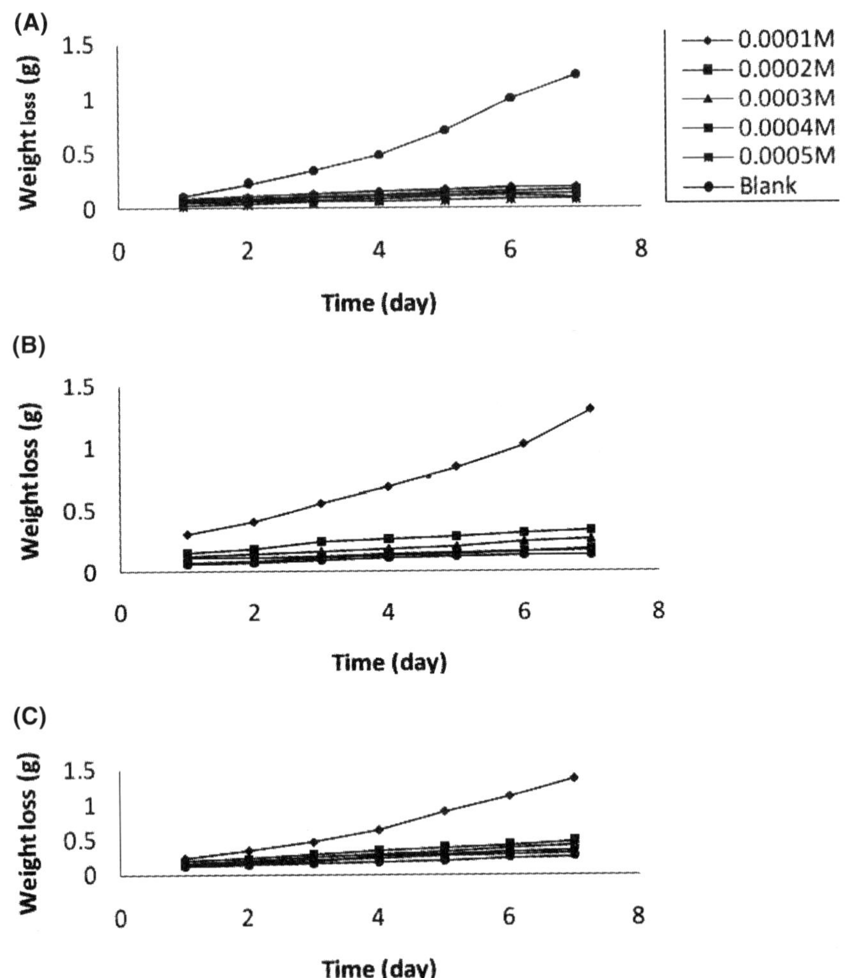

Fig. 5.2: Variation of Weight Loss with Time for the Corrosion of Zn in 0.01M H_2SO_4 Containing Various Concentrations of Clindamycin at (a) 303K, (b) 313K, and (c) 323K

Values of inhibition efficiency of clindamycin and the corrosion rates of zinc in various concentrations H_2SO_4 of are presented in Table 5.1. The table portrays that the corrosion rate of zinc increases with increase in temperature and with increasing concentration of H_2SO_4. From the table, results indicate that the inhibition efficiency increases with increase in concentration of clindamycin, but decreases with increase in temperature.

Table 5.1: Corrosion Rates (in $gcm^{-2}\ h^{-1}$) of Zinc and Inhibition Efficiencies (%) of Clindamycin (clin) in Various Concentrations of H_2SO_4

Systems	Corrosion Rate x 10^{-4} ($gcm^{-2}\ h^{-1}$)			Inhibition Efficiency (%)		
	303K	313K	323K	303K	313K	323K
0.01M H_2SO_4	3.61	3.87	4.08	-	-	-
$1x10^{-4}$M Clin + 0.01M H_2SO_4	0.57	1.01	1.43	66.94	51.54	37.96
$2x10^{-4}$M Clin + 0.01M H_2SO_4	0.51	0.87	1.22	68.60	56.92	43.07
$3x10^{-4}$M Clin + 0.01M H_2SO_4	0.39	0.68	1.04	71.90	63.08	47.45
$4x10^{-4}$M Clin + 0.01M H_2SO_4	0.30	0.56	0.93	74.38	65.35	50.36
$5x10^{-4}$M Clin + 0.01M H_2SO_4	0.28	0.51	0.77	76.03	68.51	54.01
0.02M H_2SO_4	3.93	4.44	4.61	-	-	-
$1x10^{-4}$M Clin + 0.02M H_2SO_4	0.68	0.95	1.52	59.85	53.69	32.89
$2x10^{-4}$M Clin + 0.02M H_2SO_4	0.54	0.77	1.28	62.12	54.36	38.26
$3x10^{-4}$M Clin + 0.02M H_2SO_4	0.45	0.65	1.07	64.39	56.38	42.95
$4x10^{-4}$M Clin + 0.02M H_2SO_4	0.33	0.48	0.75	67.42	57.01	50.33
$5x10^{-4}$M Clin + 0.02M H_2SO_4	0.27	0.39	0.66	68.94	58.39	52.35
0.03M H_2SO_4	4.32	4.64	4.94	-	-	-
$1x10^{-4}$M Clin + 0.03M H_2SO_4	0.82	0.98	1.46	50.71	50.64	31.88
$2x10^{-4}$M Clin + 0.03M H_2SO_4	0.75	0.87	1.22	53.71	51.28	36.88
$3x10^{-4}$M Clin + 0.03M H_2SO_4	0.72	0.81	1.04	54.29	51.92	40.63
$4x10^{-4}$M Clin + 0.03M H_2SO_4	0.60	0.65	0.71	57.14	53.85	47.51
$5x10^{-4}$M Clin + 0.03M H_2SO_4	0.45	0.53	0.63	60.71	54.49	50.10
0.04M H_2SO_4	5.15	6.55	6.88	-	-	-
$1x10^{-4}$M Clin + 0.04M H_2SO_4	0.62	0.69	0.75	51.03	42.63	38.46
$2x10^{-4}$M Clin + 0.04M H_2SO_4	0.60	0.67	0.74	51.72	43.46	38.97
$3x10^{-4}$M Clin + 0.04M H_2SO_4	0.55	0.62	0.69	53.12	43.97	39.49
$4x10^{-4}$M Clin + 0.04M H_2SO_4	0.50	0.57	0.61	54.48	44.51	41.03
$5x10^{-4}$M Clin + 0.04M H_2SO_4	0.42	0.46	0.48	57.93	45.03	43.08

Effect of Temperature

The activation energy for the corrosion of Zinc in the absence and presence of clindamycin was estimated using Arrhenius equation shown as follow:

$$CR = A\exp(-E_a/RT) \quad (4)$$

Where CR is the corrosion rate of zinc, A is the pre-exponential factor E_a is the activation energy, R is the gas constant.

The Arrhenius plots for the corrosion of zinc in 0.01 to 0.04M H_2SO_4 containing various concentrations of clindamycin are presented in Fig. 5.3a to 5.3d. The values of Arrhenius parameters realized from the plots are presented in Table 5.2.

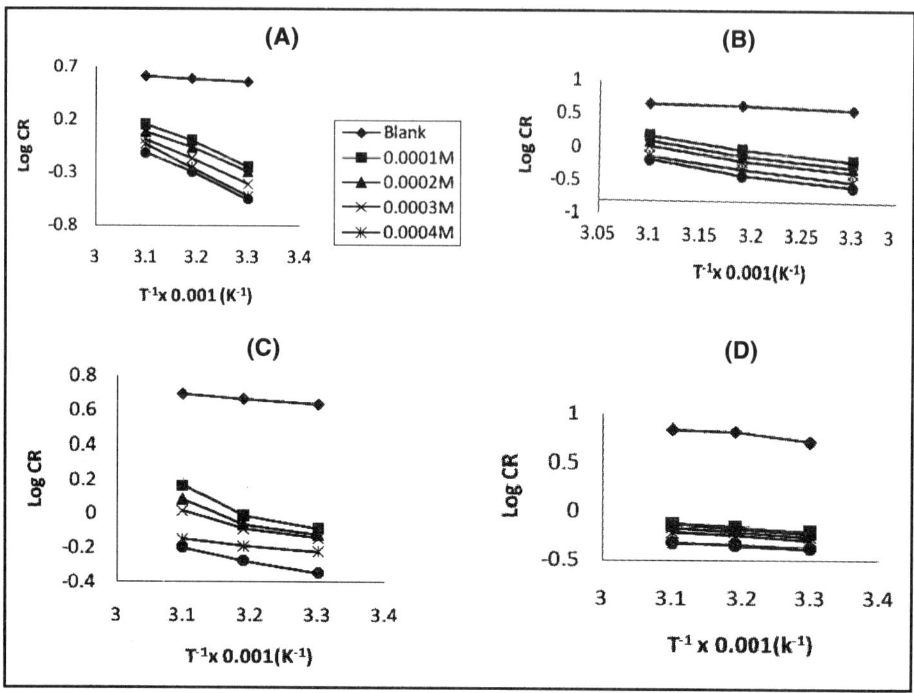

Fig. 5.3: Variation of LogCR with 1/T for the Inhibition of Zinc Corrosion [in (a) 0.01M, (b) 0.02 M, (c) 0.03 M, (d) 0.04 M H_2SO_4] by Clindamycin

Table 5.2: Thermodynamic Parameters for the Inhibition of the Corrosion of Zinc by Various Concentrations of Clindamycin

C (M)	0.01 M H_2SO_4				
	E_a(J/mol)	R^2	ΔH_{ads} (J/mol)	DS_{ads} (J/mol)	R^{2*}
Blank	3.15	0.9532	-0.87	307.94	0.9943
0.0001	38.4	0.993	35.79	-131.38	0.991
0.0002	38.5	0.995	33.64	-139.42	0.994
0.0003	40.8	0.999	38.28	-126.82	0.999
0.0004	42.19	0.997	39.48	-125.16	0.998
0.0005	47.03	0.998	48.32	-108.75	0.996

(Table Contd...)

C (M)	0.02 M H_2SO_4				
	E_a(J/mol)	R^2	ΔH_{ads} (J/mol)	DS $_{ads}$ (J/mol)	R^{2*}
Blank	4.23	0.9835	-1.57	304.77	0.9005
0.0001	33.4	0.978	30.73	-147.08	0.976
0.0002	33.9	0.989	31.31	-151.11	0.972
0.0003	35.5	0.974	32.88	-141.89	0.975
0.0004	35.7	0.977	33.01	-142.98	0.989
0.0005	36.8	0.974	34.12	-143.58	0.971
C (M)	0.03 M H_2SO_4				
	E_a(J/mol)	R^2	ΔH_{ads} (J/mol)	DS $_{ads}$ (J/mol)	R^{2*}
Blank	4.09	0.9271	-1.44	90.31	0.6203
0.0001	23.5	0.925	20.85	-178.16	0.905
0.0002	19.9	0.912	17.19	-190.97	0.901
0.0003	15.1	0.934	12.41	-206.98	0.909
0.0004	13.9	0.993	11.24	-214.60	0.978
0.0005	6.95	0.997	4.27	-235.18	0.992
C (M)	0.04 M H_2SO_4				
	E_a(J/mol)	R^2	ΔH_{ads} (J/mol)	DS $_{ads}$ (J/mol)	R^{2*}
Blank	5.12	0.9951	-7.34	284.56	0.9913
0.0001	9.56	0.997	5.26	-231.64	0.999
0.0002	9.01	0.998	6.98	-226.99	0.989
0.0003	7.93	0.995	6.33	-288.41	0.998
0.0004	8.52	0.998	5.88	-231.32	0.985
0.0005	5.71	0.982	3.12	-2.41.92	0.919

The results depict that the activation energies of the blank solutions are lower than those obtained for solutions of H_2SO_4 containing various concentrations of clindamycin. This implies that clindamycin retarded the corrosion of zinc in H_2SO_4 solutions.

However, activation energies were found to increase as the concentration of the additive increases, indicating increasing ease of adsorption of clindamycin on zinc as concentration increases.

The values of activation energies are below the threshold value of 80KJ/mol required for chemical adsorption, indicating that the mechanism of adsorption of clindamycin on zinc surface is physical adsorption.

Thermodynamic/adsorption Consideration

The transition state equation (see equation 5) was used to calculate the thermodynamic parameters for the adsorption of clindamycin on the surface of zinc.

$$CR = R/Nh\exp(\Delta Sads/R)\exp(\Delta Hads/RT) \qquad (5)$$

Where CR is the corrosion rate of zinc, R is the gas constant, N is the Avogadro's number, h is the Planck constant, T is the temperature, "Δ_{ads} and ΔS_{ads} are the entropy and enthalpy of adsorption of clindamycin on zinc surface, respectively.

Therefore, a plot of log(CR/T) verses 1/T will yield a straight line with slope and intercept equal to $\Delta Hads/2.303R$ and $(\log(R/Nh) + \Delta Sads/2.303R)$, respectively. The transition state plots for the corrosion of zinc in 0.01 to 0.04M H_2SO_4 are shown in Figs. 5.4a to 5.4d.

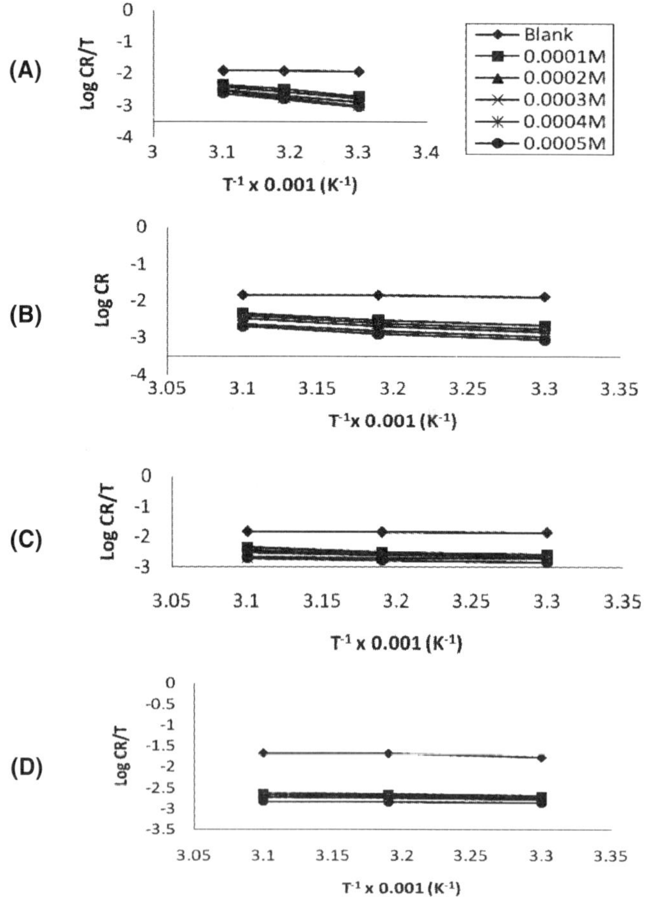

Fig. 5.4: Variation of Log(CR/T) with 1/T for the Inhibition of Zinc Corrosion [in (a) 0.01M, (b) 0.02 M, (c) 0.03 M, (d) 0.04 M H_2SO_4] by clindamycin

Similarly, values of ΔH_{ads} calculated from the slopes of lines on the transition state plots are presented in Table 5.2.

The values of ΔH_{ads} were positive indicating that the adsorption of clindamycin on zinc surface is endothermic. On the other hand, values of ΔS_{ads} calculated from the intercepts of lines on the transition state plots were negative and tend to increase with increasing concentration of clindamycin.This portrays that there is an increase in the degree of orderliness of the inhibitor's molecules.

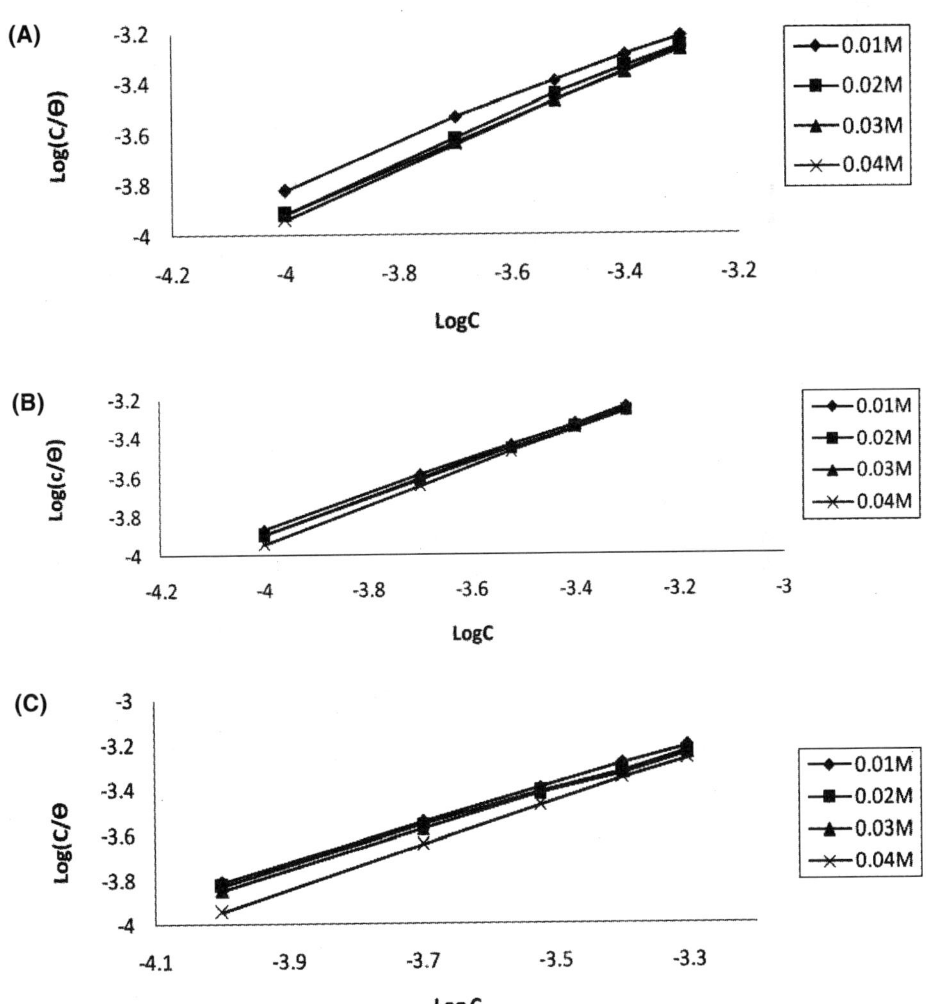

Fig. 5.5: Langmuir isotherm for the Adsorption of Clindamycin on Zinc Surface in Various Concentrations of H_2SO_4 at (a)303 K, (b) 313 K and (c) 323K

Data obtained for degree of surface coverage of the inhibitor were used to fit curves for different adsorption isotherm. Interestingly, the test reveals that the adsorption process can best be described by Langmuir adsorption isotherm. The assumptions establishing Langmuir adsorption isotherm can be expressed thus:

$$\text{Log}\ (C/\theta) = \text{Log}\ C - \log K \qquad (6)$$

Where C is the concentration (in moles/dm^3) of the inhibitor in the bulk electrolyte, θ is the degree of surface coverage of the inhibitor and K is the equilibrium constant of adsorption. The Langmuir isotherms for the adsorption of clindamycin on zinc surface were represented in Figs 5.5a to 5.5c. The values of Langmuir adsorption parameters obtained from the plots were presented in table 5.3.We can see that the slopes and R^2 values for the plots are very close to unity, which implies a strong adherence of the assumptions of Langmuir to experimental data.

Table 5.3: Langmuir Adsorption Parameters and Free Energies of Adsorption of Clindamycin on the Surface of Zinc

Temperature (K)	Concentration of H_2SO_4 =0.01M			
	slope	logK	ΔG_{ads}(KJ/mol)	R^2
303	0.872	0.332	-12.05	0.997
313	0.895	0.285	-12.16	0.999
323	0.865	0.348	-12.94	0.999
Temperature (K)	**Concentration of H_2SO_4 =0.02M**			
	slope	logK	ΔG_{ads}(KJ/mol)	R^2
303	0.957	0.081	-10.59	0.998
313	0.907	0.264	-12.04	0.999
323	0.841	0.453	-13.59	0.999
Temperature (K)	**Concentration of H_2SO_4 =0.03M**			
	slope	logK	ΔG_{ads}(KJ/mol)	R^2
303	0.925	0.212	-11.35	0.999
313	0.931	0.167	-11.46	0.999
323	0.862	0.390	-13.20	0.998
Temperature (K)	**Concentration of H_2SO_4 =0.04M**			
	slope	logK	ΔG_{ads}(KJ/mol)	R^2
303	0.973	0.043	-10.37	0.998
313	0.974	0.043	-10.71	0.999
323	0.975	0.044	-11.06	0.999

The equilibrium constant of adsorption (K) obtained from the intercepts of Langmuir adsorption is related to the free energy of adsorption (ΔGads) as follows:

$$\Delta Gads = 2.303RT \log (55.5K) \quad (7)$$

where,

55.5 is the molar concentration of the acid in the solution. The values of ΔG_{ads} calculated were presented in table 5.3.The values of ΔG_{ads} were negative, indicating that the inhibitor's molecules are strongly adsorbed on zinc surface. The values also suggest a spontaneous adsorption of inhibitor's molecules on zinc surface, which proceeded via the mechanism of physical adsorption (Eddy et al., 2008b, 2008c). The values of ΔG_{ads} obtained were below -40KJ/ mol (usually accepted as the threshold value between chemisorptions and physiosorption).

CONCLUSION

Clindamycin is a good inhibitor for corrosion of zinc in 0.01 to 0.004M H_2SO_4.The adsorption of clindamycin is spontaneous, endothermic and proceeded according to the mechanism of physical absorption. Therefore, we strongly recommend the use of clindamycin on industrial scale as inhibitor for the corrosion of zinc H_2SO_4.

REFERENCES

Abiola O.K, Oforka NC, Ebenso E.E, Nwinuka N.M (2007). Eco-friendly Corrosion Inhibitors: Inhibitive Action of Delonixregia Extract for the Corrosion of Aluminium in Acidic Medium. Anti-corrosion Methods Mater. 54(4): 219-224.

Arora, P.,Kumar, S., Sharma, M.K. and Mathur, S.P. (2007). Corrosion Inhibition by *Capparisdeciduas* in Acidic Media. E.J. Chem. 4(4): 450-456.

Chauhara L.R, Gunasekara G (2006). Corrosion Inhibition of Mild Steel in Hydrochloric Acid Solution by Zenthoxylumalatum Plant Extracts. J. Corrosion Sci. 17: 1016.

Daum R.S. (2007). "Clinical Practice. Skin and Soft-tissue Infections Caused by Methicillin-resistant Staphylococcus Aureus". *N Engl J Med* 357 (4): 380-90.

Eddy N.O, Ebenso E.E (2008). Adsorption and Inhibitive Properties of Ethanol Extracts of *Musa sapientum* Peels as a Green Corrosion Inhibitor for Mild Steel in H2SO4. J. Pure Appl. Chem. 2(6): 46-54.

Eddy N.O, Odoemelam SA, Akpanudoh NW (2008b). Synergistic Effect of Amoxicillin and Halides on the Inhibition of the Corrosion of Mild Steel in H2SO4. Research J. Pure Appl. Sci. 4(12): 1963-1973.

Eddy N.O, Odoemelam SA, Mbaba AJ (2008c). Inhibition of the Corrosion of Mild Steel in HCl by Sparfloxacin.Afri. J. Pure Appl. Chem. 2(12): 132-138.

Eddy N.O., Odoemelam S.A., Ogoko E.C, Ita B.I (2010). Adsorption and Inhibitive Properties of Lincomycin for the Corrosion of Zn in 0.01 to 0.05M H_2SO_4. *Portugaliaeelectrochimica* acta. 28(2): 73-85.

James A.O, Oforka N.C, Abiola O.K (2006). Inhibition of Aluminium (3SR) Corrosion in Hydrochloric Acid by Pyridoxol Hydrochloride. Bulletin of Electrochemistry 22: 111-116.

Odoemelam, S.A. and Eddy, N.O. (2008b). Sparfloxacin and Norfloxacin as Corrosion Inhibitors for Mild Steel: Kinetics, Thermodynamics and Adsorption Consideration. J. Mater. Sci. 4(1): 1-5.

Odoemelam S.A, Ogoko E.C, Ita B.I, Eddy N.O (2009). Inhibition of the Corrosion of Zinc in H_2SO_4 by 9-deoxy-9a-aza9a-methyl-9ahomoerythromycin A (azithromycin). *Portugaliaeelectrochimica* acta. 27(1): 57-68.

Oguzie, E.E.(2008). Corrosion Inhibitive Effect and Adsorption Behaviour of *Hibiscus Sabdariffa* Extract on Mild Steel in Acidic Media. Portug. Electrochem. Acta 26: 303-314.

Odiongenyi, A.O., Odoemelam S.A., Eddy N.O (2009). Corrosion Inhibition and Adsorption Properties of Ethanol Extract of Vernonia Amygdalina for the Corrosion of Mild Steel in H_2SO_4. *Portugaliaeelectrochimica* acta 27(1): 33-45.

Ogoko E.C, Odoemelam S.A., Ita B.I., Eddy N.O (2009).Adsorption and Inhibitive Properties of Clarithromycin for the Corrosion of Zn in 0.01 to 0.05M H_2SO_4. *Portugaliaeelectrochimica* acta. 27(6): 713-724.

S.K. Rajappa, T.V. Venkatesha, B.M. Praveen, *Bull. Mater. Sci.* 31 (2008) 37.

Rajappa, S.K., Venkatesha, T.V. and Praveen, B.M. (2008). Chemical Treatment of Zinc Sulphate and its Corrosion Inhibition Studies. Bull. Mater. Sci. 31(1): 37-41.

Umoren, S.A., Obot, I.B. and Ebenso, E.E. (2008a).Corrosion Inhibition of Aluminium Using Exudate gum from *Pachylobusedulis* in the Presence of Halide ions in HCl. E.J. Chem.. 5(2): 355-364.

Pages: 73-94

AGRICULTURE DEVELOPMENT AND SUSTAINABLE ENVIRONMENT

Edited by: Jaswant Ray; Dr. Pawan Kumar 'Bharti'

ISBN: 978-93-5056-759-3

Edition: 2015

Published by: Discovery Publishing House Pvt. Ltd., New Delhi (India)

Diversity of Vertebrates in the Campus of Institute for Social and Economic Change
A Conservation Case Study

Mahalakshmi, B.R.*[1], Imran Khan[2], Y.D and Sunil Nautiyal[2]

ABSTRACT

The faunal studies were undertaken to know the diversity and distribution of vertebrate fauna of ISEC (Institute of social and economic change). ISEC is an institute for interdisciplinary research and training in the social sciences, situated at Nagarabhavi, in the Bangalore city. The present study yields a total of 40 species of vertebrates in that 26 species of birds belonging to 20 families, 7 species of mammals belonging to 5 families, 6 species of reptiles belonging to 5 families and 1 amphibian species during a preliminary survey. Out of which birds are the most dominant in the study area because the study area comprises very good floral and faunal composition with good climatic conditions comparable to neighboring areas. The current documentation is based on field survey carried out in the campus of ISEC conducted from March and May 2013 by visual observation. Only exist species were recorded and listed. Frequency, density,

1 Department of Applied Zoology, Maharani's Science College for Women, Mysore - 570 005, Karnataka (India).

2 Centre for Ecological Economics and Natural Resources, Institute for Social and Economic Change, Bangalore - 560 072, Karnataka (India).

abundance and status of the species were done. The present study shows that a higher vertebrate diversity exists in ISEC and also provides an initial baseline of species for future research in this area. This study reveals that the academic institution play a significant role in conserving biodiversity.

Key words: ISEC, fauna, diversity, vertebrate, abundance.

INTRODUCTION

Vertebrates are the most advanced group of living organisms with backbones on earth. It includes fishes, amphibians, reptiles, mammals and birds. There are 62,305 species of vertebrates present in the world. India displays significant biodiversity. It is home to 11.7% of fishes, 4.4% of amphibians, 6.2% of reptilians, 12.6% of avians and 7.6% of all mammalian groups.

The study of vertebrate diversity is essential because they are important ecological indicators. (Alces, 2003) The role of vertebrates influence on ecosystem because they act as environmental engineers as well as ecological scavengers especially in flow of energy through food webs. (De Vault, T.L. 2003) They also impact on nutritional cycling. (Utpal Singha Roy, et.al 2012)They are essential tool for biological pest controllers. (Stebbins, R.C., et. al)

The aim of this paper is to provide baseline reference checklist of vertebrate faunal diversity (amphibians, reptiles, birds and mammals) of ISEC campus and also provides information to manage and monitor the vertebrate fauna in the study area.

STUDY AREA

This study was carried out in the ISEC campus. ISEC (Institute for Social and Economic Change) is the interdisciplinary Research and Training institute in Social sciences. It was established in 1972 by the late professor VKRV Rao at Nagarabhavi, in Bangalore, the capital of Karnataka state, is located nearby Bangalore University (Jnanabharati campus) and South - Western outskirts of city and lies between 12°57′19.6″ N and 77°30′55.2″ E and elevation of 920mts.

This institute campus covers an area of approximately 16 hectares geographical area comprising huge diversity of both flora and fauna with many different natural vegetation types include dry evergreen, scrubland, fruit trees, grasslands, open woodlands, dense forest with bushes forming a mixture of diverse habitats. This campus is home for more than 400 plant species including shrubs, grasses, orchids, trees and medicinal plants which provide food and shelter to the many faunal species. The institute campus is well maintained with sprawling gardens, lush green, lawns floral beds, huge trees with thick and dense canopy, lawns and a variety of flora and fauna. A small river vrushabavathi flows through behind ISEC. Now this river is highly polluted with sewage water.

OBSERVATION

The study sites were visited twice a day between morning 6.30-10.30 am and evening 4.00-6.30pm because those hours have remarkably less temperature and high humidity which is liked by vertebrates. Observations were made over a period of 3 months i.e., during March to May 2013.

LOCATION MAP OF INSTITUTE FOR SOCIAL AND ECONOMIC CHANGE

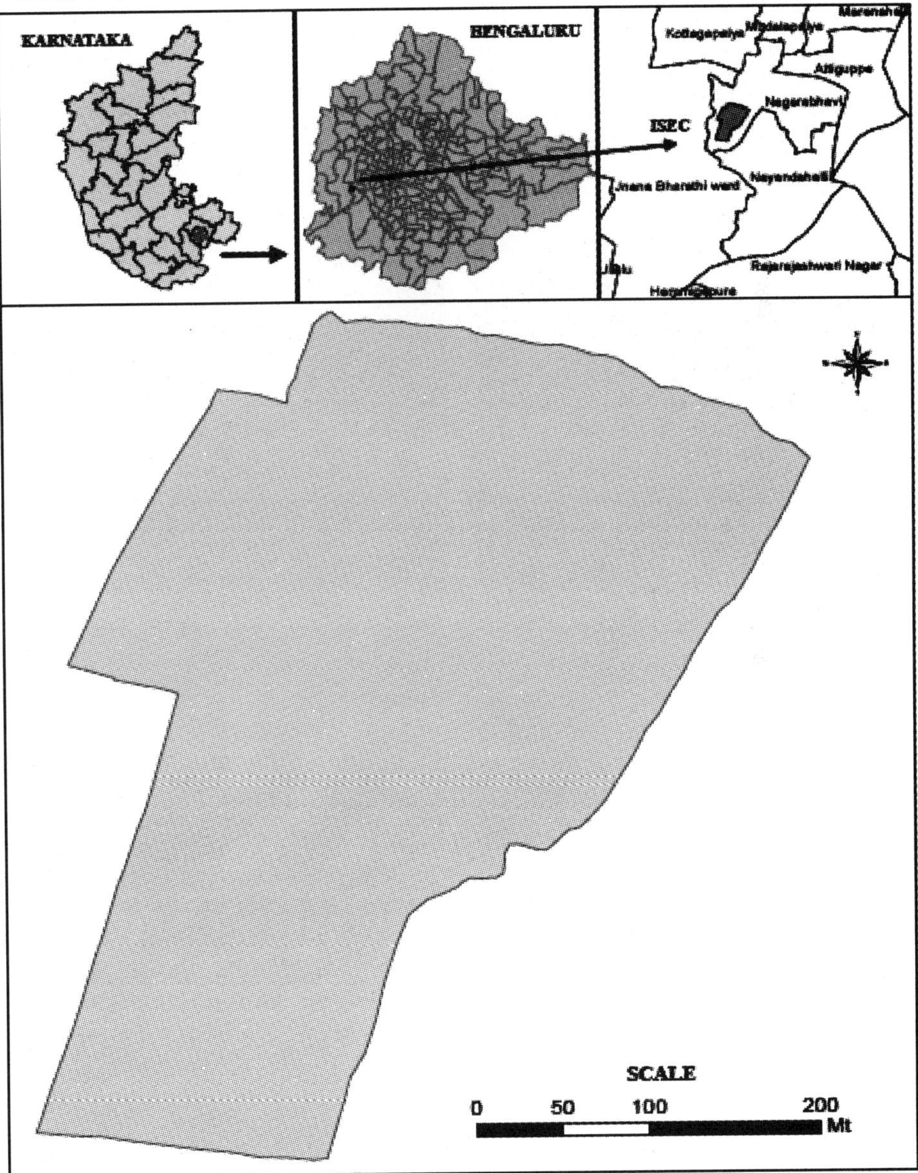

Fig. 6.1: Location of the Study Area

Fig. 6.1 (a)

Fig. 6.1 (b)

MATERIALS AND METHODS

Methodology

In this study we documented vertebrates (Amphibians, Reptiles, Birds and Mammals). For this study we followed different methods for different class of animals. These are the standard methods were suggested in protocols for surveying Flora and Fauna, which is developed by BRNS in 2009. For this sampling regular surveys were done by systematically walking on fixed routes through the study area. All vertebrates seen were recorded using a field data sheet along with the habitat type, frequency and abundance. According to the Indian Wildlife protection act (1972), we didn't collect any specimens for preservation only we have taken photographs and some are caught and identified there only by using field guides. After identification we left them into their natural habitats. And only those species with confirmed identify are reported in this paper. The checklist was prepared using standardized common names,scientific names, status and abundances and frequencies.

Methodology for Amphibians and Reptiles Documentation and Quantification

Amphibians and reptiles samplings were done in quadrate method (10m × 10m quadrates). Randomly we fixed quadrates in the study area and we quantified the species in that quadrates. Have been taken photographs of the species and some are identified there only by using field guides (Pictorial guide to Frogs and Toads of the Western Ghats by Guru Raja KV and Reptiles of India).

Methodology for Birds Documentation and Quantification

Birds can be sampled in two ways (1) Line transect method; and (2) Point count method.

We used Point count method for sampling birds. This point count method is most efficient method of estimating bird density. (Utpal Singha Roy, et.al 2012). In this point count method, observer will stand in one point randomly chosen and birds seen or heard 50m radius has to be recorded for 5 minutes. After this, 10 minutes gap should be given and then repeat observation. In one hour there will be four observations in each point. Again repeat this observation in another point. The gap between these points at least 300 meters must. Good photograph of birds were taken in the field survey. After that identification was done by using field guides.

Methodology for Mammals Documentation and Quantification

Transect method was used for mammals sampling. The entire procedure of transect method was performed by walking on local footpaths of the study area. The footpaths were monitored in morning and evening hours which generally coincide with maximum activity period of animals. Identified these mammalian species in their habitat using direct sighting and other evidences (foot prints, pellets and vocal sounds).

We have taken three variables for our study they are, Frequency, Density and Abundance. For calculating these variables we followed these formulae.

$$\text{Frequency: } \frac{\textit{Number of sampling units which a species occurs}}{\textit{Total number of sampling units studied}} \times 100$$

$$\text{Density: } \frac{\textit{Total number of individuals in all sampling units}}{\textit{Total number of sampling units studied}}$$

$$\text{Abundance: } \frac{\textit{Total number of individuals in all sampling units}}{\textit{Total number of sampling units of occurence}}$$

RESULTS AND DISCUSSION

This extensive survey of vertebrates was carried out for a period of 3 months i.e., March and May 2013. In this survey, 40 vertebrate species were found in ISEC campus that belongs to 16 orders and 31 families. Among the 40 species, one Amphibian (1 family), Six Reptiles (5 families), 26 birds (20 families) and Seven mammals (5 families) were identified (Figs. 6.1 & Fig. 6.2). Out of all species recorded, bird species were most dominant in the study area. The scientific names of the species along with their vernacular name, families and orders are listed in appendix 1.

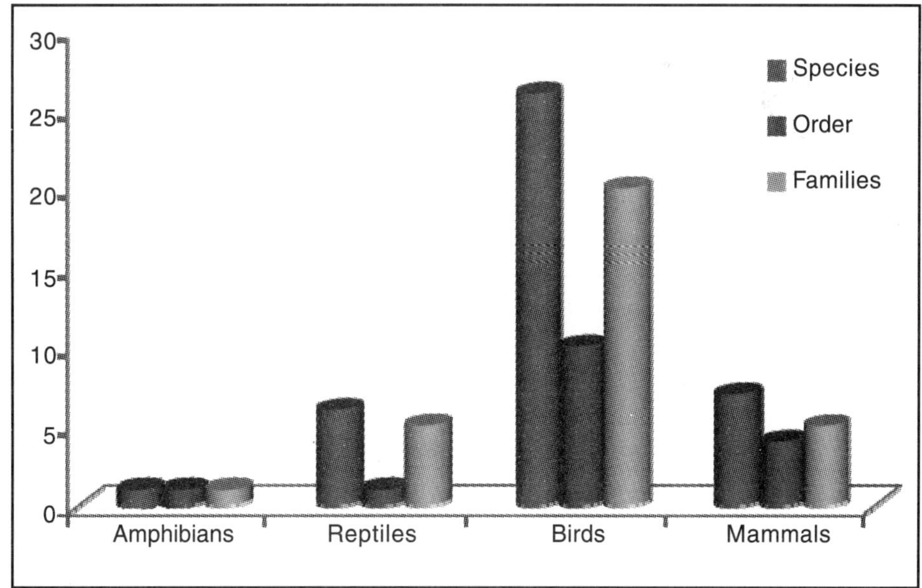

Fig. 6.2: Diversity of Vertebrates Along with Their Order and Families

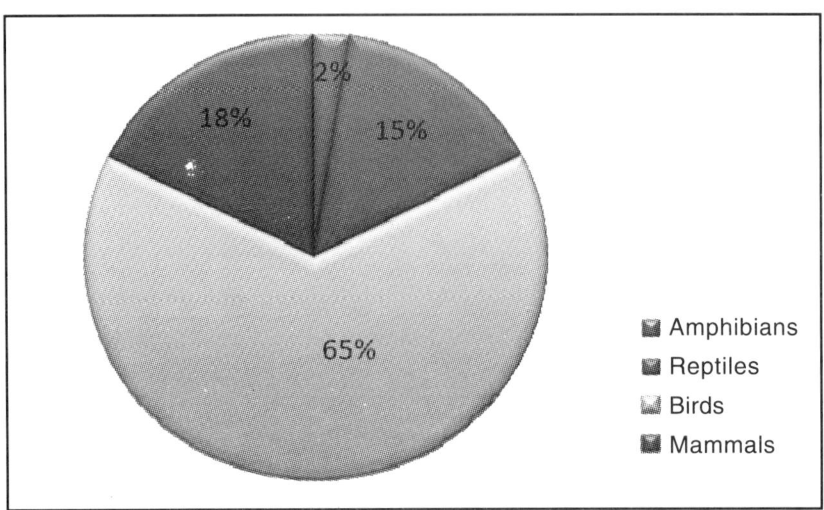

Fig. 6.3: Composition of Vertebrates in ISEC Campus

Amphibians and Reptiles

In this study, one amphibian species (*Duttaphrynus melanostictus* Schneider, 1799) i.e., common Indian toad was recorded. This species was found nearby wet places. This species is not listed in IWPA (Indian Wildlife Protection Act) and CITES (the Convention on International Trade in Endangered Species of Wild Fauna and Flora). According to IUCN (International Union for Conservation of Nature) this species was categorized under least concern status.

Total six Reptiles were recorded in ISEC campus during this study. Among them, Common house Gecko (*Hemidactylus frenatus* Dumeril & Bibron, 1836) is the most dominant species and Green vine snake (*Ahaetulla nasuta* Lacepede, 1789) is least dominant species in ISEC campus. Quantitative data (Density, Abundance and Frequency) on amphibians and reptiles from the study area are represented in the (Fig. 6.4) and listed in Appendix 2.

Out of the six species of reptiles, two are cited in CITES appendices and three species are listed under IWPA schedules. There is no threatened species according to IUCN red list category. All the details of species and their status (CITES, IWPA and IUCN) are given in appendix 5 & 6.

Birds

During the study period (March and April), 26 bird species belonging to 20 families were recorded. House crow (*Corvus splendens* Vieillot, 1817) is the most dominant species. Peafowl (*Pavo cristatus* Linnaeus, 1758) and white throated kingfisher (*Halcyon smyrnensis* Linnaeus, 1758) are the least dominant species in ISEC campus (Figure 6.5).

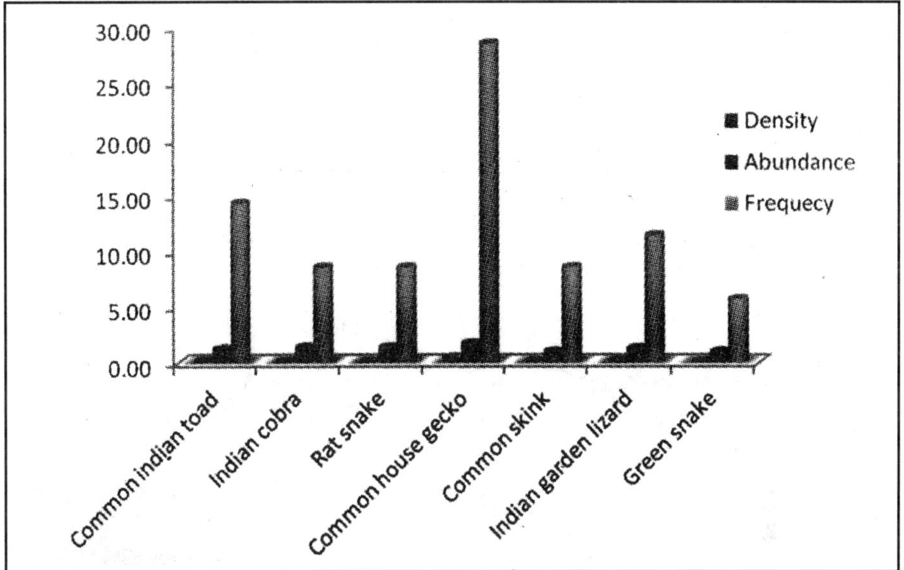

Fig. 6.4: Density, Abundance and Frequency of Amphibian and Reptiles

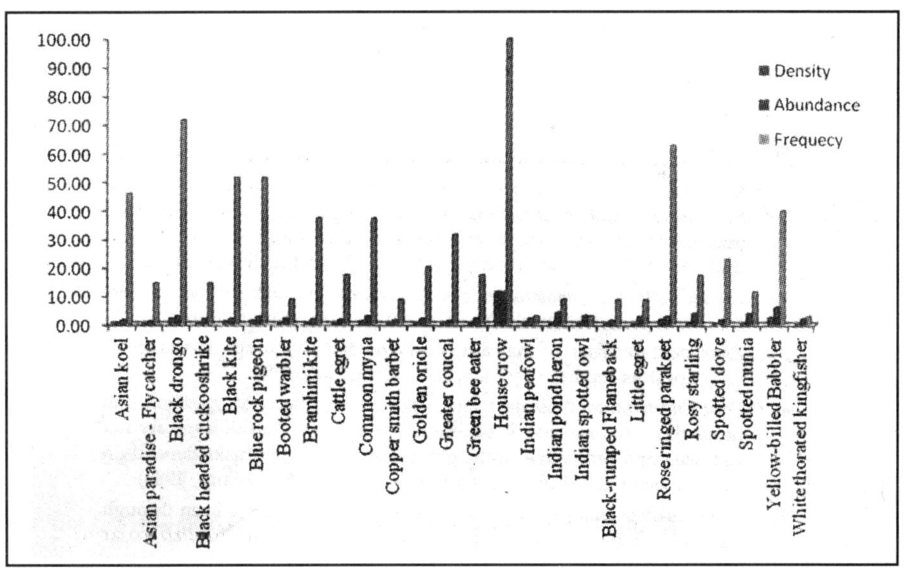

Fig. 6.5: Density, Abundance and Frequency of Birds

Quantitative data (Density, Abundance and Frequency) on birds from the study area are represented in the Figure 6.5 and listed in Appendix 3.

Among 26 bird species, two bird species are cited in CITES appendices. According to IWPA 23 bird species are listed in different Schedules. According to IUCN, there is no threatened bird species from the study area. The details of bird species and their status (CITES, IWPA and IUCN) are given in appendix 5 & 6.

Mammals

A total of seven mammal species were found in the study region and they belonging to four different orders and five families. Order wise analysis of the data revealed that order Muridae and Pteropodidae were represented by two species each whereas Leporidae, Herpestidae and Sciuridae were represented by one species each. The most dominant species is three striped palm squirrel (*Funambulus palmarum* Linnaeus, 1766) which belongs to family Sciuridae. Least dominant species is Indian black necked hare (*Lepus nigricollis* F.Cuvier, 1823) which belongs to family Leporidae.

Quantitative data (Density, Abundance and Frequency) on mammals from the study area are represented in the Figure 6.6 and listed in Appendix 4.

Among the seven mammalian species, two species are cited in CITES under different appendices. Of the two species, *Herpestes edwardsii* have been placed in app-III, and *Pteropus giganteus* have been kept under app-II. Out of a total of seven species, four species have been placed under different schedules of IWPA 1972. Four species namely *Mus musculus, Bandicota bengalensis, Pteropus giganteus* and *Cynopterus sphinx* have been kept under schedule –V. According to the global conservation status of the registered species, as per IUCN red list, all mammalian species from the study area are under least concerned category. The details of species and their status (CITES, IWPA and IUCN) are given in appendix 5 & 6.

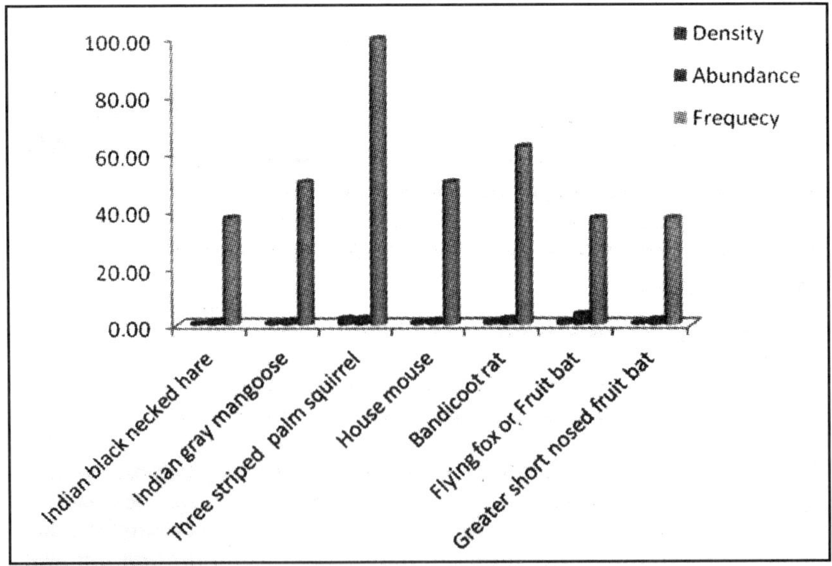

Fig. 6.6: Density, Abundance and Frequency of Mammals

The study area accommodates 0.74% of 135 species of amphibian diversity, 3.84% of 156 species of reptilian diversity, 4.61% of 563 species of bird diversity and 4% of 150 species of mammalian diversity of entire Karnataka state (Prajapati, R.C. 2010).

In the present study visibility of bird fauna was much better compared to other vertebrate. The rich diversity of the birds documented during present study may be because of adequate shelter, availability of varied sources of food as well as foraging. The high diversity of birds in this area is showed that this area is good habitats for birds. Among the 26 bird species; Ardeidae family birds were most common with 3 species. One possible reason for the availability of these bird species in the study area is the presence of Vrushabavathi Lake. House crow of Corvidae family is most abundant bird having high density and distributed throughout the study area because of abundant food source and safe habit.

Biodiversity is at the verge of extinction and also some species were extinct due to anthropogenic activities. It is our solemn duty to protect the precious beautiful gift of nature.

Today, conservation efforts are needed to protect biodiversity. The decline in the vertebrate population will greatly impact on the ecosystem that alters the food web and patterns of predation. The primary concern of conservation is to maintain balanced ecosystems, will provide greater chances to survival. Diversity is the most frequently adopted criterion for evaluating the conservation. Hence conservation is very important.

ISEC has been very cautious for conserving biodiversity.

Conservation measures followed at ISEC:

- Management of many local varieties of plants
- Protect the natural beauty
- Creating healthy environmental conditions
- Strict laws against deforestation
- Creating awareness
- Habitat preservation and restoration
- Proper protection and management of habitat
- Ceramic and clay water pots (size 2/3 feet) are arranged in the every 30 meters distance in ISEC campus for providing drinking water to birds, mammals etc.

Recommendation for further conservation

- To reduce the human interference to the maximum
- Periodic preparations of the checklist of the species and its comparison with the previous data collected.
- Conduct workshops and hands-on-training in taxonomy and field techniques.

- Initiate and encourage wide surveys.
- Identify threats and initiate action to address the issues that arise.
- Initiate programmes on conservation with assistance from relevant experts.
- Generate data that can be used to formulate conservation and management plans.
- Conduct awareness programmes on the importance of vertebrates.

Hence, this institution is rich in biodiversity and a good model for ex - situ conservation. Already several national, international, governments, nongovernmental organization and conservation groups work to protect vertebrates through protective areas, zoos and botanical garden by passing laws that preserve and restore the habitat and also a lot of work has been done in India on biodiversity conservation and most of the research data are available in website. However, only a few studies dealing with the biodiversity conservation in institution has been done. So, it can be suggested to the Government to provide space for the institutions that extend the interest in management of biodiversity, further leading to management and conservation of country's biodiversity.

CONCLUSION

From earlier days, Bangalore is considered as the Garden city because of its many beautiful parks, lakes, gardens and natural vegitations. But now a days, it is highly polluted city according to a report by the Centre for Science and Environment (CSE) due to loss of biodiversity caused by deforestation and exploitation of natural resources.

ISEC is the part of Bangalore, Hence this study report provides data on status and vertebrate diversity of ISEC would be useful for monitoring, protection and conservation of this area.

In Bangalore everyone should have to take ISEC as a role model for conserving biodiversity. Bangalore is going towards development with high speed in this busy life everyone forgotten about conserving biodiversity and importance of biodiversity in their lives. Must everyone should have to take initiate to conserve biodiversity in developing cities. The evaluation of the study area showed that the rich and undisturbed vertebrate diversity. This vertebrate diversity of ISEC campus reveals that academic institutions role in conservation. The results of this study have important implications for the assessment of biodiversity in institution. Considering this, it is recommended that this area should be added to the ecological institute. According to the results it could be concluded that ISEC has rich in biodiversity which has to be studied and we request government to declare ISEC as ecological institute to conserve vertebrate fauna. We believe that this checklist will serve as a baseline for assessing changes in species diversity and distribution.

Appendix 1: Check list of Vertebrates in ISEC campus

Sl.No.	Common Name	Scientific Name	Kannada Name	Order	Family
1.	Common indian toad	*Duttaphrynus melanostictus* (Schneider, 1799)	Kappe	Anura	Bufonidae
2.	Indian cobra	*Naja naja* (Linnaeus, 1758)	Nagara haavu	Squamata	Elapidae
3.	Rat snake	*Ptyas mucosus* (Linnaeus, 1758)	Kere haavu	Squamata	Colubridae
4.	Common house gecko	*Hemidactylus frenatus* (Dumeril & Bibron, 1836)	Halli	Squamata	Gekkonidae
5.	Common skink	*Mabuya carinata* (Schineides, 1801)	Haavurani	Squamata	Scincidae
6.	Indian garden lizard	*Calotes versicolor* (Daudin, 1812)	Uda	Squamata	Agamidae
7.	Green vine snake	*Ahaetulla nasuta* (Lacepede, 1789)	Neer haavu	Squamata	Colubridae
8.	Asian koel	*Eudynamys scolopacea* (Linnaeus, 1758)	Kogile	Cuculiformes	Cuculidae
9.	Asian paradise - Flycatcher	*Terpsiphone paradisi* (Linnaeus, 1758)	Rajahakki	Passeriformes	Muscicapidae
10.	Black drongo	*Dicrurus macrocercus* (Vierllot, 1817)	Kajaana	Passeriformes	Dicruridae
11.	Black headed cuckoo shrike	*Coracina melanoptera* (Ruppel, 1839)	Karithale kogilekeechuga	Passeriformes	Campephagidae
12.	Black kite	*Milvus migrans govinda* (Boddaert, 1783)	Haddhu	Falconiformes	Accipitridae
13.	Blue rock pigeon	*Columba livia* (Gmelin, 1789)	Parivaala	Columbiformes	Columbidae
14.	Booted warbler	*Hippolais caligata* (Lichtenstein, 1823)	Bootugaalina uliyakki	Passeriformes	Acrocephalidae
15.	Bramhini kite	*Haliastur indus* (Boddaert, 1783)	Garuda	Falconiformes	Accipitridae
16.	Cattle egret	*Bubulcus ibis* (Linnaeus, 1758)	Govakki	Ciconiiformes	Ardeidae
17.	Common myna	*Acridotheres tristis* (Linnaeus, 1766)	Goravanka	Passeriformes	Sturnidae
18.	Copper smith barbet	*Megalaima haemacephala* (Statius muller, 1776)	Kanchukutiga	Piciformes	Megalaimidae
19.	Golden oriole	*Oriolus oriolus* (Linnaeus, 1758)	Honnakki	Passeriformes	Oriolidae
20.	Greater coucal	*Centropus sinensis* (Stephens, 1815)	Kembootha	Cuculiformes	Cuculidae

(Contd...)

Sl.No.	Common Name	Scientific Name	Kannada Name	Order	Family
21.	Green bee eater	*Merops orientalis* (Linnaeus, 1766)	Kallipeera	Coraciiformes	Meropidae
22.	House crow	*Corvus splendens* (Vieillot, 1817)	Boodhukaage	Passeriformes	Corvidae
23.	Indian peafowl	*Pavo cristatus* (Linnaeus, 1758)	Navilu	Galliformes	Phasianidae
24.	Indian pond heron	*Ardeola grayii* (Sykes, 1832)	Koladha baka	Ciconiiformes	Ardeidae
25.	Indian spotted owl	*Athene brama* (Temminck, 1821)	Halakki	Strigiformes	Strigidae
26.	Black-rumped Flameback	*Dinopium benghalense* (Linnaeus, 1758)	Hombennina marakutiga	Piciformes	Picidae
27.	Little egret	*Egretta garzetta* (Linnaeus, 1766)	Sanna bellakki	Ciconiiformes	Ardeidae
28.	Rose ringed parakeet	*Psittacula krameri* (Scopoli, 1769)	Gulabi koralina gili	Psittaciformes	Psittacidae
29.	Rosy starling	*Sturnus roseus*(Linnaeus, 1758)	Gulabi kabbakki	Passeriformes	Sturnidae
30.	Spotted dove	*Streptopelia chinensis* (Scopoli, 1786)	Jorehakki	Columbiformes	Columbidae
31.	Spotted munia	*Lonchura punctulata* (Linnaeus, 1758)	Chukke raatavala	Passeriformes	Estrildidae
32.	Yellow-billed Babbler	*Turdoides affinis* (Jerdon, 1845)	Bilithaleya haratemalla	Passeriformes	Timaliidae
33.	White thorated kingfisher	*Halcyon smyrnensis* (Linnaeus, 1758)	Rajamatsi	Coraciiformes	Halcyonidae
34.	Indian black necked hare	*Lepus nigricollis* (F.Cuvier, 1823)	kaadu mola	Lagomorpha	Leporidae
35.	Indian gray mangoose	*Herpestes edwardsii* (E.Geoffroy saint, Hilaire, 1818)	Mungisi	Carnivora	Herpestidae
36.	Three striped palm squirrel	*Funambulus palmarum* (Linnaeus, 1766)	Alilu	Rodentia	Sciuridae
37.	House mouse	*Mus musculus* (Linnaeus, 1758)	Ili	Rodentia	Muridae
38.	Bandicoot rat	*Bandicota bengalensis* (Gray, 1835)	Heggana	Rodentia	Muridae
39.	Flying fox or Fruit bat	*Pteropus giganteus* (Brannich, 1782)	Baavali	Chiroptera	Pteropodidae
40.	Greater short nosed fruit bat	*Cynopterus sphinx* (Vahl, 1797)		Chiroptera	Pteropodidae

Appendix 2: Quantification Analysis of Amphibian and Reptiles

Sl. No.	Common Name	Scientific Name	Family	D	A	F
1.	Common indian toad	*Duttaphrynus melanostictus* (Schneider, 1799)	Bufonidae	0.17	1.20	14.29
2.	Indian cobra	*Naja naja* (Linnaeus, 1758)	Elapidae	0.11	1.33	8.57
3.	Rat snake	*Ptyas mucosus* (Linnaeus, 1758)	Colubridae	0.11	1.33	8.57
4.	Common house gecko	*Hemidactylus frenatus* (Dumeril & Bibron, 1836)	Gekkonidae	0.49	1.70	28.57
5.	Common skink	*Mabuya carinata* (Schineides, 1801)	Scincidae	0.09	1.00	8.57
6.	Indian garden lizard	*Calotes versicolor* (Daudin, 1812)	Agamidae	0.14	1.25	11.43
7.	Green vine snake	*Ahaetulla nasuta* (Lacepede, 1789)	Colubridae	0.06	1.00	5.71

D – Density, A – Abundance, F – Frequency

Appendix 3: Quantification Analysis of Birds

Sl.No.	Common Name	Scientific Name	Family	D	A	F
1.	Asian koel	*Eudynamys scolopacea* (Linnaeus, 1758)	Cuculidae	0.66	1.44	45.71
2.	Asian paradise - Flycatcher	*Terpsiphone paradisi* (Linnaeus, 1758)	Muscicapidae	0.14	1.00	14.29
3.	Black drongo	*Dicrurus macrocercus* (Vierllot, 1817)	Dicruridae	1.94	2.72	71.43
4.	Black headed cuckooshrike	*Coracina melanoptera* (Ruppel, 1839)	Campephagidae	0.26	1.80	14.29
5.	Black kite	*Milvus migrans govinda* (Boddaert, 1783)	Accipitridae	0.91	1.78	51.43
6.	Blue rock pigeon	*Columba livia* (Gmelin, 1789)	Columbidae	1.26	2.44	51.43
7.	Booted warbler	*Hippolais caligata* (Lichtenstein, 1823)	Acrocephalidae	0.17	2.00	8.57
8.	Bramhini kite	*Haliastur indus* (Boddaert, 1783)	Accipitridae	0.63	1.69	37.14
9.	Cattle egret	*Bubulcus ibis* (Linnaeus, 1758)	Ardeidae	0.26	1.50	17.14
10.	Common myna	*Acridotheres tristis* (Linnaeus, 1766)	Sturnidae	1.03	2.77	37.14
11.	Copper smith barbet	*Megalaima haemacephala* (Statius muller, 1776)	Megalaimidae	0.11	1.33	8.57
12.	Golden oriole	*Oriolus oriolus* (Linnaeus, 1758)	Oriolidae	0.37	1.86	20.00
13.	Greater coucal	*Centropus sinensis* (Stephens, 1815)	Cuculidae	0.34	1.09	31.43
14.	Green bee eater	*Merops orientalis* (Linnaeus, 1766)	Meropidae	0.34	2.00	17.14
15.	House crow	*Corvus splendens* (Vieillot, 1817)	Corvidae	11.29	11.29	100.00
16.	Indian peafowl	*Pavo cristatus* (Linnaeus, 1758)	Phasianidae	0.06	2.00	2.86
17.	Indian pond heron	*Ardeola grayii* (Sykes, 1832)	Ardeidae	0.34	4.00	8.57
18.	Indian spotted owl	*Athene brama* (Temminck, 1821)	Strigidae	0.09	3.00	2.86
19.	Black-rumped Flameback	*Dinopium benghalense* (Linnaeus, 1758)	Picidae	0.11	1.33	8.57
20.	Little egret	*Egretta garzetta* (Linnaeus, 1766)	Ardeidae	0.23	2.67	8.57
21.	Rose ringed parakeet	*Psittacula krameri* (Scopoli, 1769)	Psittacidae	1.69	2.68	62.86
22.	Rosy starling	*Sturnus roseus* (Linnaeus, 1758)	Sturnidae	0.66	3.83	17.14
23.	Spotted dove	*Streptopelia chinensis* (Scopoli, 1786)	Columbidae	0.37	1.63	22.86
24.	Spotted munia	*Lonchura punctulata* (Linnaeus, 1758)	Estrildidae	0.43	3.75	11.43
25.	Yellow-billed Babbler	*Turdoides affinis* (Jerdon, 1845)	Timaliidae	2.37	5.93	40.00
26.	White thorated kingfisher	*Halcyon smyrnensis* (Linnaeus, 1758)	Halcyonidae	0.06	2.00	2.86

D – Density, A – Abundance, F – Frequency

Appendix 4: Quantification Analysis of Mammals

Sl. No.	Common Name	Scientific Name	Family	D	A	F
1.	Indian black necked hare	*Lepus nigricollis* (F.Cuvier, 1823)	Leporidae	0.63	1.67	37.50
2.	Indian gray mangoose	*Herpestes edwardsii* (E.Geoffroy saint, Hilaire, 1818)	Herpestidae	0.88	1.75	50.00
3.	Three striped palm squirrel	*Funambulus palmarum* (Linnaeus, 1766)	Sciuridae	2.50	2.50	100.00
4.	House mouse	*Mus musculus* (Linnaeus, 1758)	Muridae	0.88	1.75	50.00
5.	Bandicoot rat	*Bandicota bengalensis* (Gray, 1835)	Muridae	1.50	2.40	62.50
6.	Flying fox or Fruit bat	*Pteropus giganteus* (Brannich, 1782)	Pteropodidae	1.50	4.00	37.50
7.	Greater short nosed fruit bat	*Cynopterus sphinx* (Vahl, 1797)	Pteropodidae	0.75	2.00	37.50

D – Density, A – Abundance, F - Frequency

Appendix 5: Summary Table of the Vertebrate Species Under CITES, IWPA and IUCN from the ISEC Campus

	No. of Species	No.of Families	CITES	IWPA	IUCN								
					NE	DD	LC	NT	VU	EN	CR	EW	EX
Amphibians	1	1	–	–	–	–	1	–	–	–	–	–	–
Reptiles	6	6	2	3	1	3	2	–	–	–	–	–	–
Aves	26	20	2	23	–	1	25	–	–	–	–	–	–
Mammals	7	5	2	4	–	–	–	–	–	–	–	–	–

Appendix 6: IUCN, CITES, IWPA Status of Vertebrates

Sl.No.	Scientific Name	Vernacular Name	Family	IUCN	CITES	IWPA
Amphibian and Reptiles						
1.	*Duttaphrynus melanostictus*	Kappe	Bufonidae	LC	NC	NL
2.	*Naja naja*	Nagara haavu	Elapidae	DD	Ape-II	Sch-II
3.	*Ptyas mucosus*	Kere haavu	Colubridae	DD	Ape-II	Sch-II
4.	*Hemidactylus frenatus*	Halli	Gekkonidae	LC	NC	NL
5.	*Mabuya carinata*	Haavurani	Scincidae	LC	NC	NL
6.	*Calotes versicolor*	Uda	Agamidae	NE	NC	NL
7.	*Ahaetulla nasuta*	Neer haavu	Colubridae	DD	NC	Sch-IV
Birds						
1.	*Milvus migrans govinda*	Haddhu	Accipitridae	LC	Ape-II	Sch-IV
2.	*Haliastur indus*	Garuda	Accipitridae	LC	Ape-II	Sch-IV
3.	*Bubulcus ibis*	Govakki	Ardeidae	LC	NC	Sch-IV
4.	*Ardeola grayii*	Koladha baka	Ardeidae	LC	NC	Sch-IV
5.	*Egretta garzetta*	Sanna bellakki	Ardeidae	LC	NC	Sch-IV
6.	*Columba livia*	Parivaala	Columbidae	LC	NC	NL
7.	*Streptopelia chinensis*	Jorehakki	Columbidae	DD	NC	Sch-IV
8.	*Corvus splendens*	Boodhukaage	Corvidae	LC	NC	Sch-IV
9.	*Centropus sinensis*	Kembootha	Cuculidae	LC	NC	Sch-IV
10.	*Eudynamys scolopacea*	Kogile	Cuculidae	LC	NC	Sch-IV

(Contd...)

Sl.No.	Scientific Name	Vernacular Name	Family	IUCN	CITES	IWPA
11.	*Dicrurus macrocercus*	Kajaana	Dicruridae	LC	NC	Sch-IV
12.	*Lonchura punctulata*	Chukke raatavala	Estrildidae	LC	NC	Sch-IV
13.	*Halcyon smyrnensis*	Rajamatsi	Halcyonidae	LC	NC	Sch-IV
14.	*Megalaima haemacephala*	Kanchukutiga	Megalaimidae	LC	NC	NL
15.	*Merops orientalis*	Kallipeera	Meropidae	LC	NC	NL
16.	*Terpsiphone paradisi*	Rajahakki	Muscicapidae	LC	NC	Sch-IV
17.	*Oriolus oriolus*	Honnakki	Oriolidae	LC	NC	Sch-IV
18.	*Coracina melanoptera.*	Karithale kogilekeechuga	Campephagidae	LC	NC	Sch-IV
19.	*Pavo cristatus*	Navilu	Phasianidae	LC	NC	Sch-I
20.	*Psittacula krameri*	Gulabi koralina gili	Psittacidae	LC	NC	Sch-IV
21.	*Athene brama*	Halakki	Strigidae	LC	NC	Sch-IV
22.	*Acridotheres tristis*	Goravanka	Sturnidae	LC	NC	Sch-IV
23.	*Hippolais caligata*	Bootugaalina uliyakki	Acrocephalidae	LC	NC	Sch-IV
24.	*Dinopium benghalense*	Hombennina marakutiga	Picidae	LC	NC	Sch-IV
25.	*Sturnus roseus*	Gulabi kabbakki	Sturnidae	LC	NC	Sch-IV
26.	*Turdoides affinis*	Bilithaleya haratemalla	Timaliidae	LC	NC	Sch-IV

(Contd…)

Sl.No.	Scientific Name	Vernacular Name	Family	IUCN	CITES	IWPA
Mammals						
1.	*Lepus nigricollis*	Kaadu mola	Leporidae	LC	NC	NL
2.	*Herpestes edwardsii*	Mungisi	Herpestidae	LC	Ape-III	NL
3.	*Funambulus palmarum*	Alilu	Sciuridae	LC	NC	NL
4.	*Mus musculus*	Ili	Muridae	LC	NC	Sch-V
5.	*Bandicota bengalensis*	Heggana	Muridae	LC	NC	Sch-V
6.	*Pteropus giganteus*	Baavali	Pteropodidae	LC	Ape-II	Sch-V
7.	*Cynopterus sphinx*	Baavali	Pteropodidae	LC	NC	Sch-V

REFERENCES

Abere, S.A. and Oguzo, N.S. (2011). Adaptation of Animals to Arid Ecological Conditions. *World journal of Zoology* 6 (2): 209-214. ISSN 1817-3098.

Al- Eisawi, D. (2003). Effect of Biodiversity Conservation on Arid Ecosystem with a Special Emphasis on Bahrain. *Journal of Arid Environments* (2003) 54: 81-90.

Check List of Indian Mammals (2008). *ZOOS' PRINT,* Volume XXIII, Number 8, August 2008 (RNI 9: 11)

DeVault, T.L. (2003). Scavenging by Vertebrates: Behavioral, Ecological and Evolutionary Perspectives on an Important Energy Transfer Pathway in Terrestrial Ecosystems. *Oikos*- 102: 225-234.

Dunne, G.W. and Eisenbeis, R.F. (1973). Forest Preserves District of Cook Country. *Nature bulletien* – 486.

Geier, A.R. and Best, L.B. (1980). Habitat Selection by Small Mammals of Riparian Communities: Evaluating the Effects of Habitat Alterations. *The Journal of Wildlife Management,* Vol. 44, No. 1 (Jan., 1980), pp. 16-24.

Gigannettino, B. *Bird Migration in Unpredictable yet Exciting.*

Gund, M. and Bang, A. (2012). Classification of Bird species. *International Journal of Electronics, Communication & Soft Computing Science and Engineering* ISSN: 2277-9477, Volume 2, Issue 4.

Hunt, P.D., M.B. Watkins, and R.W. Suomala. (2011). The State of New Hampshire's Birds – *A* Conservation Guide. *New Hampshire Audubon,* Concord, NH.

Joyson, E.A., and Mathew., D.W.(2000). Diversity and Species- abundance Distribution of Birds in the Tropical Forests of Silent Valley, Kerala: *Journal, Bombay Natural History Society,* 97(3) Dec. 2000.

McNeely, J.A. (2003). Biodiversity in Arid Regions: Values and Perceptions. *Journal of Arid Environments* (54): 61-70.

Mallick, J.K. (2012). Mammals of Kalimpong Hills, *Darjeeling District, West Bengal, India.* JOTT Review 4(12): 3103-3136.

Nair. T. and Krishna.C.Y., (2013). Vertebrate Fauna of the Chambal River Basin, with Emphasis on the National Chambal Sanctuary, India. *Journal of Threatened Taxa* (2013) 5(2): 3620-3641.

NRCS. (1999). Grassland Birds. *Fish and Wildlife Habitat Management Leaflet – 8. United States Department of Agriculture.*

Prajapati, R.C. (2010). Biodiversity of Karnataka: at a Glance. *Karnataka Biodiversity Board.* 1-96.

Prakash, S. (2011). Feathered Friends of JNU. *Jawaharlal Nehru University,* New Delhi.

Pullaiah, T. (2013). Biodiversity in India and its Conservation. *Souvenir and abstracts*: 27-29.

Rajashekara, S. and Venkatesha, M.G. (2011). Community Composition of Aquatic Birds in Lakes of Bangalore, India. *Journal of Enviornmental Biology* 32(1): 77-83(2011).

Reddy. K.H. and Natraj. K. *Preserving Biodiversity – Need of the Hour.*

Roy. U.S., Banerjee. P., and Mukhopadhyay, S.K., (2012). Study on Avifaunal Diversity from Three Different Regions of North Bengal, India. *Asian Journal of Conservation Biology,* December 2012. Vol. 1 No. 2, pp. 120-129.

Singh, V., Banyal, H.S. (2012). Diversity and Ecology of Mammals in Kalatop-Khajjiar Wildlife Sanctuary, District Chamba (Himachal Pradesh), India. *International Journalof Science and Nature.* ISSN 2229-6441, Vol.3 (1): 2012: 125-128.

Sinclair, A.R.E. (2003). The Role of Mammals as Ecosystem Land Scapers. *Centre for Biodiversity Research,* University of British Columbia, Canada. ALCES Vol. 39: 161-176 (2003).

Subramanian, AN. Sethuraman, A. and Murugan, S. *Mammals.* 463-467.

Vijay Kumar, K.M., and Kumara, V. (2011). Avifaunal Diversity of Mangrove Ecosystem, Kundapura, Udupi District, Karnataka, India. *Recent Research in Science and Technology* 2011, 3(10): 106-110: ISSN: 2076-5061.

Willoughby, E.J. (2011). Field Study of Migratory Behaviour. Department of Biology. *St. Mary's college of Maryland.* Maryland.

Zimmerman, L. 1998). Migration of Birds. Division of Biology, *Kansas State University,* Manhattan, KS. Revised Circular 16.

Pages: 95-104

AGRICULTURE DEVELOPMENT AND SUSTAINABLE ENVIRONMENT

Edited by: Jaswant Ray; Dr. Pawan Kumar 'Bharti'

ISBN: 978-93-5056-759-3

Edition: 2015

Published by: Discovery Publishing House Pvt. Ltd., New Delhi (India)

Effects of Pesticides on Aquatic and Aerial Oxygen Consumption in an Air Breathing Murrel Fish, *Channa gachua*

Qaisur Rahman* and D.N. Sadhu

ABSTRACT

The metabolic rate of fishes in term of oxygen uptake depends on many factors including pesticides. The present paper deals with the effect of three different pesticides namely Metacid-50 (Organophosphate), Dithane M-45 (Carbamate) and Kelthane (Organochlorine) were studies on changes in dual mode of oxygen consumption of an air breathing murrel fish, *Channa gachua*. The mean values of aquatic, aerial and total oxygen uptake of control group of fish (40.0 ± 1.5g) were recorded as 52.44, 61.56 and 114.0 ml/kg/hr respectively. This group of fish obtained 46% and 54% oxygen respectively from aquatic and aerial route. Exposure of fish to above noted pesticide brought significant decrease in aquatic as well as total oxygen uptake percent while it increases in oxygen consumption through aerial route as compared to control one due to the action of pesticides on acetylcholenesterase enzyme on respiratory muscles paralysis, finally respiratory failure and death occurs.

Key words: *Channa gachua,* air-breathing organ, pesticides.

Post Graduate Department of Zoology, Vinoba Bhave University, Hazaribag - 825 301, Jharkhand (India).

INTRODUCTION

Aquatic environment is the ultimate sink for all pollutants where they are going to affect the zones more than their counterparts in the two environs of land and water. The agricultures and aqua ventures necessitates the use of chemicals as contaminants where ever damage the living inhabitance. To contemplate a clean environment in a policy and planning unless possible on aquatic inhabitants are assessed it can be a dream only. Fish bioassay experiments, the tropic level connection in aqua systems are indices to determine the acute toxicity and possible effect on oxygen consumption due to the toxicant stress. Metabolic activities of animals on earth are dependent upon its ability to utilize oxygen and eliminate carbon dioxide. Respiration is one of the most important physiological parameters on which many of the vital functions like growth and reproduction of fish depend (Holden, 1973), which in turn has a direct bearing on the productivity of freshwater ecosystems in terms of fish production per unit area also indicator of fish health and environment. The freshwater air breathing fishes of tropical countries inhabit waters of low oxygen contents and experience hypoxic water in summer and normoxic water during winter and rainy season. In accordance with the fluctuations in the physico chemical characteristics of the ambient waters, the air breathing fishes are equipped with dual mode gas exchange machinery, employing two modes of respiration using highly vascularised air breathing organs to combat the adverse ecological conditions of their habitat while brachial and/or integument exchange gases with water.

These days pesticides are used indiscriminately to fulfill the different needs, which affect the aquatic environment including fishes. One of the early symptoms of acute pesticide poisoning is the alteration or failure of respiratory metabolism (Holden, 1973). Changes in oxygen uptake of fishes in response to pesticide exposure are varying in different fishes exposed to a variety of pesticides (Karuppiah, 1996). The effect of pesticides on oxygen consumption has been extensively studied in a number of water breathing fishes (Mount, 1962; Waiwood and Johansen, 1974; Vasanthi, 1985). However the above investigators estimated only the changes in aquatic respiration even though the air breathing fishes like, *Mystus vitttus* (Gopalakrishna Reddy and Gomathy, 1977) and *Channa punctatus* (Sambasiva Rao *et al.* 1984) were used in their investigations. A review of literature indicates that the effects of pesticides on the proportion of oxygen uptake from water and air by air breathing fishes were studied by only a few investigators (Bakthavathasalam, 1980; Natarajan, 1981; Ganapathyraman, 1987 and Karuppiah, 1996), as such the present work has been undertaken in an air breathing fish, *Channa gachua* to advance our information in this regard.

MATERIAL AND METHODS

Channa gachua also known as an air breathing fish belong to the family Channidae of the order Channiformes. It is found in estuaries and freshwaters of India. It has a very good flavour and is popular as food. This fish has dual mode gas exchange mechanism as it extracts oxygen from water through gills and from air by accessory respiratory organs. The accessory respiratory organs comprise one pair of supra branchial chambers.

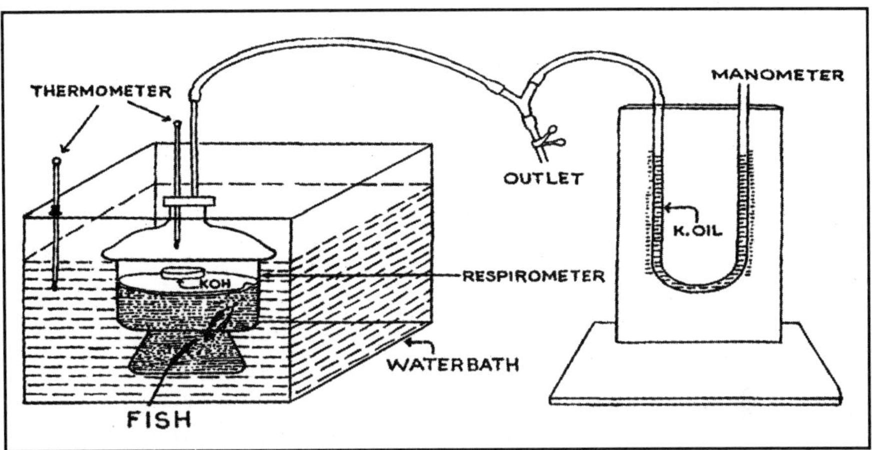

Fig. 7.1: Experimental Set up for the Measurements of Dual Mode of Oxygen Uptake in *Channa gachua*

Live specimens of *Channa gachua* were procured from Local fish dealers at Hazaribag (Latitude 25° 59′N and longitude 85° 22′E) and maintained in large glass aquaria size (90 × 60 × 60cm) with continuous flow of water. The fish were fed on chopped goat liver daily during a minimum acclimation period of 15 days in the laboratory. Routine oxygen consumption from air and still water was measured in a closed glass respirometer containing 3 litres of water (initial 02 content = 6.5 mg oxygen/Iitre; pH = 7.2) and 0.51 ML of air (Fig. 7.1). The fish had free access to air through a small semi circular hole (10 cm diameter) in a disc float. Carbosorb (B.D.H) or KOH in a petridish placed on the float absorbed Co_2, Thus the fish could exchange gases with water by way of its gills as well as with the air using the suprabranchial chamber. The air phase of respirometer was connected to a differential manometer. Movement of the manometer fluid follow uptake of oxygen when the CO_2 is absorbed by "Carbosorb" (KOH). The fish were acclimatized to the respirometers at least 12 hours before the reading were taken. The concentration of dissolved oxygen in the water was estimated by Winkler's volumetric method (Welch, 1948). The oxygen uptake through gills was calculated from the difference between the oxygen levels of the ambient water in the respirometer before and after the experiment and the reading of volume of water in the respirometer. Oxygen uptake from air was measured and calculated the reading volume change in the manometer and by the use of the combined gas law equations and vapour's pressure (Dejour's 1975). Mean values of oxygen consumption of a series of observations, on each fish at STPD and standard errors were calculated. The experiments were conducted at 29.0 ± 1.5°C. The pH of the ambient water was measured by an electronic pH meter (systronics). The respiratory chambers were thermostated by immersion in a temperature controlled water bath.

Acute toxicity tests were performed with one pesticide of each group (i.e. one each from organophosphate, organochlorine and carbamate). The pesticide's technical or trade name, active ingredients and manufacturing concerns are as follows:

1. Metacid-50 (organophosphate) 50%, methyl parathion = O-O dimethyl O-P-Nitrophenyle phosphorothionate : Bayers India Ltd. Mumbai.
2. Dithane M - 45 (Carbamate): 75% mancozeb as zinc ion and manganese ethylene bis dithio-carbamate. Indofil chemical Ltd., Mumbai.
3. Kelthane E.C (organochlorine) 18.15%, 1, 1 bi-chlorophenyl, 2, 2, 2 trichloroethanol (DICOFOL): Indofil chemical Ltd., Mumbai.

Metacid and Kelthane were purchased in liquid form but Dithane M-45 was soluble in distilled water. The desired degrees of concentrations were prepared by adopting the dilution techniques of APHA *et.al.* (1971). The 96 hours bio assay tests were performed employing the technique of static bio assay tests (Doudoroff *et. al.*, 1951). The (median tolerance limit) or LC50 (96h) values were 11.0 mg/l for Metacid, 14.0 mg/I for Kelthane and 20.0 mg/I for Dithane M-45. The determination of aquatic, aerial and total oxygen consumption in the experimental fishes were made at sublethal concentration of pesticides (as recorded in table 7.1). Values of oxygen uptakes were expressed as (ml /kg/hr). Five fish were used for each set of experiment. The mean values of oxygen uptake of all the fish of each set of experiment were taken and compared. The difference of significance, if any, between the control and experimental groups of fish, was calculated by student's t-test at the level of 5%.

RESULTS

The data showing the effect of sublethal concentrations of Metacid-50, Dithane M-45 and Kelthane on aquatic, aerial and total oxygen uptake (ml/ kg/hr), percent aerial and aquatic oxygen uptake and aquatic/aerial oxygen uptake ratio are summarized in Table 7.1. The mean values of aquatic, aerial and total oxygen uptake of control group of fish was recorded as 52.44 ± 0.93, 61.56 ± 1.08 and 114.0 ± 1.93 respectively. This group of fish obtained 46% and 54% oxygen respectively from aquatic and aerial route. The aquatic/ aerial oxygen uptake ratio was calculated to be 0.852 in this group of fish. Exposure of fish to different sublethal concentrations of all the above noted three pesticides brought significant decrease both in aquatic and total oxygen uptake. The experimental fish obtained 30.0-38% oxygen through aquatic route as compared to 46% in control group of fishes while in the experimental group of fishes the oxygen uptake through aerial route ranged from 62-70% as compared to 56% in the fishes of control group. The ratio of aquatic/

aerial oxygen ranged from 0.428-0.613 in experimental animals as compared to 0.852 in the control group of fish. Thus a shift in the dependency towards air-breathing was clearly marked out in fishes exposed to different concentration of above noted all the three pesticides. The effect of these pesticides was dose dependent and the Kelthane was found to be more effective as compared to Dithane M-45 and Metacid 50 respectively.

DISCUSSION

Different water bodies with varied physico chemical qualities are present in tropical India. Various piscine organizations, including gills are modified to suit these water bodies. The dual breathers can survive in hypoxic and hyper carbic swampy waters or even pesticides polluted water due to the presence of air breathing organs supplementary to gills. However, such water bodies are unsuitable for purely water breathing fishes for the lack of air breathing organ.The commonly used pesticide such as organochlorine, organophosphate and carbamate which were used to control different kind of pest in a biological community respectively. It is very interesting to note that all the different groups of pesticides or even the different pesticides of the same group do not have the same effect on fishes. The mode and site of action of different pesticides also differ as reported by Qaisur (2011) and therefore, it is very difficult to generalize the effect of different pesticides in fishes unless a detailed investigation is carried out.

One of the early symptoms of acute pesticide poisoning is the alteration of respiratory metabolism in fishes. A perusal of relevant literature on the effect of pesticides on oxygen uptake of purely water breathing fishes and of air breathing fishes indicate that the effects of pesticides on oxygen uptake are varied. Waiwood and Johanson (1974) in white sucker, *Catastomus commersoni* after the treatment of methoxychlor, Huner *et.al.* (1967) in *Lepomis macrochirus* after the exposure of endrin, Bakthvathsalam (1980) in *Anabas testudineus* Peer Mohammed and Gupta (1984) in *Cirrhinus mrigala* after the treatment of ethyl parathion, Jabde and Ansari (1993) in *Nemechillus aureus* after the exposure of Cyper methrin and Karuppiah (1996) in *Channa striatus* after the treatment of carbamate pesticide, sevin have reported elevated oxygen uptake following exposure of different insecticides. On the other hand Uthaman (1977) in *Colisa lalia* following exposure of ã-BHC, Gopalakrishna Reddy and Gomathy (1977) in thiodon exposed *Mystus vittatus*, Pandey *et al.* (1979) in DOT, metacid and unizeb exposed *Channa punctatus*, Vasanthi and Ramaswamy (1987) in thiodon exposed *Sarotheroden mossambicus*, Velavan (1992) in Cuman L-exposed *Oreochronis mossambicus*, Kumar (1998) in metacid exposed *Heteropneustes fossilis* and Pandey *et.al.* (1989) in sevin exposed *Clarias batrachus* (Linn) have reported 21% to more than 50% decrease in oxygen uptake following exposure to different pesticides and those investigators are of the opinion that the dual mode breathers predominantly relies more on aerial gas exchange as compared to aquatic gas exchange following exposure to different concentrations of pesticides and this may be assumed as an adaptation towards hypoxic water conditions. The above noted investigators have stated that the dependency on aquatic and aerial respiration is different in different concentration of pesticides indicating a survival values for the fish.

The results obtained in the present study, on the dual mode oxygen uptake of control fish indicates that the air breathing fish, *Channa gachua* predominantly relies on aerial gas exchange obtaining 54% of its total oxygen uptake by their air breathing organ where as only 46% was contributed by gills. Similar trends have been reported by Karuappiah (1996) in *Channa striatus* and Munshi *et. al.,* (1979) in *Channa marulius* (84.5%) *Channa striatus* (67.7%) *Channa gachua* (53.4%) and *Channa punctatus* (86.8%). In the present study in *Channa gachua* the contribution of gas exchange through aerial route increased between 62-70% following exposure of different concentration of Metacid-50, Dithane M-45 and Kelthane which is consistent with the findings of Karuppiah (1996) and Pandey *et. al.,*(1999) respectively.

In the present study in *Channa gachua* significant decrease in both aquatic and total oxygen uptake was observed following exposure to different concentrations of Metacid-50, Dithane-M-45 and Kelthane (Table 7.1) which is consistent with the findings of Pandey *et. al.,* (1999; 2005). Though the exact reason for the decrease in oxygen uptake in fish *Channa gachua* could not be understand but Chambers (1976) has stated that the mode of action of organophosphate pesticides is the irreversible inhibition of acetylcholinesterase, with death in vertebrates usually attributed to respiratory failure from paralysis of respiratory muscles. Similar explanations may be followed here. The increased dependency on aerial respiration in *Channa gachua* following exposure to Metacid, Dithane and Kelthane probably indicates that the fish tries to avoid the aquatic medium containing sublethal concentration of pesticides. Qaisur (2011) reported that respiratory activity of a fish is often the first physiological response to be affected by the presence of contaminants in the aquatic environment. Although many biological early warning systems monitor abnormal opercular movement as an indicator of respiratory stress, a more direct measurement of stress in this sense necessitates the quantification of oxygen consumed by the fish. The oxygen consumption is not often used as a bioindicator of pollution associated stress in biological early warning systems. Respiratory responses were found to be less sensitive, but also could be successfully used in bioassay testing of treated industrial and municipal effluents before they are discharged into receiving waters. Gill ventilation frequency and coughing rate are intimately associated with respiratory demands and gill irritation or blockage. Oxygen consumption measurements provide a robust indicator of whole animal stress and concomitant water quality respectively.

Table 7.1: Effects of Three Different Pesticides on Oxygen Consumption in *Channa gachua*

N=5, Bodyweight = 40.0 ± 1.5 gm Water temperature = 29.0 ± 1.5ºC SEM* = Significant

Sl. No.	Condition	Doseg/l	Oxygen Uptake (ml/kg/h)			Percent O_2 Uptake		Aquatic	% Decrease in O_2 Uptake	
			Aquatic	Aerial	Total	Aquatic	Aerial	Aerial Ratio	Aquatic	Total
1.	Control	–	52.44 ± 0.93*	61.56 ± 1.08	114.0 ± 1.93	46.0	54	0.852	–	–
2.	Metacid-50	2.0	24.98 ± 1.64*	46.37 ± 1.24*	71.35 ± 1.08*	35.0	65	0.538	52.36	37.41
3.	-Do-	4.0	26.65 ± 1.04*	43.47 ± 1.33*	70.12 ± 1.04*	38.0	62	0.613	49.17	38.49
4.	Dithane M-45	4.0	26.20 ± 1.23*	56.65 ± 1.28*	82.85 ± 1.12*	31.6	68.4	0.462	50.04	27.32
5.	-Do-	8.0	30.9 ± 1.12*	50.42 ± 1.12*	81.32 ± 1.48*	38.0	62	0.613	40.50	28.67
6.	Kelthane	5.0	25.0 ± 2.68*	58.32 ± 0.61*	83.32 ± 1.93*	30.0	70	0.428	52.33	26.91
7.	-Do-	8.0	29.06 ± 1.36*	52.09 ± 0.28*	80.15 ± 1.04*	35.0	65	0.538	44.58	29.69

Fig. 7.2: Showing Groups *Channa gachua* Used in the Present Investigation

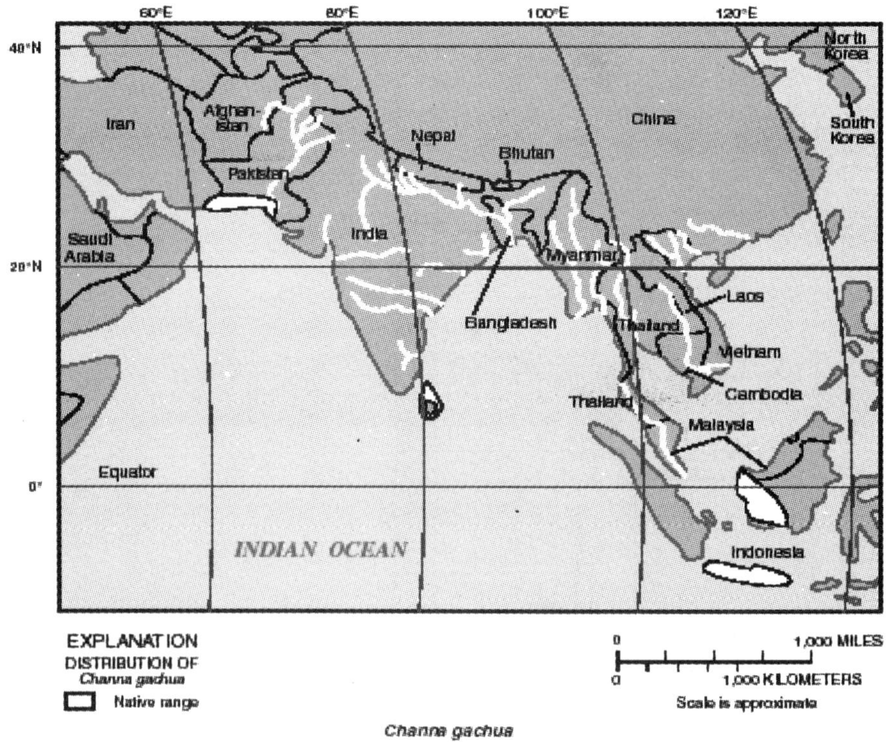

Fig. 7.3: Showing the Distribution of *Channa gachua* in Different Areas of the World

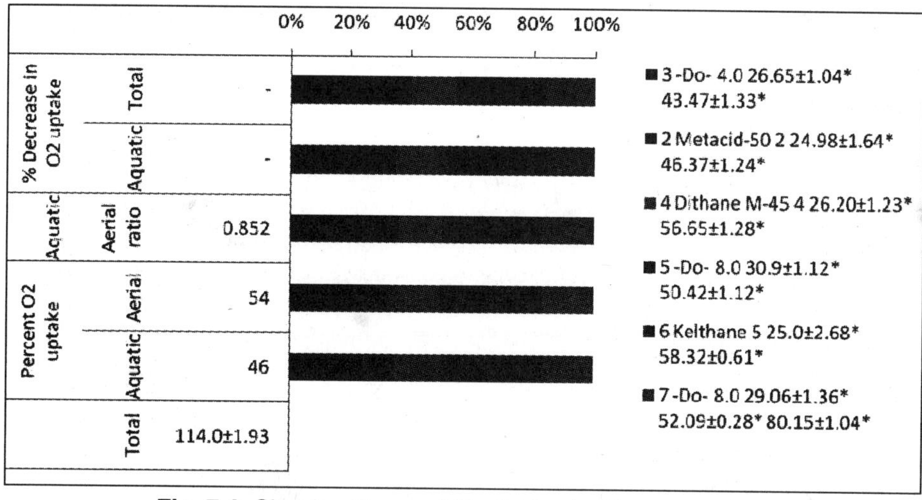

Fig. 7.4: Showing Doses of Pesticides in *Channa gachua*

REFERENCES

APHA, AWWA and WPCF (1971): *In* Standard Method for the Examination of Water and Waste Water. 14th, Edition *Am. Publ. Health. Assoc.* Washington, INC, p. 1193.

Bakthavathsalam, R., (1980). Toxicity and Physiological Impact of Three Selected Pesticides in an Air Breathing Fish, *Anabas Testudineus*. Ph.D. Thesis. Annamalai University, Tamilnadu. India.

Chambers, J.E. (1976). The Relationship of Esterates to Organophosphorous Insecticides Tolerance in Mosquito Fish. *Pestic. Biochem. Physio.* 6: 517-222.

Dejours, P., (1975): Principles of Comparative Respiratory Physiology. North-Holland Publishing Co. Amesterdam, p. 253.

Doudoroff, P; Anderson, B.G; Burdick, G.E; Goltsoff, W.B. ; Hart, W.B.; Patrick, R; Strong, E.R.; S.urbur, E.W. and Van Horn, W.M. (1951). Bioassay Methods for the Evaluation of Acute Toxicity of Industrial Wastes to Fish. *Sewage Ind. Wastes.* 23: 1380-1397.

Ganapathyraman, S (1987): Impact of Organophorous Pesticides, Monocrotophos on Dual Mode Respiration and Protein Metabolism in the Air Breathing Fish, *Channa punctatus* (Bloch). M. Phil. Dissertation. Annamalai University, Tamil Nadu.

Gopalkrishna Reddy, T and Gomathy, S., (1977): Toxicity and Respiratory Effects of Pesticide, Thiodon on Catfish, *Mystus vittatus. Indian J. Environ. Hlth*, 19(4): 360-363.

Holden, A.V. (1973): The Effects of Pesticides on Life in Freshwater. *Proc, R. Soc. London.* 180: 383-394.

Hunner, J.V; Dowden, B.F. and Bennett, H.J (1967): The Effects of Endrin on the Oxygen Consumption of Blue Gills, *Lepomis macrochirus. Proc. La. Acad. Sci*, 30: 80-86.

Jabde, P.V. and Ansari, M., (1993): Effect of Acute Exposure of Cypermethrin on the Oxygen Consumption in a Fresh Water Fish, *Naemechillus aureus* (Day). *Proc. Acad. Environ. Biol.* 2 (1): 95-98.

Karuppiah, D (1996): Toxicity and Effects of a Carbamate Pesticide Sevin on some Physiological Aspects in a Freshwater, Edible Air Breathing Fish, *Channa striatus* (Bloch). Ph.D. Thesis. Bharathiar University, Coimbatore, Tamil Nadu.

Kumar Arun; B.N. Pandey; Arshi Rana and Ranjan Kumar (1998): Toxic Effect of Metacid on Dual Mode Oxygen Uptake in an Air Breathing Fish, *Heteropneustes Fossilis* (Bloch). *Columban. J. Life Sci.* 6 (2): 339-341.

Mount, D.I. (1962): Chronic Effects of Endrin on Bluntnose Minnows and Guppies, U.S. *Fish Wild. Ser. Rept.* 58: 1-38.

Munshi, J.S.D., Ajoy K. Patra ; Niva Biswas and Jagdish Ojha (1979): Interspecific Variations in the Circadian Rhythm of Dual Mode Oxygen Uptake in Four Species of Murrerls. *Jap. J. Ichthyol.* 26(1): 69-74.

Natarajan, G.M. (1981): Changes in the Dual Mode Gas Exchange and Some Blood Parameters in the Air Breathing Fish, *Channa striatus* (Bleeker) Following Lethal Exposure to *Metasystok* (Dimeton) *Curre. Sci.* 50 (I): 40-41.

Pandey, B.N. A K. Chanchal; S.B. Singh; S. Prasad and M.P. Singh (1979): Effect of Some Biocides on the Blood and Oxygen Consumption of *Channa punctatus* (Bloch). *Proc. Symp. Environ. Biol.* 23: 343-348.

Pandey, B.N; Arun Kumar, Ram Pyare Singh; Dhananjay Kumar, Ranjan Kumar and Arshi Rana (1999): Toxic Effect of a Carbamate Pesticide, Sevin on Gas Exchange in an Air Breathing Fish, *Clarias batrachus* (Linn). *Him. J. Env. Zool.* 13: 103-106

Panday, B.N., Rumana Perween: W.Ahsan: S.N Akhtar and R.K.Singh (2005): Changes in Bimodal Oxygen Uptake of Obligate Air-breathing Fish *Anabas testudineus* (Bloch.) Exposed to Pesticides. *Proc.Zool.Soc. India* (4): 71-78.

Peer Mohammed, M and Gupta, R.A., (1984): Effects of Sub-lethal Concentration of Ethyl parathion on Oxygen Consumption and Random Swimming Activity of *Cirrhinus mrigala* (Hamilton) *Indian. J. Exp. Biol.* 22: 42-44.

Qaisur Rahman (2011): Studies on Some Factors Affecting on Aerial and Aquatic Respiration in an Air Breathing Fish *Channa gachua* (Ham.) Ph.D.Theses, Vinoba Bhave University, Hazaribag, Jharkhand, India.

Sambasiva Rao, K.R.S.; Siva Prasad Rao and Raman Rao, K.V. (1984): Impacts of Technical and Commercial Grade Phenothoate on Some Selected Parameters of Oxidative Metabolism in the Fish, *Channa punctatus* (Bloch.) *Indian. J. Ecol.* 11 (1): 6-11.

Uthaman, M (1977): Toxicity and Respiratory Effects of the Pesticide Y-BHC in the Anabantid Fish, *Colisa lalia.* M.Sc. Dissertation, Annamalai univ, Tamil Nadu.

Vasanthi, M (1985): Effect of Thiodon (endosulfan) on Oxygen Consumption, Glycogen Content and SDH Activity of a Freshwater Teleost, *Sarotherodon mossambicus* (Peters). M. Sc. Dissertation. Bharathiar University, Coimbatore, Tamil Nadu.

Vasanthi, M and Ramaswamy, M (1987): A Shift in Metabolic Pathway of *Sarotherodon mossambicus* (Peters) Exposed to Thiodon (Endosulfan). *Proc. Ind. Acad. Sci.* 96 (1): 55-61.

Velavan, P (1992): Toxicity and Sublethal Effect of Carbamate, Cuman L on Respiration and Biochemical Aspects in the Freshwater Fish, *Oreochromis mossambicus* (Peters). M.Phil, Dissertation. Annamalai University, Tamil Nadu.

Waiwood, K.G. and Johansen, A H., (1974): Oxygen Consumption and Activity of the White Sucker (*Catastomus commersioni*) in Lethal and Non Lethal Levels of Organochlorine Insecticide, Methoxychlor. *Water Res.* 8 (7): 401-406.

Welch, P.S., (1948): Limnological Methods Mc. Graw Hill. Co. Inc. New York, London. pp. 20-213.

Pages: 105-116

AGRICULTURE DEVELOPMENT AND SUSTAINABLE ENVIRONMENT

Edited by: **Jaswant Ray; Dr. Pawan Kumar 'Bharti'**

ISBN: 978-93-5056-759-3

Edition: **2015**

Published by: **Discovery Publishing House Pvt. Ltd., New Delhi (India)**

8

Biotechnological Production of Poly Lactic Acid (PLA) Biopolymer and its Applications

Amit Kumar

ABSTRACT

Poly lactic acid (PLA) is extensively applicable bioplastic, this is a polymer of lactic acid which is an aliphatic acid (2 hydoxy propeonic acid), PLA is a best alternative of petroleum based plastics and this is produced from renewable sources and is very ecofriendlly with having good biocompatibility than petroleum based plastic. PLA have number of unique properties which make it excellent for use in different fields like due to its degradable nature and good biocompatibility it become the first choice of biomedical engineers for the production of different biomaterials used in medical field.

90% of total production of lactic acid is done by fermentative processes as it gives optically pure isomers (separate D and L form) of lactic acid, which is highly desirable for the use of lactic acid based polymers in different industries. In fermentative production, a number of genetically engineered strains of microbes are being used.

Department of Biotechnology, Delhi Technological University, New Delhi - 110 042, (India).

In this review, recent development in the fermentation strategies and different molecular approaches, vectors and recombinants have been discussed, which are being used to overproduce the PLA with low cost and to improve its qualities.

Key words: Poly Lactic Acid (PLA), Biotechnological production, Biopolymer, Desalting electrolysis, Microbial fermentation, Bio-medical applications

INRODUCTION

Common plastics which are used now a days is derived from fossil fuels like petroleum based plastics, on decomposition these plastics produces high amount of green house gases which are causing serious problems to environment so to avoid this problem and to save our future the best alternative are biodegradable bioplastics which can be hydrolyzed at temperature approximate at 50'c in few months to one year with the production of little or no green house gases.

Bioplastics are generally derived from renewable biomass sources like oils of vegetables, starch of pea and corn, waste of paper and pulp industries and most useful from microorganisms like microalgae and different bacteria. The current world wide demand of lactic acid is approximate 130,000-150,000 tons per year, to fulfill the increasing demand of lactic acid which is a monomer of poly lactic acid (PLA), different biotechnological techniques are being used. Different molecular approaches have been used to overproduce the lactic acid and to increase its quality by maintaining the properties like thermo stability elasticity and many more.

On the basis of their source and method of production bioplastics are of different types like Poly hydroxy alkanoates (PHA), Poly hydroxy butarate (PHB) and Poly lactic acid (PLA).

Poly lactic acid (PLA) or polylactide is aliphatic polyester; which is biocompatible thermoplastic and derived from different renewable sources like corn, wheat, sugar beet and from different waste products like banana peel, agriculture waste, paper pulp industries waste, forest waste etc.

PLA is most useful type of biodegradable polymers as lactic acid can be easily produced by biotechnological process using strain of lactic acid bacteria (LAB) and easily available cheep raw materials. The decomposition of PLA can be done by hydrolyzing the ester bond simply without action of any enzyme, the most important advantage of PLA is that it produces lactic acid as a result of degradation which is not toxic to organisms as lactic acid is itself occurs in the metabolism.

METHODS OF PRODUCTION

Lactic acid is an organic acid (2-hydroxy Propionic acid), exist in three possible stereo forms D-Lactic acid, L-Lactic acid and Meso lactic acid, they are used in different industries like pharmaceutical, textile, food, lather, chemical and in medical fields, by its polymerization in the form of poly lactic acid.

Lactic acid can be synthesized by two major approaches:

(a) Chemical synthesis of lactic acid

(b) Biological synthesis of lactic acid

Chemical Synthesis of Lactic Acid

Chemically lactic acid can be synthesized by hydrolysis of lactonitrile with strong acids but as a result of this process a recimic mixture of D-lactic acid and L-lactic acid obtained.

Biological Synthesis of Lactic Acid

Biologically lactic acid is produced by fermentations of starch and other polysaccharides which are easily available from different renewable sources. For the fermentative production of lactic acid sugar cane, bagasse, pea starch, wheat, barley and waste of potato, paper and pulp and dairy industry, waste of algal biofuel and banana peel are being used as a substrate for microorganisms.

There are several advantages of this method over chemical synthesis of lactic acid due to low requirement of temperature and energy, the cost of production get decreases, this method is environment friendly as it uses renewable sources not the fossil flues which produces harmful gases on decomposition, apart from these the main advantage is this method gives optically pure product that is separate D and L lactic acids which is very important for industrial use of lactic acid as nowadays main challenge with PLA is to increase its melting point.

Microbial Production of Lactic Acid

Microbes like different algae and bacteria are being used to produce lactic acid at industrial level. Due to a number of advantages approximate 90% of total lactic acid lactic acid is produced by bacterial fermentation.

Lactic Acid Production from Micro Algae

Micro algae are easy to grow and due to short life span (1-10 days) they are cheaper than other sources. Nguyen et al. (2012)[1] have done a study on a microalgae *Hydrodictyon reticulatum* (HR) this is a fresh water algae which is containing glucose and mannose, due to high polysaccharide this is having many advantages as a feed stock over other sources of biomass like sugarcane, rice, corn and cassava etc., this algae is having ability to produce lactic acid quickly and cheaply with the productivity of 20 ton/ha. Simentenious saccharification and co-fermentation (SSCF) through *lactobacillus coryiformis* sub sp. torquens which is a homo fermentative D-LA producer have been used to produce D-Lactic acid from HR (Yanez et al. 2003)[2].

Fermentative Production of Lactic Acid

Lactic acid exist in two stereo isomers D and L forms these both can found in bacterial system for the synthesis of lactic acid pyurvate is used in oxygen limiting condition by action of enzyme dehydrogenase, the specificity of this enzyme determines the stereo isomeric ratio of D and L lactic acid.

For the fermentative production of lactic acid mostly species of lactic acid bacteria are used which convert hexose into lactic acid. For the production of lactic acid fermenter can be operated either in batch or in continuous mode, operating fermentor in continuous mode gives high productivity in comparison to batch mode. While operating batch fermentor, pH is kept constant by adding neutralizing agents like during fermentative production of lactic acid pH has an inhibitory effect as the no. of LAB cannot survive well below the pH level of 4 (Adachi et al. 1998)[3], to avoid this problem neutralizing agents like NaOH, $Mg(OH)_2$, $CaCO_3$ are added to maintain the constant pH in batch reactor.

While operating batch reactor for lactic acid production have a major problem of substrate inhibition of sugar concentration (Ding and Tan 2006[4]; Gatje and Golt schalk 1991[5]), to avoid this problem of inhibition and to increase viable cell concentration and prolonged culture life the fermenter can be operated under the fed batch mode. To produce highly concentration of lactic acid (Ding and Tan 2006) [4] developed four different fed batch feeding strategies, these are Poly fed batch, Continuous feed rate fed batch, Exponential feed rate fed batch and compact residual glucose concentration fed batch.

A new method was developed by Zuhang et al.2010 [6] to control the concentration of substrate through automatic adjustment of pH as result of this method 96.3 g/l lactic acid was obtained with *lactobacillus lactis*. To get high productivity of lactic acid with *Lactobacillus shamnosus* a new production approach, multi stage continuous high cell density culture was developed by Chang et al 2011[7].

MOLECULAR APPROACH FOR PLA PRODUCTION

For the overproduction of PLA and obtaining highly pure isomers different molecular approaches have been used, in this review some of them have been summarized.

A metabolic engineering have been performed on *Synechocystis* sp. PCC 6803 to produce optically pure lactic acid from a sustainable source CO2 and a recent developed enzyme that is a mutated glycerol dehydrogenase GlyDH. For the improvement in D-lactic acid synthesis, codon optimization and blending of a co factor NADH availability through hetrologus expression of a soluble trans-hydrogenase (Varman et al. 2013)[8].

Use of Recombinant for the Production of Lactic Acids

For the production lactic acid an UV- Induced mutated strain of recombinant *Bacillus subtilis* 1-A304(Φ105MU331) was used, this recombinant was using glucose as carbon source for the production of lactic acid, on studying the effect of N2 source on lactic acid production by this recombinant, it was found that inorganic nitrogen was having some inhibitory effect as when the concentration of nitrogen decreased in the medium there was increase in the production, 79 g/l and 93g/l was produced in 24 hr and 51 hr respectively (Wong, Yuk-ki 2010).

Similarly when the effect of cell density and oxygen transfer was studied, it was found that on increasing the cell density and culture volume in shake flask level (low oxygen concentration), the production of lactic acid get increased. An important feature of this recombinant is that Bacillus subtilas have capability of producing alpha amylases which is used in liquefaction of starch. hence for the production of lactic acid is followed by sccharification liquefaction of starch as on using liquefied starch there are no lactic acid production, for the optimization of scarification process different temperatures and forms of *Aspergillus niger* (mycelium, pellet and supernatant of the culture) was used (Wong and Yuk-ki 2010). Starch can be used for the production of lactic acid by a mix culture of recombinant *Bacillus subtilis* and *Aspergillus niger*.

Vectors Used of Production of Lactic Acid

Due to the increasing demand of PLA different genetic approaches are being used to improve its properties and to over produce it, shuttle vector pMBLTO2 can used as a stable plasmid vector to overproduce D lactate which is monomer of PLA.

This vector pMBLTO2 was constructed from the pMBLT00 replicon and an erathrosynin resistance gene of pE194. For the overproduction of D lactate dehydrogenase this vector is used to engineer *Luconostoc citereum*95, this engineered strain overexposes D-lactate dehydrogenase and exhibit the enhance production of optically pure D lactate (Han Seung Chae et al. 2012).

For the efficient production of lactic acid, a metabolically engineered yeast have developed in which coding region for pyurvate decarboxylase (PDCE) on chromosome No. 12 is replaced by L lactate dehydrogenase gene (LDH). These recombinant yeast cells which are over expressing LDH were producing both lactate and ethanol on cane sugar glucose as carbon source approximate 62.7% glucose is being converted to lactic acid under naturalizing conditions (Nobuhiro Ishida et al. 2004).

ISOLATION AND PURIFICATION STRATEGIES

As in the conventional fermentation process organic acids are produced in the form of salt of calcium ammonium or sodium hence to recover free acid from some purification and acidification steps are used.

Chemical Separation Process for Purification of Lactic Acid

This is a traditional process for separation of lactic acid from fermentation broth in which first $caco_3$ is used to neutralize the fermentation broth and then calcium lactate containing broth is filtered to remove cells, carbon treated, decolored, evaporated, and acidified with sulfuric acid to produce lactic acid and insoluble calcium sulfate (Datta and Henry 2006) [9] for further purification hydrolysis, estrification and distillation is done.

This process has disadvantages like production of large amount of caso4 as a byproduct and high concentration of H_2So_4 (Qin et al. 2010)[10]. Apart from this traditional method a number of processes for lactic acid recovery for fermentation broth like recovery by solvent extraction method (Yabannavar et al.1991)[11], by absorb in ion exchange chromatography (Kaufman and Cooper et al. 1994)[12], by direct distillation process (Cockrem and Johnson et al.1993)[13], and most promising by electro dialysis (Hongo et al.1986)[14], although these process can help in increasing the recovery of lactic acid and reducing the amount of waste generated but all the above mentioned methods have some kind of disadvantages like solvent extraction process was having problem of un favorable distribution coefficient and have economical problem which result in high cost of product similarly in absorption process, ion exchange resin regeneration and large amount of chemical requirement for adjustment of pH to increase the sorption efficiency and in indirect distillation process high boiling intend esters can form dimmers and polymers.

However eletrodialysis most suitable method for recovery of lactic acid as this method gives efficient removal of non ionic molecules concentration of product and less time consuming and most useful that in this method no byproduct generation take place.

Recovery of Lactic Acid by Electro Dialysis

This is an electrochemical process in which certain cation and anion membrane are used these membrane allow to pass through positive and negative ions respectively.

Desalting Electrolysis

Nanofiltration is a noble technique to remove the impurity of magnesium, and calcium ions from sodium lactate fermentation broth, this method is used before the concentration of fermentation broth and converted in to lactic acid by electro dialysis. There are two main type of electro dialysis method are being used for recovery of lactic acid, conventional electro dialysis (CED) consisting of cation- and anion-exchange membrane and ion substitution electrodialysis (ISED) consisting of only cation-exchange membrane. When a comparative study between CED and ISED was done by Seung-Hyoen Moon et al. 2002[15], it was found at to remove the lactic acid from sodium lactate ISED technique was more efficient in compression to CED as there was negligible loss of lactic acid in removal of sodium ion from feed.

Although both the process are capable of removing impurities of sodium ions from feed up to 95% but there is a problem with ISED technique is sodium ion get accumulated in acid compartment and process efficiency get decreased when these ions in acid compartment started going back to the feed stream to cope up with this problem they have suggested to used proton permselective cation exchanger.

Two Stage Electrodialysis Method

For the recovery of lactic acid a two stages electro dialysis method is used in which the 1st step is the concentration of sodium lactate was done with desalting electrodialysis which uses ion exchange membrane while the second stages related with electro conversion of sodium lactate to lactic acid by electro dialysis with the help of a bipolar membrane, before the electrodialysis some pretreatment processes like ultrafiltration, deconcentration and removing the multivalent metal ions are required, in the very 1ststep of clarification large impurity like bacterial cells, high molecular weight residue are eliminated by the help of micro filtration, after it the fluid is concentrated by the help of conventional electro dialysis CED which is based on the principle of electro-migrartion of ions, now the acid salt is converted in to free organic acid form by bipolar electrodialysis (Yong Keun Chang et al.1998)[16], to improve the overall efficiency of this process nano-filtration membrane are used before and after BED process.

PROPERTIES OF POLY LACTIC ACID (PLA)

Thermoplastic Properties

Pure PLA is a semicrysteline polymer which is having melting point 180 degree centigrade while meso lactide has an amorphous nature. In 1968 Samits and Kovaus produced pseudo orthorhombic crystal structure of PLA. The melt enthalpy estimated for enatiopure PLA of 100% crystalnity by Fisher et al [17] is 93 j/g, the value most rottenly refferd in the literature although high values up to 148 j/g also have been reported, the melting temperature and degree of crystalinity are depend on the thermal history, molar mass and the purity (blending ratio) of the polymer. To get a crystalline form of PLA atleast 72-75% of optical purity corresponding to approximate 30 isolactic lactile units is required, however Sarasua et al.[18] have though been able to crystallize a polysaccharide of as low as 43% optical purity.

Rheological Properties of PLA

When compared with polyfins, it was found that the polymer of lactic acid has low melt elasticity, this property causes problems during extrusion process when used for cast film, paper coating and blown-film manufacture, the reason behind this low elasticity is low degradation of molecular chains entanglement, to acid this problem, branching in the polymers can be introduce by adding low level of an epoxide natural oil during polymerization James Lunt et al. 1997[19], Gruber, P. R., Kolstad 1994 [20].

Solubility of Lactic Acid Based Polymers

The solubility of lactic acid based polymers in different organic solvents like chlorinated and floronated organic solvents dioxolane, furane, acetone, pyridine and ethyl lactate is highly depend on the molar mass, degree of crystalinity and different comonomers present in the polymers, while lactic acid polymers are typically insoluble in water alcohol and undistributed hydrocarbons (Anders sodergards et al. 2002)[21].

Blending Effect on Properties of PLA

To improve the properties like degradation rate, drug release properties permeability characteristics and different thermal and mechanical properties, the polymer of lactic acid are blended with other polymers.

No. of researchers are studying different sterioforms of poly lactic acid based polymers[22], due to increased melting temperature and improved molecular properties the stereocomplaxation of enatiomers have been highly studied[23]. The blending of PLA with poly vinyl acetate[24], poly vinyl chloride, poly ethylene oxide, poly ethylene glycol, poly acrylate, poly vinyl phenol and many more have been studied by researchers.

Mechanical Properties

For getting high mechanical properties semi crystalline polymer of lactic acid are used in place of amorphous polymers as for semi crystalline PLA the value of tensile modulus and flexural modulus is approximate 3Gpa and 5Gpa respectively and the tensile strength and flexural strength is about 50-70Mpa and 100Mpa respectively[25].

The degree of crystalinity 226and molar mass 221of the polymer are two major factor which affect the mechanical properties of PLA. On increasing the molar mass from 50 to 100 KDa, it has been seen that tensile strength of poly lactic acid gets increased by two times [26].

APPLICATIONS OF POLY LACTIC ACID

Due to their unique properties like thermoplastic nature, processability, biodegradable and eco-friendly nature lactic acid based polymer (PLA) have potential applications in different fields like manufacturing of disposable materials, agriculture products, in production of packaging materials and as a commodity plastic apart from this they are also used in biomedical fields as bone fixing material, in drug delivery and in tissue engineering.

Application of PLA in Biomedical Fields

PLA is most preferred choice of engineers for its biomedical use as it results lactic acid on degradation, which is totally biocompatible and biodegradable.

PLA has growing multidimensional application as a biomaterial like:

Use of PLA as Suture Material

They are filaments used to cover the wound which can be fabricated in different shape as per requirement, the basic function of sutures is that they hold up the tissue and provide support to wound tissue until heeling is not done. (Gupta et al. 2007)[25]. FDA has been approved PLA as a suture material as it offers crucial advantages (Benicewicz et al. 1990)[26]

There are some limitations of using PLA as suture material due to its intrinsic properties like high crystalinity, slow degradation and high rigidity to avoid these problems copolymerization of lactic acid is done with other biodegradable monomers like Glycolic acid. Ethicon has commercialized a copolymer with a ratio of 90:10 mole of glycolic acid lactide by the name of 'Vicryl' which has a high rate of degradation in comparison to PLA filaments.

Use of PLA in Drug Delivery System

Due to its biodegradability PLA is highly used polymer in designing of drug delivery system.

Eerink et al.[27] have produced biodegradable hollow fibers from polymer of lactic acid by a dry wet phase inversion spinning from DLLA-PVR dioxane spinning dope, a pours sponge like wall of fiber was generated, which external and internal surface remained covered with skin ca.0.3 0.4 micro meters thick. To study the release behavior of drug a hormone Levonorgestrenol was filled in it due to the pours nature of wall, a high release of hormone was obtained.

Use of PLA in Tissue Engineering and Bone Fixation

One of the most important applications of PLA is in tissue engineering; tissue engineering approach is used for treatment of malfunctioning/lost organs. In this patient's own cells are grown on a polymer support to regenerate the tissue 5, this polymer is basically a scaffold provide the physical support to guide the growth of new organ. A three dimensional scaffold of poly lactic acid are being used in culturing of different type of cell based gene therapy for cardiovascular disease, muscle tissue and in the regeneration of bone and cartilage and in the treatment of neurological and orthopedical conditions [28] [29] [30].

Bioabsorable polymer are highly used in tissue engineering because they can be easily hydrolyzed in to products which can be metabolizes by body, the degradation period of poly lactic acid is ranges from 10 months to 4 years, this depends on no. of factors like chemical composition crystallinity and processing of PLA.

Due to its suitable mechanical properties profile, thermoplastic processabilty and biological properties like biodegradability and biocompatibility PLA is highly used as a bone fixing material among all other biopolymers used for medical applications.

Application of PLA in Packaging Material

Apart from physical safety and maintaining the of quality of product, a packaging material must be eco-friendly as it should not cause the waste deposal problems hence the demand of petroleum based polymers for packaging material is shifting towards the biodegradable bioplastics which are made up of renewable sources. Among the different bioplastic available, poly lactic acid is highly used at industrial level [31][32].

There are no. of advantages of using of PLA in place of PET for packaging material is like transparency of PLA is higher than PET, PLA can easily be degraded in biological environment like soil or compost in two steps hydrolysis and enzymatic degradation, in hydrolysis water get diffused in polymer and results in the random breakdown of ester bonds due to which molecular weight of polymer get decreased and formation of oligomer and lactic acid take place which can be assimilated by different microorganisms like fungi and bacteria [33].

Application of PLA in Production of Sports Wear

PLA is also used in the production of some type of sportswear by different companies worldwide like - A Japan based company Kanebo Ltd., has produced fibers of PLA under the brand name LACTRON these fibers were exhibited in garments at the time of Nagano Olympics [34], and a French company Fiberweb have developed web and laminations which are made up of 100% poly lactic acid under the brand name Deposa [35].

CONCLUSION

Due to its unique properties many researchers are highly interested and working on poly lactic acid (PLA) and hence its applications in different fields are increasing day by day, further research is needed to improve its properties like to decrease the degradation time, increase its thermo stability, melting point and many more. For completely fulfilling the increasing demand of PLA new molecular approaches can be developed to overproduce it with low cost and good quality.

There are number of copolymers and blends of PLA have been developed, which are having excellent application of PLA in different fields, In future new copolymer and blends can be produced to use it in many unexplored applications.

REFERENCES

1. Nguyen CM, Kim JS, Hwang HJ, Park MS, Choi GJ, Choi YH, Jang KS, Kim JC (2012) Production of L-Lactic acid from a Green Microalga, Hydrodictyon Reticulum, by Lactobacillus Paracasei LA104 Isolated from the Traditional Korean Food, Makgeolli. Bioresour Technol 110: 552-559.
2. Yanez R, Moldes AB, Alonso JL, Parajo JC (2003) Production of D-(-)-Lactic Acid from Cellulose by Simultaneous Saccharification and Fermentation Using Lactobacillus Coryniformis subsp. Torquens. Biotechnol Lett 25: 1161-1164.
3. Adachi, E., Torigoe, M., Sugiyama, M., Nikawa, J., Shimizu, K., 1998. Modification of Metabolic Pathways of Saccharomyces Cerevisiae by the Expression of Lactate Dehydrogenase and Deletion of Pyruvate Decarboxylase Genes for the Lactic Acid Fermentation at Low pH Value. J. Ferment. Bioeng. 86, 284-289.
4. Ding, S.F., Tan, T.W., 2006. L-Lactic Acid Production by Lactobacillus Casei Fermentation using Different Fed-batch Feeding Strategies. Process Biochem. 41, 1451-1454.
5. Gatje, G., Gottschalk, G., 1991. Limitation of Growth and Lactic Acid Production in Batch and Continuous Cultures of Lactobacillus Helveticus. Appl. Microbiol. Biotechnol. 34, 446-449.
6. Zhang, Y., Cong, W., Shi, S., 2010b. Application of a pH Feedback-controlled Substrate Feeding Method in Lactic Acid Production. Appl. Biochem. Biotechnol. 162, 2149-2156.
7. Chang, H.N., Kim, N.J., Kang, J., Jeong, C.M., Choi, J.D., Fei, Q., Kim, B.J., Kwon, S., Lee, S.Y., Kim, J., 2011. Multi-stage High Cell Continuous Fermentation for High Productivity and Titer. Bioprocess Biosyst. Eng. 34, 419-431.
8. Arul M Varman, Yi Yu, Le You and Yinjie J Tang.2013. Photoautotrophic Production of D-lactic Acid in an Engineered Cyanobacterium. *Microbial Cell Factories*,12: 117 doi:10.1186/1475-2859-12-117
9. Datta, R., Henry, M., 2006. Lactic Acid: Recent Advances in Products, Processes and Technologies a Review. J. Chem. Technol. Biotechnol. 81, 1119-1129.
10. Qin, J., Wang, X., Zheng, Z., Ma, C., Tang, H., Xu, P., 2010. Production of l-lactic Acid by a Thermophilic Bacillus Mutant Using Sodium Hydroxide as Neutralizing Agent. Bioresour. Technol. 101, 7570-7576.
11. V.M. Yabannavar, D.I.C. Wang, Extractive Fermentation for Lactic Acid Production, Biotech. Bioeng. 37 (1991) 1095±1100.
12. E.N. Kaufman, S.P. Cooper, B.H. Davison, Screening of Resins for Use in a Biparticle Fluidized-bed Bioreactor for the Continuous Fermentation and Separation of Lactic Acid, Appl. Biochem. Biotech. 45 46 (1994) 545±554.
13. M.C.M. Cockrem, P.D. Johnson, Recovery of Lactate Esters and Lactic Acid from Fermentation Broth, USP 5 210 296, 1993.
14. M. Hongo, Y. Nomura, M. Iwahara, Novel Method of Lactic Acid Production by Electrodialysis Fermentation, Appl.Environ. Microbiol. 52(2) (1986) 314±319.
15. Jae-Hwan Choi, Sung-Hye Kim, Seung-Hyeon Moon. 2002. Recovery of Lactic Acid from Sodium Lactate by Ion Substitution Using Ion-exchange Membrane. Separation and Purification Technology 28 69-79.
16. Eun Gyo Lee, Seung-Hyeon Moon, Yong Keun Chang, Ik-Keun Yoo, Ho Nam Chang.1998. Lactic Acid Recovery Using Two-stage Electrodialysis and its Modeling. Journal of Membrane Science 145 53±66.
17. Fischer EW, Sterzel HJ, Wegner G. 1973. Investigation of the Structure of Solution Grown Crystals of Lactied Copolymer by Mean of Chemical Reactions. Kolloid ZZ Polym 251: 980 90.
18. Sarasua J.R, Prud'homme RE, Wisniewski M, Le Borgne A, Sparsky N. Crystallization and Melting Behaviour of Polylactieds. Macro Molecules 1992; 25: 5719 23.

19. James Lunt.1997. Large-scale Production, Properties and Commercial Applications of Polylactic Acid Polymers. PII: 50141-3910(97)00148-I 0148 1.
20. Gruber, P.R., Kolstad, J.J. and Witzke, D.R., US Patent 5,539,026, 1994.
21. Anders Sodengard, Mikael Stolt. 2002. Properties of Lactic Acid Based Polymers and Teir Correlation with Composition. Prog. Polym.sci.27 1123-1163.
22. Tsuiuji H, Iada Y.Crystallization from the Melt of Poly Lactied with Different Optical Parties and Their Blends. Macro mol Chem Phy 1996; 197: 3483 99.
23. Tsuiuji H, Iada Y, Hyon S-H, Kimura Y, Kito J. Stereocomplex Formation Between Enantiomers Poly(lactic acid). 8 Complex Fiber Spun from Mixed Solution of poly(D-lactic acid) and poly (L-lactic acid).J Appl polym Sci 1994; 51: 337 44.
24. PiH Ch, Cha y, Shah SS, Zhu KJ. blends of PVA and PGLA: Controle of Permeability and Degradiabilty of Hydrogels by Blending. J Control Rel 1992; 19: 189 200.
25. Bhuvanesh Gupta, Nilesh Revagade, Jo¨ ns Hilborn. 2007. Poly(Lactic Acid) Fiber: An Overview. Prog. Polym. Sci. 32 (2007) 455-482.
26. Benicewicz BC, Hopper PK. Polymers for Absorbable Surgical Sutures. J Bioact Compat Polym 1990; 5: 453-72.
27. Eenink MJD, Feijien J, Olijslager J, Albers JHM, Rieke JC, Greidanus PJ. Biodegradable Hollow Fibers for the Controlled Release of Hormones. J Contr Rel 1987; 6: 225 47.
28. Kim K, Yu M, Zong X, Chiu J, Fang D, Seo YS, et al. Control of Degradation Rate and Hydrophilicity in Electrospun Non-woven Poly(DL-lactide) Nanofiber Scaffolds for Biomedical Applications. Biomaterials 2003; 24: 4977-85.
29. Zong X, Bien H, Chung CY, Yin L, Kim K, Fang DF, et al. Electrospun Non-woven Membranes as Scaffolds for Heart Tissue Constructs. ACS Polym Preprint 2003; 44: 96 7.
30. Kenawy E, Bowlin G L, Mansfield K, Layman J, Simpson D G, Sanders E H, et al. Release of Tetracycline Hydrochloride from Electrospun Poly(ethylene-co-vinylacetate), poly(lacticacid) and a blend. J. Contr Rel 2002; 81: 57-64.
31. Kalb B, Pennings AJ. General Crystallization Behaviour of Poly (L-lactic Acid). Polymer 1980; 21: 607-12.
32. Penning JP, Dijikstra H, Pennings AJ. Preparation and Characterization of Absorbable Fibers from L-lactide Copolymers. Polymer 1993; 34: 942-51.
33. Lowe CE. Preparation of High Molecular Weight Polyhydroxyester, US Patent, 2,668, 162, 1954.
34. Lunt J, Shafer A L. Polylactic Acid Polymers from Corn: Applications in the Textiles Industry. J Ind Text 2000; 29: 191-205.
35. Crop-based Polymers for Nonwovens. Insight Conference, Toronto. Calvin Wooding Coulting Ltd.; 2000.

Pages: 117-133

AGRICULTURE DEVELOPMENT AND SUSTAINABLE ENVIRONMENT

Edited by: Jaswant Ray; Dr. Pawan Kumar 'Bharti'

ISBN: 978-93-5056-759-3

Edition: 2015

Published by: Discovery Publishing House Pvt. Ltd., New Delhi (India)

9

Safe Use of Chlorine with Special Reference to Production, Storage, Handling and Emergency Preparedness in Case of Leakage/Accident

G.C. Kisku

INTRODUCTION

Chlorine is a yellowish-green, non-combustible heavy gas element at atmospheric pressure in group VIIA of the periodic table with a pungent, irritating, suffocating odour. It is shipped as a liquefied compressed gas. It is the commonest of the 4 halogens which are among the most chemically reactive of all the elements. It is not flammable but it is a strong oxidizer. Although classified as a non-flammable gas, chlorine deserves special attention because of its widely used and has been involved in many health-related incidents. It reacts explosively or forms explosive compound with many organic compound and common substance such as acetylene. Chlorine reacts with water to form hypochlorus acid. It condenses to an amber liquid at-35°C. In the 1920s, chlorine was introduced as a bleaching agent. Subsequently, it was used in many industrial processes as well as household bleaching and water purification. At present, chlorination is the primary measure employed in disinfecting community pools.

Environmental Monitoring Division, CSIR-Indian Institute of Toxicology Research, MG Marg, Lucknow - 226 001, U P (India).

Table 9.1: Chlorine Concentrations Associated with Odour Perception and Irritation

Cl_2 Concentration		Subjective
(ppm)	(mg/m³)	
0.02-2	0.06-5.8	Odour perception and irritation
1	2.9	Burdensome
2-3	5.8-8.7	Annoying
4	>11.6	Intolerable

PHYSICAL PROPERTIES

Gross formula: Cl_2

Atomic weight:35.453

Melting point: -101°C

Vapour pressure: 6.8 atm

Solubility in water, g/100 ml at 20°C: 5168

Relative vapour density (air=1): 2.5

Density: 14085 at 20°C and 6.864 atm (liquid)

Atomic number: 17

Molecular weight: 70.906

Boiling point: -34°C

Soluble in alcohol and chlorides

CHEMICAL PROPERTIES

Chlorine has the potential to react with most of other elements. Mixture of chlorine and hydrogen can react violently to form hydrogen chloride. Chlorine reacts with alkalis and alkaline earth metal hydroxides to form soda and lime bleaches. Chlorine reacts with ammonia or ammonium compounds to form various mixtures of chloramines (NH_2Cl, NCl_3^- is dangerously explosives). Chlorine reacts with organics to form chlorinated derivatives and hydrogen chlorides. Some of these reactions are explosives.

HAZARDOUS POTENTIALS

(i) Flammability

Non-combustible in air but most combustible materials will burn in chlorine as they do in oxygen. Flammable gases and vapours will form explosive mixtures with chlorine. Reacts explosively or forms explosive compounds with many common chemicals, especially ether, turpentine, acetylene, fuel gas, ammonia gas, hydrocarbons, hydrogen and finely pulverized metals except the noble gases and carbon (in the absence of combined hydrogen).

(ii) Toxicity

OSHA: TWA 0.5 ppm (1.5 mg/m^3) STEL: 1 ppm (2.95 mg/m^3)

ACGIH: TWA 0.5 ppm (1.5 mg/m^3) STEL: 1 ppm (not classified as a human carcinogen)

DFG: 0.5 ppm NIOSH : 0.5 ppm

Threshold Toxicity Limit: 3 mg/m^3 of air for solids

USE OF CHLORINE

Chlorine and hydrochlorides have broad application as bleaching agents in the textile and paper industries. Indispensable reagent in synthetic chemicals, manufacture of chlorinated organic materials and inorganic chlorides and chlorates. Chlorine itself is used extensively to purify water supplies. It is an intermediate in the production of many products - specifically plastics, refrigerants, vitamins, medicines, solvents, synthetic rubbers, high-test gasoline's, insecticides and herbicides. Chlorine is used as an intermediate in the synthesis of common antifreeze (ethylene glycol).

SAFE DRINKING WATER ACT AND SMCL

The US-EPA established Secondary Maximum Contaminant Levels (SMCL) for chlorine is 250 mg/L. SMCL guidelines correspond to approximate concentrations at which chlorine will not cause aesthetic problems such as coloured water, turbidity, staining and bad taste that would impact public acceptance. EPA has also issued a chlorine health advisory at the 250 mg/L SMCL, where potential chronic health concerns at or below this level are unlikely to occur.

MANUFACTURING PROCESS

According to Alkali Manufactures Association of India (AMSI) chlorine could be produced in three different processes which are described below:

(A) Mercury Cell Process

In this process, the mercury cell cathode comprises of a slowly flowing layer of mercury across the cell bottom. In this, sodium ions at the cathode are converted into sodium, which forms an amalgam with the mercury at the cathode. The amalgam reacts with water in a separate reactor called a decomposer, where hydrogen gas and a caustic soda solution of 50% concentration are produced. Chlorine, which is also produced as a byproduct in the process is collected separately and then cooled, dried, compressed and liquefied. Mercury is pumped back into cell. As the brine is usually re-circulated, solid salt is required to maintain the saturation of the salt water. The brine is first de-chlorinated and then purified by a precipitation filtration process.

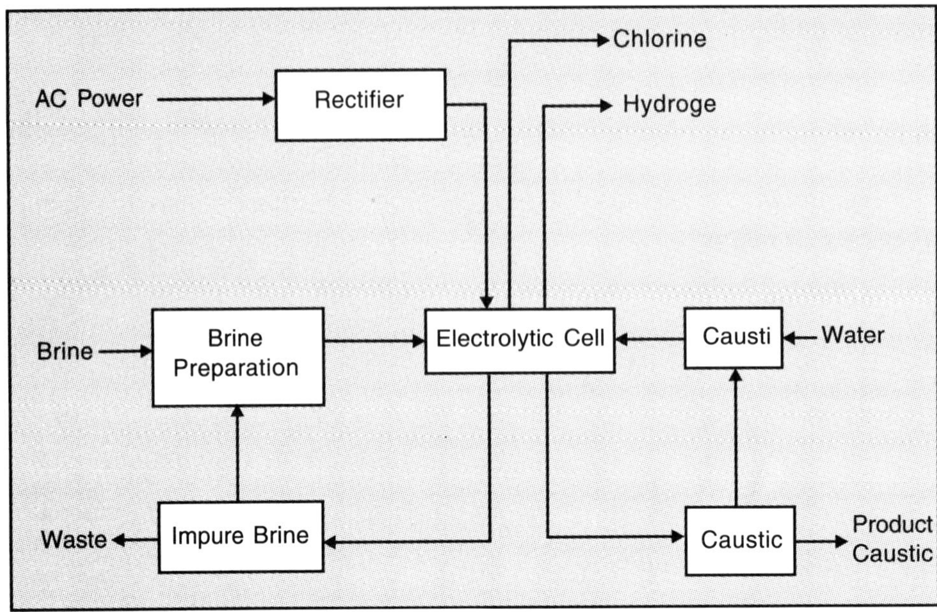

Fig. 9.1: Schematic Diagram of Chlor-Alkali Plant and Chlorine Production

(B) Membrane Cell Process

In the membrane cell process, the anode and the cathode are separated by an ion exchange membrane that selectively transmits sodium ion and some amount of water but restricts the hydroxyl ions from the cathode section into the anode section. Diluted brine is fed into the anode compartment, where chlorine gas is generated and sodium ions migrate into the cathode section through the membrane. In the cathode section, hydrogen is evolved at the cathode, leaving behind hydroxyl ions, which along with sodium ions, producing caustic soda. The caustic solution leaves the cell with about 30-33% concentration. This 33% caustic soda is further concentrated to 50% at a later stage as per the market requirement. The chlorine gas, generated from this process contains some oxygen and must be purified by liquefaction and evaporation. The brine is de-chlorinated and re-circulated. Solid salt is usually needed to re-saturate the brine. After purification by precipitation - filtration, the brine is further purified with an ion exchange.

(C) Diaphragm Process

A diaphragm cell contains a porous diaphragm, which is used to separate two halves of the cell, to allow a flow of brine and to prevent chlorine and hydrogen gas from mixing. The brine is introduced into the anode compartment. Chlorine gas is formed at the anodes, whereas the sodium hydroxide solution and hydrogen gas are formed directly at the cathode. A diluted caustic brine leaves the cell, after which the caustic soda must usually be concentrated to 50% and the salt be removed by an evaporative process. The salt separated from the caustic brine can be used to saturate diluted brine. It is estimated that, approximately three tons of steam is required for each ton of caustic soda. The chlorine gas generated contains oxygen and must be purified by liquefaction and evaporation. This process also uses asbestos which has serious environmental implications.

The main raw materials for the caustic soda manufacture are power and common salt. The solution of salt in water is prepared and is purified by addition of sodium carbonate, lime etc. The impurities of calcium and magnesium are precipitated and removed from the process fluid by setting and filtration. The purified brine solution is acidified and electrolysed in cells. D.C. from anode to cathode decomposes common salt into sodium and chlorine ions, sodium ions combine with mercury to form mercury amalgam.

The chlorine is a byproduct of caustic soda plant. After its dissociation from common salt in the electrolyser, it is taken to the liquefication section, where it is first scrubbed with water to remove impurities of sodium chloride in scrubbing towers. So washed chlorine gas, which is saturated with water vapours, is dried in contact with sulphuric acid in drying towers. The dried chlorine is non-corrosive, but, if wet, it becomes very corrosive. In the liquefication operation of chlorine no chemical reaction takes place as such, but care is taken to ensure that chlorine is absolutely dry after the drying operation. This is being done by constant monitoring of the concentration of sulphuric acid in the drying towers and the chlorine compressors, which are checked at every hour interval and proper operating record maintained. After compressing the gas to 3 kg/cm^2, it is liquefied in refrigeration system by cooling it to about minus 10 °C. The liquefied product is taken to the main storage tank.

Chlorine and caustic solution (sodium or potassium hydroxide) are produced simultaneously by means of decomposition of a salt solution in water. Along with chlorine and caustic solution, hydrogen is produced. The raw materials used in the process are NaCl or KCl, water, electricity, *etc.* Most of the time, NaCl is used in the process as a raw material and less frequently KCl. Other processes such as the electrolysis of hydrochloric acid (HCl) or the electrolysis of molten NaCl are also applied, but rarely. In all processes, the NaCl is dissolved in water:

The overall process is based on reaction:

$$NaCl = Na^+ + Cl^-$$

$$2Na^+_{(aq)} + 2Cl^-_{(aq)} + 2H_2O = 2Na^+_{(aq)} + 2OH^-_{(aq)} + Cl_{2\,(g)} + H_{2\,(g)}$$

Following chemical equation:

$$2NaCl_{[58.5g]}\ (\text{or KCl}) + 2H_2O_{[18g]} \longrightarrow Cl_{2[35.5g]} + H_{2\,[1g]} + 2NaOH_{[40g]}\ (\text{or KOH})$$

The basic principle in the electrolysis of chloride solutions of NaCl proceed according to the following equations:

- At the Anode:

The chloride ions are oxidized and chlorine is formed based on the following reactions

$$2Cl^-_{(aq.)} \longrightarrow Cl_{2\,(g)} + 2e^-$$

- At the Cathode:

In this mercury cell process, sodium/ mercury amalgam is formed and hydrogen (H_2) and hydroxide ions (OH^-) are formed by the reaction of the sodium in the amalgam with water in the denuder. The cathode reaction is:

$$2Na^+_{(aq.)} + 2H_2O + 2e^- \longrightarrow H_{2\,(g)} + 2Na^+_{(aq.)} + 2OH^-_{(aq.)}$$

Overall process: $2NaCl$ (or KCl) $+ 2H_2O \longrightarrow Cl_2 + H_2 + 2NaOH$ (or KOH)

Whereas, in case of Membrane Cell Process and Diaphragm cell Process, water decomposes to form Hydrogen (H_2) and hydroxide ions (OH^-) at the Cathode.

At the Cathode:

$$2H^+_{(aq)} + 2e^- \longrightarrow H_{2\,(g)}$$

The caustic soda and hydrogen are produced more or less in a fixed ratio. Independent of the technology used.

Per 1 ton of chlorine produced.

- 1128 kg of NaoH (100%) is produced if NaCl is used as the raw material.
- 1577 kg of KOH (100%) is produced if KCl is used as the raw material (the Mol. Wt. of KOH is higher than the NaOH)
- 28 kg of hydrogen is produced.

CHLOR-ALKALI PLANTS IN INDIA AND PRODUCTION

(a) India Chlorine production (2012-2013)

Indian capacity is only 3.2 million tones. i.e. 4% of the World capacity. The chlor–alkali plants of India are tabulated in Table 9.2.

(b) World Chlorine production (2012-2013)

World production of caustic soda is 80 million MTPA

MEASUREMENT OF CHLORINE IN AMBIENT AIR

According to Stahl, there are no specific methods of chlorine measurement; most methods used rely on the oxidizing property of chlorine.

SAMPLING METHODS OF CHLORINE

Chlorine gas samples are collected either in impinger containing a reactive liquid solution or on a solid. The common liquid solution used is NaOH solution. Commonly used absorber solutions react with Cl_2 gas to directly or indirectly produce a colour change in the solution which is taken as an indication of the amount of Cl_2 in the sampled air or gas. This basic solution converts the Cl_2 gas to equal amounts of chloride ions and hydrochlorite ions. When the solution made acidic, the reaction is reversed and the Cl_2 gas is generated.

Table 9.2: Chlor-Alkali Plants in India

Sl. No.	Chlor-Alkali Plants	Capacity (MTPA)
1.	M/s. Rayalseema Alkalies & Alied Chemicals Ltd., Kumool	92600
2.	M/s. Gujarat Alkalies & Chemicals Ltd., Bharuch	116500
3.	M/s. Gujrat Alkalies & Chemicals Ltd., Vadodara	153500
4.	M/s. Shriram Alkali & Chemicals Bharuch	62500
5.	M/s. Indian Rayon & Industries Ltd., Junagarh	37950
6.	M/s. The Travancore – Cochin Chemicals Ltd., Kochi	52250
7.	M/s. Grashim Industries Ltd., Nagda	108000
8.	M/s. Jayshree Chemicals Ltd., Ganjam	225000
9.	M/s. Chamfab Alkalis Ltd., Kalapet	38700
10.	M/s. Punjab Alkalies & Chemicals Ltd., Roper	99000
11.	M/s. Siel Chemical Complex Patiala Ltd., Patiala	82500
12.	M/s. Shriram Vinyl & Chemical Industries, Kota	39550
13.	M/s. DCW Ltd., Tuticorin	60000
14.	M/s. ABCIL Ltd., Renukut, Sonebhadra	52000
15.	M/s. Durgapur Chemical Ltd., Burdwan	10050
	Total capacity	**1250200**

QUALITATIVE AND SEMI-QUALITATIVE METHODS

Many types of Cl_2 indicator papers have been developed. The most common one is starch–iodide papers. The basic reaction of chlorine gas with the potassium iodide of the paper yields free iodine, which then reacts with the starch to produce a blue colour. The limit of detection is ~2 to 6 ppm. A starch–iodide paper also coated with glycerine and sulfurous acid is reported to turn brown or black and to have sensitivity of 0.25 to 12 ppm. Other common papers used include bromide–fluoresce in papers which change from yellow to red or rose red with a sensitivity of ~10 ppm and o-tolidine papers which turn yellow to bluish green with a sensitivity of ~2 ppm.

Rapid semi quantitative determination of Cl_2 gas can be made with commercially available gas-detecting tubes. These tubes contain a solid–coated reactive material which changes calorimetrically when exposed to a specific gas or to a certain types of gases. A given volume of the gas sample is passed over the absorbent and the amount of absorbent that changes colors (measured by the length is affected) is used to determine the amount of particular gas being tested (in this case Cl_2 gas). Reactive substances that have been used as indicators for Chlorine are o-toluidine, bromide-florescence and tetraphenylbenzidine.

QUANTITATIVE METHODS FOR CHLORINE

Most quantitative methods of analysis for Cl_2 gas are based on colorimetric reactions. A sensitive reagent commonly used is o-toluidine. The air sample can either be passed directly into an acid solution of o-toluidine or collected in dilute NaOH which can later be acidified and the o-toluidine then added. The latter method has the advantage that the time allowed for the development of colour can be controlled and maximized. Acidification yields a more stable yellow to orange colour. Colour comparisons can be made with standardized colour solutions.

By visual methods or in a spectrophotometer at 435 and 490 mμ, atleast 3 L of air must be sampled to detect CI_2 concentration of 3000 μg/m^3. This method is reported to be better than 99% efficient. However, the presence of other oxidants such as chlorine dioxide, ozone, ferric and magnetic compounds and nitrates may interfere with this method. Continuous sampling instruments for detection of Cl_2 gas have been developed. An alarm system can be used with the instruments to warm when a certain limit has been reached. Sensitivity ranges from 300 to 9000 μg/m^3 (0.1 to 3 ppm) of Cl_2.

STORAGE OF CHLORINE

Prior to working with chlorine you must be trained on its proper handling and storage. Use cylinders with special fittings. Protect containers against physical damage. Cylinders and ton containers should be stored in cool, dry, relatively isolated area, protected from weather and extreme temperature changes. Keep cylinders upright and secure them tightly so as they will remain upright. Store ton containers in such a fashion so all are accessible in case of emergency. Except when containers are connected, keep valve outlet caps and valve protection hood in place. Do not store full and empty containers together and keep the storage area well ventilated. Make certain that no escaping chlorine can enter a general ventilating system because chlorine vapour is heavier than air, make sure areas are arranged so that escaping gas will not accumulate in low areas. Separate from combustible, organic or easily oxidizable materials and especially isolate from acetylene, turpentine, ether, ammonia gas, fuel gas, hydrocarbons, and hydrogen and finely pulverized. Store outdoors or in well-ventilated non-combustible construction, detached or segregated areas. Chlorine cylinder should be used on a first-in-first-Out because valve packings can harden during prolonged storage and cause leaks when containers are finally used. In case of fire contaminators may explode. From a secure, explosion-proof location, use water spray to cool exposed containers.

HANDLING OF CHLORINE

There must be proper safety instruction, intelligent supervision and safe equipment. Workers should be completely informed of the hazards that can result from improper handling. Each person should know what to do in an emergency and should be trained in first aid. Wear chemical goggles, chemical cartridge respirator.

- Cylinders should be transported on a properly balanced hand truck having a claim. Never lift a cylinder by its valve-protection hood.
- Valves on both cylinders and ton containers are to do design to deliver full volume after one complete counter clock wise turn. Never apply heat to containers to increase the discharge rate.
- Extra heavy seamless steel pipe, connected with drop forged steel fittings and flange unions should be used for chlorine pipe lines. Design the system so that liquid chlorine will not be trapped between valves.
- Properly designed emergency showers and eye baths should be places in convenient locations outside the chlorine room wherever chlorine is used. Equipment should be inspected frequently to make sure it is in proper working condition.

LEAKES OF CHLORINE

- Any leakage in lines, equipment or containers must be given prompt attention. Clear the contaminated area of personal and keep them upwind on higher ground than the leak. Only specially trained and equipped men should be permitted in the area.
- Good safety practice requires a check for leak daily. A rag dipped in ammonia water and tied to a stick or an atomizer filled with ammonia water will help to locate a leak because white smoke (ammonium chloride) forms.
- A valve leak of a cylinder or ton containers can usually be stopped by tightening the packing unit.
- Leakage on the wall/containers, turn the unit so that vapour not liquid escapes.
- Emergency kits are available for handling leaks in cylinders/containers.
- Do not use water on a leak to reduce the flow. Neutralize the chlorine in an alkaline solution. Never immerse the container, but pass the chlorine into the solution through an iron pipe or weighed rubber hose.
- It can be absorbed in solutions of NaOH, Na_2CO_3, and Ca (OH) 2. A suitable tank should be conveniently available.

Table 9.3: Recommended Alkaline Solutions for Absorbing Chlorine

Container Capacity (lbs)	Caustic Soda		Soda Ash		Hydrated Lime	
	Solid (lbs.)	Water (lbs)	Solid (lbs.)	Wate (lbs.)	Solid (lbs.)	Water (lbs.)
100	125	40	300	100	125	125
150	188	60	430	150	188	188
2000	2500	800	6000	2000	2500	2000

FIRE AND EXPLOSION HAZARDS OF CHLORINE GAS

- Although Cl_2 vapours are non-flammable, non explosives and non-conductor of electricity, it is a powerful agent and at room temperature may react directly with many oxidizable elements and compounds.
- For fire near Cl_2 cylinders, the best possible procedure is to keep the cylinders cool. Water on a chlorine leak only makes it worse.
- In case of fire, remove containers from the fire zone immediately. Disconnect tank cars or trucks and full out of danger area.
- If containers cannot be moved away and if no chlorine is escaping, apply water to keep containers cool. Keep unauthorized persons at a safe distance.

POISONING SYMPTOMS

The three major routes of human exposure are inhalation, eye and skin contact. Inhaled chlorine usually attack lungs and respiratory system. Chlorine vapour irritates the mucous membrane, the respiratory system and the skin. The high concentrations irritate the eyes and cause coughing and labored breathing. Symptoms of high exposure are retching and vomiting followed by difficult breathing. Liquid chlorine may cause skin and eye burning upon contact. Chlorine produces no known cumulative effects. Chlorine vapours have an intense smell at 3-5 ppm in air. Based on time period the chlorine concentration is given in below.

Table 9.4: Exposure Limits of chlorine Exposure Level (Parts per Million) Exposure Limit

Exposure Level (Parts per million)	Exposure Limit
0.5 ppm	Maximum allowable concentration averaged over an 8 hr period
1 ppm	Maximum allowable short-term exposure (15 minutes)
10 ppm or more	Immediately Dangerous to Life and Health (as published by NIOSH)

Note: The Immediately Dangerous to Life and Health (IDLH) exposure level is the point at which a person without appropriate respiratory protection could be fatally injured or could suffer irreversible or incapacitating health effects. NIOSH is the National Institute for Occupational Safety and Health in the United States.

Table 9.5: Following symptoms have also been mentioned in Toxic and Hazardous Industrial Chemicals Safety Manual Irritation of eyes, eye burns, difficult breathing, cough, pain behind breast bone, hemoptysis, headache pain, nausea, vomiting, weakness, cyanosis, pulmonary edema, epigastric (Upper Stomach)

HAZARDOUS SYMPTOMS			
Hazardous Symptoms		Preventive Measures	Fire Extinguishing/First Aid
Fire	Non-combustible, many chemical reactions can cause fire and explosion.	Avoid contact with combustible substances, hydrogen, acetylene, anhydrous ammonia, metal powder's and phosphorus.	In case of fire in immediate vicinity: use any extinguishing agent.
Explosion	Contact with hydrogen, acetylene, anhydrous ammonia, metal powders or phosphorus can cause explosion.	Special equipment.	In case of fire keep cylinder cool by spraying with water.
		Strict Hygiene	In all these cases call a doctor
Inhalation	Corrosive, store, throat, cough, shortness of breath, severe breathing difficulties.	Ventilation, local exhaust or respiratory protection.	Fresh air, rest, place in half sitting position, take to hospital.
Skin	Corrosive, redness, pain, serious burns.	Insulated gloves, protective clothing.	Remove contaminated clothing, flush skin with water or shower, and call a doctor.
Eyes	Corrosive, redness, pain, impaired vision.	Acid goggles or combined eye and respiratory protection.	Flush with water, take to a doctor.

Table 9.6: The Physiological Effects of Chlorine

Sl. No.	Response to Various Concentrations of Gas in Air	Ppm, Cl_2 in Air by Volume
1.	Least amount required to produce slight symptoms after several hours.	1
2.	Least detectable odour.	3.5
3.	Max. concentration can be inhaled for 1 hr without serious disturbances.	4
4.	Noxiousness, impossible to breath several minutes.	5
5.	Least amount required to cause irritation of throat.	15.1
6.	Least concentration required to cause coughing.	30.2
7.	Amount dangerous in 30 min. to 1 hr.	40-60
8.	Kill most animals in very short time.	1000

THE BASIC MACHENISM OF CHLORINE TOXICITY

In 1915, first toxic exposures to chlorine were reported when chlorine was used as a chemical warfare agent in Ypres, Belgium. It is intermediate water-soluble and can cause acute damage to both upper and lower respiratory tracts. Its toxicity is thought to be mediated by the generation of hydrogen chloride upon contact with moist mucous membrane and by the formation of free radicals at the cellular level. Chlorine, once inhaled, dissolves in water and generates hydrochloric acid upon contacting moist mucous membrane. Toxicity of chlorine however is not limited to the effects attributable to hydrochloric acid because chlorine is approximately 20 times more toxic to the respiratory tract than hydrochloric acid. Chlorine is a highly irritant gas with inter-mediate water solubility. Therefore, it can damage large airways as well as small airways and lung parenchyma. Toxicity following chlorine gas exposure appears to get worsened with longer duration and higher concentration of exposure. With considerable consistency around the world, chlorine gas has a time-weighted average exposure standard of 0.5-1 ppm. The basic mechanism of toxicity is related to the solubility of chlorine in water, with chlorine forming hydrochloric and hypochlorous acids, which subsequently undergo ionization. This reaction occurs in moist environments such as eyes, nasal mucosa, and respiratory epithelium. Injury begins with edema of the upper airway and lung parenchyma, followed by development of cellular exudates in alveoli. As injury progresses, severe edema, hemorrhage, and destruction of the bronchiolar mucosa can develop.

FIRST AID IN CASE OF CHLORINE EXPOSURE

- Remove the victims from the contaminated area. Loosen constrictive clothing around the neck.

- If breathing has stopped or is exceptionally labored, start artificial respiration immediately and continue until the patient is breathing normally.
- Someone should call a physician.
- If oxygen inhalation apparatus is available, it may be administered with the instruction of a physician. Instructions come with equipment must be followed carefully.
- Keep the patient warm and quite wrap him in a blanket and apply warm water bottles. Do not allow him to move. He is apt to become panicky, so reassure him.
- Remove contaminated clothing and flush with water those skin areas which have been exposed. Do not attempt to neutralize the CI_2 with chemicals.
- In case of eyes, eyes should be flushed immediately with copious quantities of running water for at least 15 min. Never attempt to neutralize with chemicals. The eyelids should be held apart during this period to make sure water contacts all accessible tissues of the eye and lids. Call a physician/ophthalmologist.
- If this chemical has been inhaled, remove from exposure; begin rescue breathing (using universal precautions).
- When this chemical has being swallowed, get medical attention. Give large quantities of water and induce vomiting.

PHYSICAL EXAMINATIONS

Medical surveillance: Special emphasis should be given to the skin, eyes, teeth and cardiovascular status in placement and periodic examination. Physical examinations including chest X-ray should be given applicants for jobs where exposure to CI_2 vapours might occur. Chest X-ray should be taken and pulmonary function followed. Persons handling CI_2 should be examined periodically for asthma, bronchitis, chronic lung conditions or irritation of the upper respiratory tract that becomes aggravated upon exposure to CI_2 vapours.

FIRE EXTINGUISHING

Although, chlorine is non-combustible gas, but it will increase the intensity of a fire and may cause fire upon contact with combustible materials. Therefore, combustible substance and reducing agents are to be kept away from chlorine. Vapors are heavier then air and will collect in low areas. Chlorine may combine water or steam to produce toxic and corrosive fumes of hydrochloric acid, which is corrosive to many metals. Hydrogen chlorine mixtures (5: 95 %) are exploded by almost any form of energy (heat, sun light, sparks etc.). If employees are expected to fight fire, they must be trained and equipped in as per OSHA 1910.156.

Fig. 9.2: A Self-contained Breathing Apparatus

PERSONAL PROTECTING METHOD

Personnel should wear appropriate personal protective clothing to prevent the skin from contact with the evaporating liquid or from contact with vessels containing the liquid. Where very high gas concentration or liquid chlorine may be present, full protective clothing, gloves and eye protection should be used. Whenever there is likelihood of excessive gas levels, workers should use respiratory protection in the form of full-face gas masks with proper canisters or supplied air respirators.

Fig. 9.3: A Full-facepiece Respirator with Cartridges (a) and an escape respirator (b)
Source: Chlorine safe work practices

A CASE STUDY OF CHLORINE EXPOSURE IN TAIWAN

Min PO Hol et. al. (2010) nicely reported a case study of a seven persons (6+1) exposed to chlorine gas and afterwards treatment in Taiwan. Seven persons (6+1) including a nonsmoking, previously healthy 15-yearold girl were presented in the hospital emergency room after an unintentional exposure to chlorine gas at a community swimming pool. They were exposed to chlorine gas for some 6 minutes in a shower room after while a swimming pool workers mixing sodium hypochlorite with hydrochloric acid outside the room. The exact concentration of inhaled chlorine was unknown. All of them were sent to the emergency room with dyspnea, dry cough, and throat and eye irritation. They were treated with supplemental 100% oxygen, intravenous fluid and corticosteroid, and an inhaled â2 agonist therapy every 6 hour. On the next day, 6 of them were asymptomatic and did not require oxygen therapy. All 6 were discharged on that day.

While the girl was hospitalized due to persistent dyspnea. In her case, mild hypoxemia immediately developed after exposure to chlorine for 6 minutes. Initial chest radiograph revealed pneumonitis-like opacities over right middle and lower lungs. She received supplementary oxygen, oral prednisolone 10 mg and inhaled budesonide 2 puff every 8 hour for 4 days. Her clinical manifestations improved 3 days later. She was discharged on 5th hospital day. A follow-up chest radiograph was normal 8 days post-exposure (Figs. 9.4 and 9.5).

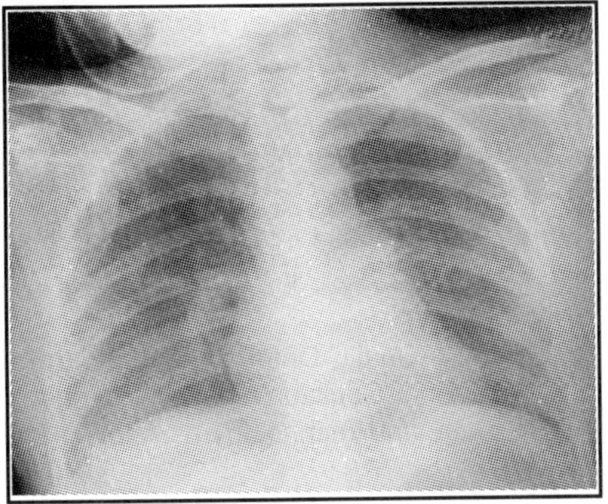

Fig. 9.4: Chest radiograph showing increased infiltrates over right middle and lower lung fields

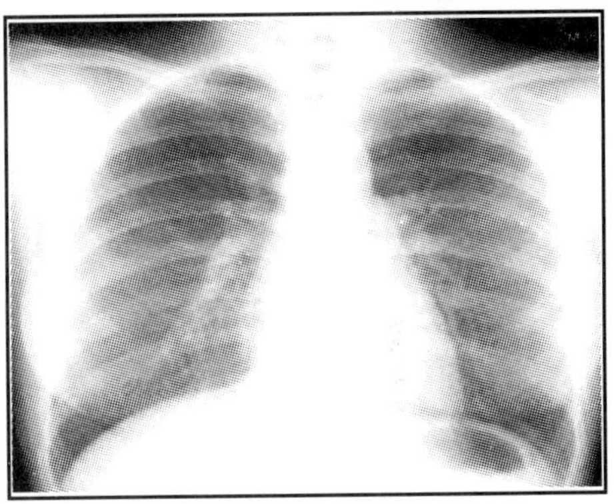

Fig. 9.5: Follow-up chest radiograph 8 days post-exposure demonstrating normal findings in both lungs
Source: Min-Po Ho et al. 2010

Although in this case showed much improvement after receiving both β2 agonist and steroid therapy, the efficacy of such treatment in human with chlorine poisonings has not been confirmed and needs further evaluation.

Treatment of acute chlorine injury with aerosolized terbutaline followed by aerosolized budesonide improved lung function. Combined treatment was more effective than treatment with either drug alone. The doses of inhaled budesonide and intravenous betamethasone were chosen as recommended for treatment of toxic gas exposure by the Swedish Poison Information Center (Wang et al 2005).

METHOD SUGGESTED FOR WASTE DISPOSAL

Where a chlorine-consuming process discharges of a waste gas containing appreciable amounts of CI_2 special disposal equipment may be required, Use solution of reducing agent (bisulfites or ferrous salts with 3M H_2SO_4 or hypo). Neutralize with soda ash or dilute HCl. Drain into the sewer with abundant water. If material or contaminated runoff enters waterways, notify downstream user of potentially contaminated waters.

REFERENCES

American Conference of Governmental Industrial Hygienists (ACGIH); Cincinnati, OH, Publication No. 4542, 1990.

American Conference of Government Industrial Hygienists (ACGIHR) Worldwide Documentation of the TLVsR and BEIsR with Other Worldwide Occupational Exposure Values CD-ROM, Cincinnati, OH, 2003.

Fundamentals of Air Pollution, Edited by Daniel Valuro, 4th Edn. Chapter 34, pp. 852, 2008.

Health and Safety [available at http://www.worksafebc.com/ ublications/health_ and_safety/bytopic/ assets/ pdf/chlorine.pdf], 2008.

Herbert F. Lund, Research Programmes for Air and Water Pollution Control, In: Industrial Pollution Control Handbook, Edited by Herbert F. Lund, Mc Graw Hill, Inc. chapter-9, pp. 9-9, 1971.

Herman Koren, Occupational Environment In: Handbook of Environmental Health and Safety, Principles and Practices, edited by Herman Koren, V-I. Pergamon Press Inc., pp. 283, 1980.

Identification of Workers Exposed Contaminantly of Heat Stress and Chemicals. Industrial Health, Edited by Robert Bourbonnais, Joseph Zajed, Martine Levesque, Marc-Antonine Beesque, Patrice Duguay and Ginette Truchon. 51-25-33, 2013.

J.H. Futrell: Safe Handling of Toxic Chemicals In: Human and Environmental Risks of Chlorinated Dioxins and Related Compounds, Edited by Richard E. Tucker, Alvin L. Young and Allan P. Grat, Environmental Science Research, London, Vol. 26, 1981.

J.H. Knelson, The Roll of Clinical Research in Establishing Air Quality Criteria and Standards, In: EQS Environmental Quality and Safety, Edited by. Frederick Coulston Albany/N.Y. Frledhelm Korte, Munich-global Aspects of Chemistry, Toxicology and Technology as Applied to the Environmental Vol. 3, pp. 207-211, 1973.

L.G. Taft, P.R. Beltz and B.C. Garrett: Laboratory Handling and Disposal of Chlorinated Dioxin Wastes, In: Human and Environmental Risks of Chlorinated Dioxins and Related Compounds, Edited by Richard E. Tucker, Alvin L. Young and Allan P.Grat, Environmental Science Research, London, Vol. 26, 1981.

Liviu–Daniel Galatchi, Environmental Risk Assessment, In: Chemicals as Intentional and Accidental Global Environmental Threats, Edited by Lubomir Simeonor, Elisabeta Chiria, pp. 1-6, 2006.

Min-Po Ho1, Chen-Chang Yang, Wing-Keung Cheung, Chang-Ming Liu, and Kuang-Chau Tsai1, Chlorine Gas Exposure Manifesting Acute Lung Injury, 內科學誌□21□210-215, 2010.

NIOSH Manual of Analytical Methods, 3rd Edn.; U.S. Department of Health and Human Services, Center for Disease Control, National Institute of Occupational Safety and Health; Cincinnati, OH, Method 2537, DHHS (NIOSH) Publ. No. 84-100, 1984.

NIOSH (National Institute for Occupational Safety and Health) NIOSH Manual of Analytical Methods (NMAM (R) (DHHS (NIOSH) Publ. No. 94-113), 4th Edn., Cincinnati, OH, pp. 2539-1–2539-10, 1994a and 1994b.

Occupational Safety and Health Administration, OSHA Analytical Methods Manual, 2nd Edn. Part 1, Vol. 2 (Methods 29-54), Salt Lake City, UT, Method 52, 1990a.

OSHA Analytical Methods Manual, 2nd Edn.; U.S. Department of Labor, Occupational Safety and Health Administration; OSHA Analytical Laboratory; Salt Lake City, UT, Method 56.

Peter Brimblecombe, The Upper Atmosphere in Air Composition and Chemistry, 2nd Edn., Cambridge University Press, London, pp. 173, 1986.

Quade R. Stahl: Air pollution aspects of chlorine gas, National Air Pollution Control Administration, Consumer Protection and Environmental Health Service, Department of Health Education of Welfare. Sep. 1969.

R.B. Philp, Environmental Hazards and Human Health, Lewis Publisher, London. pp. 100, 1995.

R.D. Ross: Selection of equipments for Gaseous Waste Disposal, In: Air Pollution and Industry, Van Nostrand Reinhold Company, New York, pp. 440, 1972.

Remy Bouscaren, Marie - Jeanne Brun, Arthur C. Stern, Rene Wunenburger: Air Pollution Standards, In: Air Pollution, Supplement to Management of Air Quality, Arthur C. Stern, vol. VIII, 3rd Edn. Academic Press, London, pp. 163-164, 1986.

Sara Visentin Lessons Learned from Industrial Chemical Accidents: In Chemicals as Intentional and Accidental Global Environmental Threats, Edited by Lubomir Simeonor, Elisabeta Chiria, pp. 29-44, 2006.

Stanley E. Manahan: Gaseous Inorganic Air Pollutants In: Environmental Chemistry, 8th Edn. CRC Press LLC, pp. 318, 2005.

Wang J, Winskog C, Edston E, Walther SM. Inhaled and Intravenous Corticosteroids both Attenuate Chlorine Gas Induced Lung Injury in Pigs. Acta Anaesthesiol Scand 49: 183-90, 2005.

Pages: 134-158

AGRICULTURE DEVELOPMENT AND SUSTAINABLE ENVIRONMENT

Edited by: Jaswant Ray; Dr. Pawan Kumar 'Bharti'

ISBN: 978-93-5056-759-3

Edition: 2015

Published by: Discovery Publishing House Pvt. Ltd., New Delhi (India)

10

Biodiesel Production from Microalgae

Farouk K. El-BAZ*[1]; Amal A. Mohamed[1] and Sami I. ALI[1]

ABSTRACT

Due to increasing oil prices and climate change concerns, biodiesel has gained attention as an alternative energy source. Biodiesel derived from microalgae is a potentially renewable and carbon–neutral alternative to petroleum fuels. One of the most important decisions in obtaining oil from microalgae is the choice of algal species to use. When the oil is pressed out of the algal biomass, the oils can be burned directly in diesel engines. It is called clean or green diesel because it burns with almost no pollutants. Biodiesel offers several advantages over ethanol besides avoiding engine modification or redesign. Biodiesel yields about 30% more energy than gasoline and runs much cleaner. Results gained in the last few years highlighted the promising potential of microalgae-based biofuels compared with traditional terrestrial feedstock. Future possible implementation of the green economy initiative in more Arab countries might shift the whole regional economy throughout the Middle East and North Africa into a green economy, which is much more sustainable than the current economy. Only through small concrete and effective steps that big progress can be achieved in the interests of the future generations.

Keywords: Microalgae, biodiesel, fatty acids, oil, transesterification.

[1] Plant Biochemistry Dept., National Research Centre (NRC), Dokki-Cairo, Egypt.

INTRODUCTION

Continued use of petroleum sourced fuels is now widely recognized as unsustainable because of depleting supplies and the contribution of these fuels to the accumulation of carbon dioxide in the environment. Now, global demand for petroleum is predicted to increase 40% by 2025. Higher oil prices erode revenues by increasing costs throughout the economy. Renewable, carbon neutral, transport fuels are necessary for environmental and economic sustainability (National Energy Technology Laboratory, 2005). The only way to insulate the economy from petroleum price shocks is to lower the dependence on petroleum in the economy. The most practical and least disruptive strategy to achieve this objective is to use alternative fuels. Biodiesel derived from oil crops is a potential renewable, carbon neutral alternative to petroleum fuels and as a solution to the problem of peak oil (Kulkarniand Dalai, 2006). There are two demerits associated with this approach: first, growing more oilseed crops would displace the food crops grown to nourish mankind. Second, traditional oilseed crops cannot be considered as most efficient source of vegetable oil (Chisti, 2007).

The insufficiency of fossil based fuels and an adverse environmental impact produced by the conventional sources of energy has resulted new research work tofind the sustainable sources of clean energy. Microalgae appear to be the only source of renewable biodiesel that is capable of meeting the global demand for transport fuels. Like plants, microalgae use sunlight to produce oils but they do so more efficiently than crop plants. Biodiesel is defined as the mono-alkyl esters of fatty acids derived from vegetable oils or animal fats. In simpler terms, biodiesel is the product you get when a vegetable oil or animal fat is chemically reacted with methyl or ethyl alcohols to produce a new compound that is known as a fatty acid methyl or ethyl esters.

Because the cells grow in aqueous suspension, where they have more efficient access to water, CO_2 and dissolved nutrients, microalgae are capable of producing large amounts of biomass and usable oil in either high rate algal ponds or photobioreactors. This oil can then be turned into biodiesel which could be sold for use in automobiles. Regional production of microalgae and processing into biofuels will provide economic benefits to rural communities. Oil productivity of many microalgae greatly exceeds the oil productivity of the best producing oil crops (Camacho et al., 1992). Algae can be grown in ponds or inplastic tanks called bioreactors with little more sunlight, heat and water (Ana et al., 2006). Additionally, algae can be very efficient in absorbing carbon which is generated by fossil fuel power plants which makes it a carbon neutral biofuel.

In Egypt with sun intensity available during the whole year, the presence of different saline water sources and vast plain desert areas, the production of biodiesel from algae would be favored, especially if compared to Germany where 60 % of the algal biodiesel oil is produced (Spolaore et al., 2006 and Afify et al., 2010). The entrance of Industrial cultivation of algae in Egypt is to be considered of national security importance; as a source of oil and a unique source of bioactive phyto-nutrients and food additives. With the expectation of depletion of oil sources in Egypt within 15 years, Egypt is expected to turn into oil importing country.

In the last decades, several researches work has revealed that algae are potential source of new bioactive compounds of pharmaceutical importance as found by El-Baz et al, (2002), El-Baz et al., (2004), El-Baz et al., (2013). Petroleum-based fuels are limited reserves concentrated in certain regions of the world. These sources are on the verge of reaching their peak production. Microalgae, as biomass, are a potential source of renewable energy, and they can be converted into energy such as Biofuel oil and gas. Scientists have identified thousands of forms of algae, but certain algae strains are more suitable for biofuels use than others because of their high oil yield and other qualities. The characteristics of the strain (growth rate, oil content, salinity tolerance) should be taken into consideration along with the climate in which the algae will be grown.

Algae Strains

Algae have a clear potential to be used as a source for the production of renewable energy. Since there are many species of algae with varying characteristics, a diversity of options for the production of algae-based energy have been analyzed. Also, genetically modified strains of algae are being developed for algae biofuels, especially high lipid-content algae. Certain companies have developed algae strains with unique characteristics. Subsequently, the inputs and conditions needed for growing algae are examined. The preference for microalgae has come about due largely to their less complex structure, fast growth rates, and high oil-content (for some species). However, some research is being done into using seaweeds for biofuels, probably due to the high availability of this resource (Guschina and Harwood, 2006). The following species (some of them presented in Fig. 10.1) commonly used for their suitability as a mass oil-producer:

- *Botryococcusbraunii*
- *Chlorella*
- *Scenedesmusobliquus*
- *Dunaliellatertiolecta*
- *Gracilaria*
- *Pleurochrysiscarterae* (also called CCMP647).
- Sargassum, with 10 times the output volume of Gracilaria.

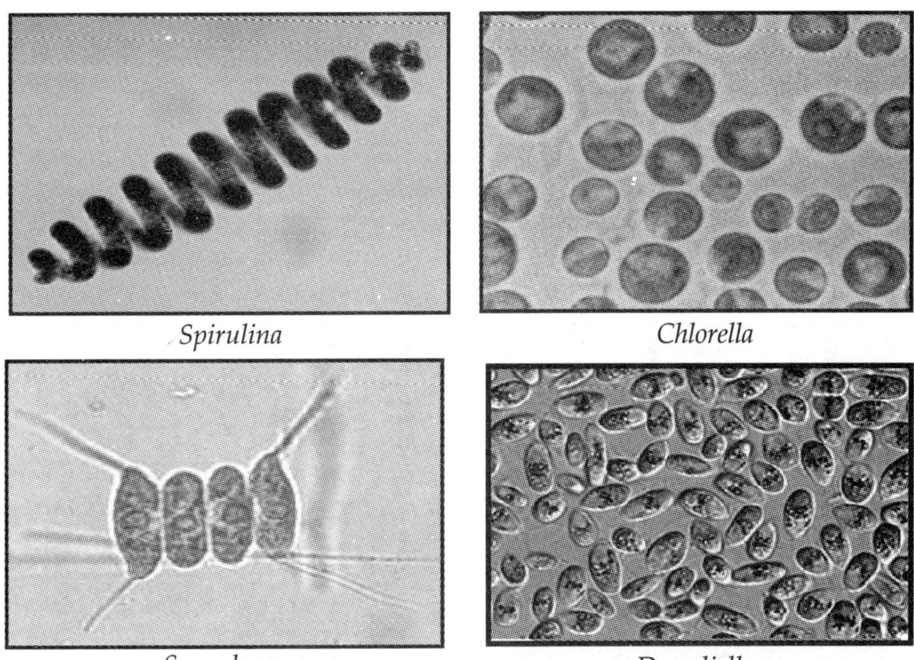

Spirulina Chlorella

Scenedesmus Dunaliella

Fig. 10.1: Example of Some Major Algae Strains

The amount of oil each strain of algae produces varies widely as presented in (Table 10.1).

Table 10.1: % Oil Yield of Some Microalgae (DW)

Microalgal Species	Oil Yield%
Ankistrodesmus TR-87	28-40%
Botryococcusbraunii:	29-75%
Chlorella protothecoides	15-55%
Chlorella sp.	29%
Crypthecodiniumcohnii	20%
*Cyclotella*DI-35	42%
Dunaliellatertiolecta	36-42%
Hantzschia DI-160	66%
Nannochloris	6-63%
Nannochloropsis	31-68%
Neochlorisoleoabundans	35-54%
Nitzschia TR-114	28-50%
Phaeodactylumtricornutum	31%
Scenedesmus TR-84	45%
Tetraselmissuecica	15-32%
Thalassiosirapseudonana	21-31%

Isolation of the strains is a necessary process to obtain pure cultures and presents the first step towards the selection of microalgae strains with potential for biodiesel production. Traditional isolation techniques include the use of a micropipette for isolation under a microscope or cell dilution followed by cultivation in liquid media or agar plates. Single cell isolation, based on traditional methods from the original sample is time-consuming and requires sterilized cultivation media and equipment, but the result of this elaborate process is always a pure culture that is usually easily identifiable. Algae grow lab developed a series of tubular as in Fig. 10.2.

Fig. 10.2: Lab Scale for Algal Cultivation

Cultivation of Algae: Open Pond (Op) and Photobioreactor (PBR)

Like plants, algae use the sunlight for the process of photosynthesis. Photosynthesis is an important biochemical process in which plants, algae, and some bacteria convert the energy of sunlight to chemical energy. Algae capture light energy through photosynthesis and convert inorganic substances into simple sugars using the captured energy. There are two main methods of cultivation:

- Ponds
- Photobioreactors

(a) Open ponds

Open pond systems (Fig. 10.3) are the most common system of algae cultivation, already used commercially to produce nutritional products and treat wastewater (Oswald, 1969). Algae can be grown in natural or man-made ponds. Cultivation of algae in open ponds has been extensively studied. The most commonly used systems include shallow big ponds, tanks, circular ponds and raceway ponds.

Furthermore, contamination by predators and other fast growing heterotrophs have restricted the commercial production of algae in open culture systems to only those organisms that can grow under extreme conditions. Also, due to inefficient stirring mechanisms in open cultivation systems, their mass transfer rates are very poor resulting to low biomass productivity. The ponds in which the algae are cultivated are usually what are called the "raceway ponds". In these ponds, the algae, water and nutrients circulate around a racetrack. With paddlewheels providing the flow, algae are kept suspended in the water, and are circulated back to the surface on a regular frequency. The ponds are usually kept shallow because the algae need to be exposed to sunlight, and sunlight can only penetrate the pond water to a limited depth. The ponds are operated in a continuous manner, with CO_2 and nutrients being constantly fed to the ponds, while algae-containing water is removed at the other end.While this is indeed the simplest of all the growing techniques, it has some drawbacks owing to the fact that the environment in and around the pond is not completely under control. Bad weather can stunt algae growth. Contamination from strains of bacteria or other outside organisms often results in undesirable species taking over the desired algae growing in the pond. The water in which the algae grow also has to be kept at a certain temperature, which can be difficult to maintain (Carlsson et al., 2007; Rodolfi et al., 2009).

Fig. 10.3: Open Cultivation Systems (Open Pond)

(b) Closed pond

An alternative to open ponds are closed ponds where the control over the environment is much better than that for the open ponds (Figs. 10.4-10.6). Closed Pond systems cost more than the open ponds, and considerably less than photobioreactors for similar areas of operation. As a variation of the open pond system, the idea behind the closed pond is to close it off, to cover a pond or pool with a greenhouse. While this usually results in a smaller system, it does take care of many of the problems associated with an open system. It allows more algae species to be grown, it allows the species that are being grown to stay dominant (Rosenberg et al., 2008). It is also possible to increase the amount of carbon-di-oxide in these quasi-closed systems, thus again increasing the rate of growth of algae. Usually closed ponds are used in Spirulina cultivation. These closed systems are constructed using plexiglass. Closed systems (not exposed to open air) avoid the problem of contamination by other organisms blown in by the air. The problem for a closed system is finding a cheap source of sterile CO2.Closed reactors require artificial light to drive the photosynthetic process when they are operated indoors. Indoor lighting is usually provided by florescent bulbs, halogen lamps and light emitting diodes (LED) coupled with fiber optic cables and reflectors that rely on the power from the grid or other sources such as solar panels etc.

Fig. 10.4: Closed Pond of Cultivation System

(c) Cultivation of algae in photobioreactor (PBR)

A photobioreactor is closed equipment which provides a controlled environment and enables high productivity of algae. As it is a closed system, all growth requirements of algae are introduced into the system and controlled according to the requirements. PBRs facilitate better control of culture environment such as carbon dioxide supply, water supply, and optimal temperature, efficient exposure to light, culture density, pH levels, gas supply rate, and mixing regime.

Types of Photobioreactors

There are different types of photobioreactor such as Horizontal tubular reactor (Fig. 10.5) and Vertical stacked tubular reactor (Fig. 10.6).

Horizontal/vertical tubular photobioreactors and flatbed photobioreactors are the most commonly-used closed reactors because of their high biomass production compared to raceway pond reactors.

Fig. 10.5: Horizontal Tubular Reactor

Fig. 10.6: Vertical Stacked Tubular Reactor

Horizontal photobioreactors are not considered for carbon capture because of the higher costs associated with the larger land requirements and lower effective gas-to-liquid transfer which leads to lower biomass yields. Horizontal reactors are tubes of 5-30 ft. in length which are connected in parallel to each other. The algae grown in the reactor water are circulated by pumps. Typically, the pumps force a pig composed of a spongy plastic to clean the internal surface of the reactor as it passes through the reactor tubes. The advantage of horizontal bioreactors is that not only is they suitable for growing algae cultures both indoors and outdoors but also because of their larger illuminated surface area compared to open ponds. Vertical photobioreactors are compact, inexpensive, simple to construct, and easy to operate. Vertical photobioreactors are generally cylindrical vessels in which gas is spared into the liquid. They vary in length and diameter. Vertical photobioreactors have higher yields than horizontal photobioreactors because of the hydrodynamics, the amount of gas in dispersion, and their gas–liquid mass transfer characteristics (pH, pCO_2, pO_2). The vertical reactors upright orientation allows gas to be introduced at the bottom of the reactor and travel to the top. The gas rises rapidly along the axis of the column and disperses as it reaches the reactor surface and causes liquid to circulate in the entire column - upward near the cylinder axis and downward near the walls. This process allows for improved gas–liquid exchange due to its inherent design.

Running of Photobioreactor (PBR)

This microalgae growth model is based on the work of Jonker (2010). The model is a simulation model based on parameters such as: irradiance, respiration, temperature, limitation by factors such as CO_2 and O_2 concentration, pH, nutrients and mixing. This model was rebuild and tested in order to assess if it was a model with sufficient level of sophistication and reliable results for further environmental analysis.

The following steps summarize the running of photobioreactor:

1. From the feeding vessel, the flow progresses to the diaphragm pump which moderates the flow of the algae into the actual tube. Built into the pump is the CO_2 inlet valve.
2. The photobioreactor itself is used to promote biological growth by controlling environmental parameters including light. The tubes are made of acrylic or polycarbonate and are designed to have light and dark intervals to enhance the growth rate.
3. The photobioreactor has a built-in cleaning system that internally cleans the tubes without stopping the production.
4. After the algae have completed the flow through the photobioreactor, it passes back to the feeding vessel. As it progresses through the hoses, the oxygen sensors determine how much oxygen has built up in the plant and this oxygen is released in the feeding vessel itself. It is also at this stage that the optical cell density sensor determines the harvesting rate.
5. When the algae are ready for harvesting, they pass through the connected filtering system. This filter collects the algae that are ready for processing, while the remaining algae passes back to the feeding vessel.

Photosynthesis is a process comprising two steps, light reactions that only occurwhen the cells are illuminated, and carbon-fixation reactions, also known as dark reactions, that occur both in the presence and absence of light. Thus in the first step the cells transform light energy into chemical energy, which is stored in high-energy compounds for later use in the carbon-fixation reactions. The use of these photosynthetic pathways in environmental engineering processes requires the use of solar energy so as to develop clean technology processes. Thus the cells use the light energy byway of exergonic reactions, producing energy that is used in the synthesis of compounds as from carbon dioxide fixation by way of endergonic reactions (Fig. 10.7).

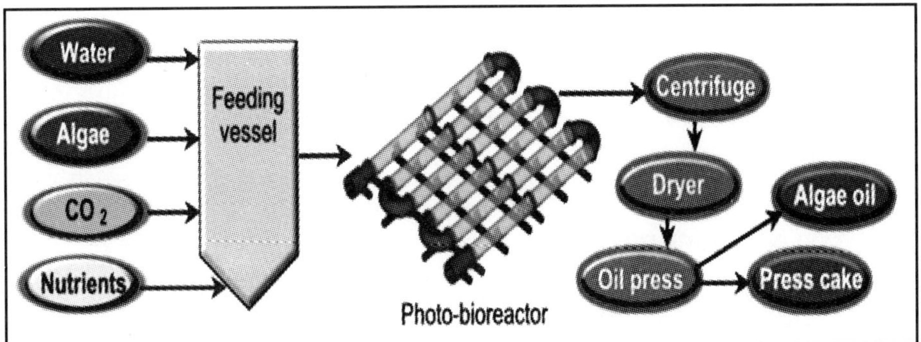

Fig. 10.7: Requirements for the Biomass and Oil Production Process

Advantages of photobioreactors

- Cultivation of algae is in controlled circumstances, hence potential for much higher productivity.
- Large surface-to-volume ratio. PBRs offer maximum efficiency in using light and therefore greatly improve productivity. Typically the culture density of algae produced is 10 to 20 times greater than bag culture in which algae-culture is done in bags - and can be even greater.
- Better control of gas utilization.
- Reduction in evaporation of growth medium.
- More uniform temperature.
- Better protection from outside contamination
- Space saving - can be mounted vertically, horizontally or at an angle, indoors or outdoors.
- Reduced fouling - recently available tube self-cleaning mechanisms can dramatically reduce fouling.

Covering ponds does offer some of the benefits that are offered by photobioreactors, but enclosed systems will still provide better control of temperature, light intensity, better control of gas transfer, and larger surface area-to-volume ratio. An enclosed PBR design will enhance commercial algal biomass production by keeping algae genetics pure and reducing the possibility of parasite infestation.

Disadvantages of Photobioreactors

Capital cost is very high. This is one of the most important bottlenecks that are hindering the progress of algae fuel industry.

Despite higher biomass concentration and better control of culture parameters, data accumulated in the last two decades have shown that the productivity and production cost in some enclosed photobioreactor systems are not much better than those achievable in open-pond cultures.

The technical difficulty in sterilizing these photobioreactors has hindered their application for algae culture for specific end-products such as high value pharmaceutical products. Also this system is difficult to control temperature. The disadvantages of photobioreactors could be summarized as follows:

- Cost/complexity
- Thermal management
- Oxygen accumulation
- Biofouling
- Cell damage by shear stress
- Deterioration of materials

Harvesting and Drying of Algal Biomass

The choice of harvesting methodology, likely to be a combination of individual methods, depends highly on the biomass type and requirements of the down-stream processing. Thekey harvesting and dewatering operations, currently used, are sedimentation in gravity field, centrifugation, flotation and filtration. The costs of harvesting microalgal biomass can be a major component of production (Molina-Grima et al., 2003). The first challenge is to concentrate the cells from relatively dilute solutions. A question that arises when considering the logistics of moving harvested algae to a central processing plant is whether the lipid content remains stable or how long the lipids remain stable.

It is possible that microalgae or associated bacteria could consume components of the algae, including the stored triglyceride. Lipid stability in biomass during production, extraction, and storage is important for maintaining the integrity of lipids and fatty acids for future conversion to fuels. Drying is the final processing step that may be necessary to ensure stable storage of algal biomass if the material does not go through extraction following harvesting. Methods that have most commonly been employed for drying microalgae include spray-drying, drum-drying, freeze-drying, and sun-drying. Given the high water content of algal biomass, sun-drying becomes problematic, and spray-drying is often too expensive for low-value commodities. Dehydration represents a significant cost to processing algal biomass, and when added to the cost of growth and harvesting, it poses a major economic barrier to the large-scale production of algal. Example of two drying system discuss below:

Solar Drying

A low-cost drier with perforated trays was built for solar drying of algae. Drying was aided by burning biogas at the bottom of the drier. Thin layers of algae were placed on the trays. The dried algae had a solids content of about 30% TTS; but the nutritive value was limited because the cell walls had not been ruptured (Fig. 10.8).

Fig. 10.8: Solar Energy Drier for Algae

Drumdrier

In the drum drier, the algal slurry was subjected to a shock temperature of up to 120°C for a short time. The high temperature caused instant vaporization of the protoplasmic water. The sudden increase in pressure ruptured the cell walls and released the cytoplasm.

Attempts to view the phenomenon under the microscope were unsuccessful. The drum drier was heated with supersaturated steam to give a surface temperature of 110-120 °C. When the algal slurry was sprayed on the rotating drum, it spread into a thin layer. The blades constantly scraped the dried algae flakes off the drum surface before they burned. The final moisture content of the algal flakes had to be 8% for safe storage.

Extraction of Algal Oil

Extracting lipids is one of the most key and limited processes for biofuel production based on microalgae at large scale. The conventional methods for lipid extraction generally involve dewatering before extracting lipids since residual water in wet microalgal biomass hindered mass transfer of the lipids from the cell and then lead to a decrease in the efficiency of lipids extraction. There are a few different ways to extract the oil from algae. The oil press is the simplest and most popular method. It's similar tothe concept of the olive press. It can extract up to 75 per cent of the oil from the algae being pressed. Basically a two-part process, the hexane solvent method (combined with pressing thealgae) extracts up to 95 per cent of oil from algae. First, the presss queezes out the oil. Then, left over algae is mixed with hexane, filtered and cleaned so there's no chemical left in the oil (El-Kinawy et al., 2009 & Mercer et al., 2011). For microalgal oil extraction, although an appropriate technique of cell disruption is a prerequisite, the efficient extraction of lipids is highly dependent on the polarity of the organic solvent or solvent mixture used. In general, solvent mixtures containing a polar and a non-polar solvent could extract a greater amount of lipids. For example, a combination of chloroform (non-polar), methanol (polar) and water, known as the Bligh & Dyer method, has been used for lipid extraction from a wide range of biological samples (Ryckebosch et al., 2012). However, concerns about biosafety issues using extraction solvents has driven a demand for biocompatible and less or non-toxic solvents (e.g., dichloromethane). Alternative solvent methods for lipid extraction thereby have been studied; for instance, saponification has resulted in significant lipid recoveries from several types of microalgae. Different strains of algae have different structures and compositions. In some, theoil can easily be extracted, while in some others, the oil may be contained with in the cells, enveloped by tough cellwalls, which need to be cracked a priori. Among several extraction methods, maceration is the most traditional and the simplest extraction procedure.

Some drawbacks of this method include long extraction time, low mass transfer and low yield, despite the low cost of production. Other tan maceration, several extraction techniques have lateron been developed. Among those, cavitational effects from ultrasound assisted extraction (UAE) and intracelular heating from microwave assisted extraction (MAE) have been found to cause damage to cell walls, shortening the time needed for extractions. As for biodiesel production via transesterification, for the past decade, there has been an exponentially rising number of studies aiming to improve the design of the transesterification process as well as optimizing the operating parameters, e.g. reaction conditions, alcohol to oil ratio, choices of catalyst. While these work are in search of efficient methods for extraction of microalgal lipids for the generate biodiesel, others propose quite interesting alternative approach of an insitu or single step transesterification without a need of prior tediousextraction step (Johnson and Wen, 2009).

Enhance Lipids Content in Microalgae

Microalgae contain lipids and fatty acids as membrane components, storage products, metabolites and sources of energy.Lipids produced by microalgae can be grouped into two energies categories, storage lipids (non-polar lipids) and structural lipids (polar lipids). Storage lipids are mainlyin the form of triacylglycerols (TAG) made of predominately saturated fatty acids (FAs) and some unsaturated FAs which can betransesterified to produce biodiesel. Structural lipids typically have a high content of polyunsaturatedfatty acids (PUFAs), which are also essential nutrients for aquatic animals and humans. Microalgal TAGs are generally characterized by both, saturated and monounsaturated FAs. Hence, PUFA-rich TAGs are metabolically active and aresuggested to act as a reservoir for specific fatty acids. In response to a sudden change in theenvironmental condition, when the de novo synthesis of PUFA may be slower, PUFA-rich TAG maydonate specific acyl groups to mono-galactosyl-diacylglycerol (MGDG) and other polar lipids to enable rapid adaptive membrane reorganization.

The ability of microalgae to survive in diverse and extreme conditions is reflected in the tremendous diversity and sometimes unusual pattern of cellular lipids obtained from thesemicroalgae. Some microalgae can also modify lipid metabolism efficiently inresponse to changes in environmental conditions. Under optimal growth conditions, large amounts of algal biomass are produced but with relatively low lipid contents, which constitute about 5-20% of their drycell weight (DCW), including glycerol-based membrane lipids. Under unfavorable environmental or stress conditions manymicroalgae alter their lipid biosynthetic pathways towards the formation and accumulation of neutrallipids (20-50% DCW), mainly in the form of TAG, enabling microalgae to endure these adverseconditions. Microalgal lipids are the oils of future for sustainable biodiesel production. However, relatively high production cost due to low lipid productivity has been one of the major obstacles impeding their commercial production. Also, producing biofuels from microalgae requires a balance of tradeoffs between species with high biomass productivity and high lipidcontent that can be reliably manipulated and are tolerant or recover easily from a range of environmental perturbations to continue growing. Therefore, a combination of environmental parameters can affect microalgae growth and lipid accumulation of which, the type and availability of nutrients play a major role (Chen et al., 2011).

Nutrient Starvation

Nutrient availability has a significant impact on growth and propagation of microalgae and broad effects on their lipid and FA composition. Environmental stress condition when nutrients are limited, invariably cause a steadily declining cell division rate (Thompson, 1996). Surprisingly, active biosynthesis of fatty acids is maintained in some algae species under such conditions, provided there is enough light and CO_2 available for photosynthesis. When algal growth (as measured by cell divisions) slows down and there is no requirement for the synthesis of new membrane compounds, the cells instead divert and deposit fatty acids into TAG. Under these conditions, TAG production might serve as a protective energies mechanism. When cell growth and proliferation is impaired due to the lack of nutrients the pool of the major electron acceptor for photosynthesis, NADP+ can become depleted.

Since photosynthesis is mainly controlled by the abundance of light, and cannot be shut down completely, this can lead to a potentially dangerous situation for the cell, damaging cell components. NADPH is consumed in FA biosynthesis, therefore, increased FAs production (which in turn are stored in TAGs) replenishes the pool of NADP+ under growth-limiting conditions. Nutrient starvation is one of the most widely used and applied lipid induction techniques in microalgal TAG production and has been reported for many species (Table 10.2). Nitrogen is the single most critical nutrient affecting lipid metabolism in algae. A general trend towards accumulation of lipids, particularly TAG, in response to nitrogen deficiency has been observed in numerous species or strains of various microalgae.

A study on nitrogen stress responses of several green microalgae was conducted (El- Fouly et al., 1985). The results showed a significant rise in lipid production. A detailed and large-scale model of lipid induction by nutrient starvation (nitrogen, phosphorus) on several diatoms, green algae, red algae, prymnesiophytes and eustimatophytes was established (Roessler, 1988). However, only asmall increase in TAG levels (from 69 to 75% from total lipids) together with phospholipids from 6 to 8% was reported for the microalga *Phaeodactylum tricornutum* as a result of reduced nitrogen concentrations (Alonso et al., 2000). *Scenedesmus sp.* subjected to nitrogen or phosphorus limitation showed an increase in lipids as high as 30% and 53%, respectively (Xin et al., 2010). Lipid content of freshwater green alga *Chlorella vulgaris* could be significantly increased by 40% in low nitrogen-containing medium. With manipulated culture conditions of 1 mM KNO_3, 1.0% CO_2, 60 μmol photon $m^{-2}s^{-1}$and 25 °C lipid production of *C. vulgaris* was increased by 2.5-fold (Illman et al., 2000).

In addition, lipid stimulation in *Chlorella* was also achieved via silicon deficiency and iron supplementation (Alonso et al., 1998). Moreover, it was found for *C. vulgaris* that changing from normal nutrient to nitrogen depletion media gradually changed the lipid composition from free FA-rich lipids to lipid mostly contained as TAG (Widjaja et al., 2009). Nitrogen starvation in microalgae not only affects the fatty acid metabolism, but also affects pigment composition. For *Parietochloris incise* grown in nitrogen-replete medium a considerable increase in the ratio of carotenoid and chlorophyll contents was recorded.

Additionally, phosphorus limitation resulted in increased lipid content, mainly as TAG, in *P. tricornutum*, *Chaetoceros sp.*, *Isochrysisgalbana* and *Pavlovalutheri* (Reitan et al., 1994 and Alonso et al., 2000), but decreased lipid content in *Nannochlorisatomus* and *Tetraselmis sp.* (Converti et al., 2009). Due to phosphorus deprivation, production of C16:0 and C18:1 was increased and production of C18:4ωз, C20:5ωз and C22:6ωз was decreased (Reitan et al., 1994). Hence, nitrogen starvation is the most successful lipid inducing technique at present. However, high lipid production due to nitrogen stress may take 2-5 days and is complemented with slow growth rates and low cell counts and thus finally effecting the total biomass and lipid productivity.

Table 10.2: Different Types of Nutrient Starvation Stress to Induce Lipids in Microalgae

Microalgae Species or Strain	Nutrient Stress	Changes in Lipid Profile After Induction	Reference
Nannochloropsisoculata	Nitrogen limitation	Total lipid increased by 15.31%	(Converti et al., 2009)
Chlorella vulgaris	Nitrogen limitation	Total lipid increased by 16.41%	(Converti et al., 2009)
Chlorella sp.	Nitrogen limitation	Lipid productivity of 53.96 ± 0.63 mg/L d	(Praveenkumar et al., 2012)
Phaeodactylumtricornutum	Nitrogen limitation	TAG levels increased from 69 to 75%	(Alonso et al., 2000)
Dunaliellatertiolecta	Nitrogen limitation	Five times increase in lipid fluorescence	(Chen et al., 2011)
Chlorella vulgaris	Nitrogen medium	Lipids increased by 40%	(Illman et al., 2000)
Neochlorisoleoabundans	Ammonium nitrate	Lipid productivity of 0.133 g /L d	(Li et al., 2008)
Scenedesmussp	Nitrogen and phosphorus starvation	Lipids increased 30% and 53%, respectively	(Xin et al., 2010)
Chlamydomonasreinhardtii	Sulphur limitation	PG was increased by 2-fold	(Sato et al., 2000)
Cyclotellacryptica	Silicon starvation	Increased in total lipids from 27.6% to 54.1%	(Roessler, 1988)

Fatty Acids Composition in Algal Cells

Algae produce both saturated and unsaturated fatty acids with different number and position of unsaturated bonds and various length of carboxylic chain (Rasoul- Amini et al., 2011).The suitability of microalgal biomass as biofuel feedstock is closely related to the length and degree of saturation of its fatty acids as specified by the four key figures iodine value, oxidation stability, cetane number, and the cold filter plugging point (Knothe 2005 and Miao and Wu, 2006). A high iodine number represents a high degree of unsaturation of fatty acids in biodiesel, which is unfavourable because fatty acids with higher content of double bonds are prone to oxidative damage (Jang et al, 2005; Dijkstra, 2006 and Chisti, 2007).

Otherwise, unsaturated fatty acids are beneficial for flow properties, especially at lower temperatures and therewith result in an advantageous cold filter plugging point (Prabakaran and Ravindran et al., 2012). Lipids rich in long chain fatty acids with a low degree of saturation exhibit a high cetane number (Knothe 2005 and Mallick et al 2012), indicating a short ignition delay time and high combustion quality (Damiani et al., 2010) whereas an exceeding degree of saturation might collide with the request for a reasonable cold filter plugging point by precipitation at low temperatures (Chisti, 2007).

While algae could be excellent source of PUFA in dietary supplementation, in biodiesel production the amounts of fatty acids with four or more double bonds should be as small as possible. Such acids as well as their esters are definitely more susceptible to oxidation during fuel storage decreasing their quality. It seems especially important in the case of biodiesel which is to be used in vehicles. European standards (Standard EN 14214) allow only 1% mol contents of methylic or ethylic esters of 4 or more double bonds fatty acids. Many of algae derived oils are not up to this standard.The European norm EN 14214 gives an overview of biodiesel quality requirements and test methods. Table 10.3 shows a comparison of properties of microalgal oil, petroleum diesel, and norm standards.

Strain selection can be performed with a special focus not only on generally applied selection criteria, such as lipid content and areal lipid productivity, but also on the fatty acid profiles matching biodiesel requirements. Further selection criteria for microalgae need to be considered as they mainly influence the ability to produce biomass at a large scale in the respective environments. Amongst them strain-specific optimal temperature range, salinity of the cultivation medium, and the ability to be maintained for longer periods in nonaxenic cultures need to be taken into account. Therefore, the choice of the most adequate cultivation system and process strategy will be decisive in order to achieve high areal lipid productivities.

Table 10.3: Comparison of Selected Properties of Algal Bio-oil and Typical Conventional Diesel with Respect to the European Norm for Biodiesel

Fuel Property	Algal Biodiesel	Petroleum Diesel	EN14214 Standard	Aviation Diesel
Higher heating value (MJ/kg)	41	45.9	–	–
Kinematic viscosity (mm^2/s) 40°C	5.2	1.2-3.5	3.5-5.2	1.9-6
Density (kg/L)	0.864	0.83-0.84	0.86-0.90	–
Carbon (wt%)	76	87	–	–
Hydrogen (wt%)	<12, 7	13	–	–
Oxygen (wt%)	>11, 3	0	–	–
Sulphur (wt%)	0	0.05 max	<10 max. 0,02	0.0015- 0.05
Boiling point (°C)	–	180–340	–	–
Flash point (°C)	115	60-80	>101	93 min
Cloud point (°C)	–	–15 to 5	–	–
Pour point (°C)	–12	–35 to –15	–	–
Cetane number	–	51	>51	47 min

The fatty acid composition of the feedstock used for biodiesel production also affects the ignition quality of the fuel as measured by its Cetane Number (CN). The carbon chain length and the number of double bonds in the fatty acid chain both affect the ignition quality. The Cetane Number (CN) is a dimensionless parameter related to the ignition delay period that the fuel experiences upon injection into the cylinder of a diesel engine. The higher the CN, the shorter the ignition delay period, and the lower the CN, the longer the ignition delay period. A CN scale using hydrocarbons has been established in which n-hexadecane (C16H34) is the high CN (CN=100) reference compound with a very short ignition delay period and 2, 2, 4, 4, 6, 8, 8-heptamethylnonane (HMN; also C16H34) is the low CN (CN=15) reference with a long, poor quality ignition. The ASTM D6751 standard for biodiesel requires a minimum CN of 47 and the EN 14214 requires a minimum CN of 51.The CN of a diesel fuel must be within acceptable limits for proper operation of a compression ignition engine. If the CN of the fuel is too high, combustion can occur before the fuel and are air properly mixed resulting in incomplete combustion and smoke; conversely, low CN leads to misfiring, higher combustion air temperatures, slower engine warm-up, and incomplete combustion.

Conversion of Algal Oil to Biodiesel

The transesterification of biomass derived lipids to fatty acid methyl ester (FAME) liquid fuels is well established and practised on large scales, using transesterification technology.

Transesterification of Oil

Transesterificationof natural glycerides with methanol to methylesters is a technically important reaction that has been used extensively in the soap and detergent manufacturing industry worldwide for many years. Almost all biodiesel is produced in a similar chemical process using base catalyzed transesterification as it is the most economical process, requiring only low temperatures and pressures while producing a 98% conversion yield. The transesterification process is the reaction of a triglyceride (fat/oil) with an alcohol to form esters and glycerol. A triglyceride has a glycerine molecule as its base with three long chain fatty acids attached. The characteristics of the fat are determined by the nature of the fatty acids attached to the glycerine. The nature of the fatty acids can, in turn, affect the characteristics of the biodiesel.

During the esterification process, the triglyceride is reacted with alcohol in the presence of a catalyst, usually a strong alkaline like sodium hydroxide. The alcohol reacts with the fatty acids to form the mono-alkyl ester, or biodiesel, and crude glycerol. In most production, methanol or ethanol is the alcohol used (methanol produces methyl esters, ethanol produces ethyl esters) and is base catalyzed by either potassium or sodium hydroxide. Potassium hydroxide has been found more suitable for the ethyl ester biodiesel production, but either base can be used for methyl ester production (Hawash et al., 2009, El Kinawy and Zaher, 2012; Zaher et al., 2003). The figure below shows the chemical process for methyl ester biodiesel (Fig. 10.9). The reaction between the fat or oil and the alcohol is a reversible reaction, so the alcohol must be added in excess to drive the reaction towards the right and ensure complete conversion.

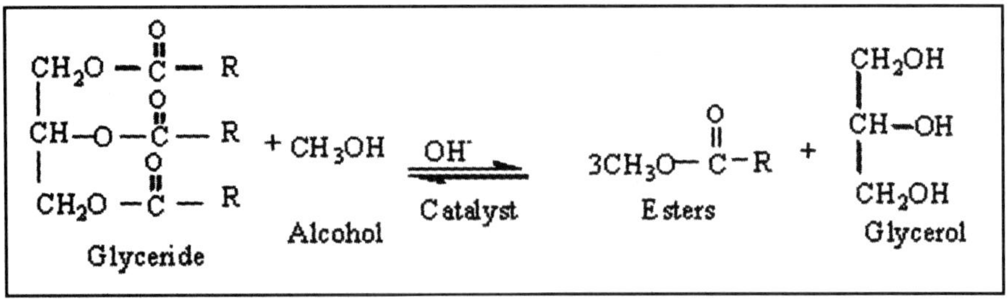

$$\begin{array}{l} CH_2O-\overset{O}{\overset{\|}{C}}-R \\ CH-O-\overset{O}{\overset{\|}{C}}-R \\ CH_2O-\overset{O}{\overset{\|}{C}}-R \end{array} + CH_3OH \xrightleftharpoons[\text{Catalyst}]{OH^-} 3CH_3O-\overset{O}{\overset{\|}{C}}-R + \begin{array}{l} CH_2OH \\ CH-OH \\ CH_2OH \end{array}$$

Glyceride — Alcohol — Catalyst — Esters — Glycerol

Fig. 10.9: Conversion of Oil to Biodiesel by Transesterification

The products of the reaction (Transesterification) are the biodiesel itself and glycerol.A successful transesterification reaction is signified by the separation of the methyl ester (biodiesel) and glycerol layers (Fig. 10.10) after the reaction time (Solimanet al., 2013, Zaher and El Kinawy 2012).

The heavier co-product, glycerol, settles out and may be sold as is or purified for use in other industries, e.g. pharmaceutical, cosmetics, and detergents (Abdoet al., 2012, and Abdoet al., 2012a).

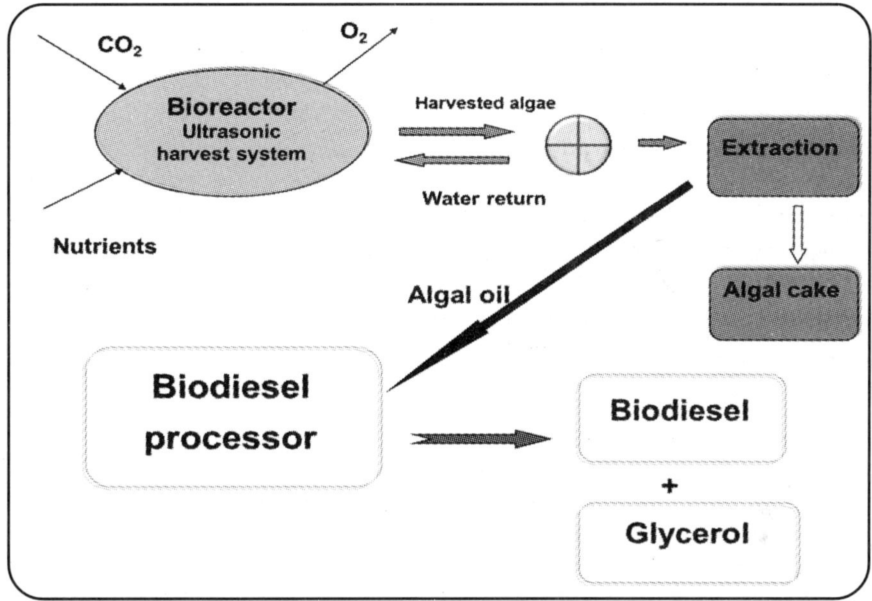

Fig. 10.10: Steps Involved in the Biodiesel Production from Algal Biomass

After the transesterification reaction and the separation of the crude heavy glycerin phase, the producer is left with a crude light biodiesel phase. This crude biodiesel requires some purification prior to use (El Kinawyand Zaher, 2012). Biodiesel has a viscosity similar to petroleum diesel and can be used as an additive in formulations of diesel to increase the lubricity. Algal biodiesel properties are so closed to the petroleum diesel properties as presented previously in table 10.3. For example, algal biodiesel can be used in pure form (B100) or may be blended with petroleum diesel at any concentration in most modern diesel engines. Biodiesel will degrade natural rubber gaskets and hoses in vehicles (mostly found in vehicles manufactured before 1992), although these tend to wear out naturally and most likely will have already been replaced with Viton type seals and hoses which are nonreactive to biodiesel.

Biodiesel's higher lubricity index compared to petroleum diesel is an advantage and can contribute to longer fuel injector life.

Biodiesel is a better solvent than petroleum diesel and has been known to break down deposits of residue in the fuel lines of vehicles that have previously been run on petroleum diesel. Fuel filters may become clogged with particulates if a quick transition to pure biodiesel is made, as biodiesel "cleans" the engine in the process. It is, therefore, recommended to change the fuel filter within 600-800 miles after first switching to a biodiesel blend.Biodiesel's commercial fuel quality is measured by the Biodiesel Specifications (ASTM) standard designated D 6751.

The standards ensure that biodiesel is pure and the following important factors such as :-complete reaction - removal of glycerin - removal of catalyst - Removal of alcohol - absence of free fatty acids - low sulfur content.Biodiesel is, at present, the most attractive market alternative among the non-food applications of vegetable oils for transportation fuels. The different stages in the production of plant/seed oil methyl ester generate by-products which offer further outlets. Oil cake, the protein rich fraction obtained after the oil has been extracted from the seed, is used for animal feed. Glycerol, the other important by-product, has numerous applications in the oil and chemical industries such as the cosmetic, pharmaceutical, food, and painting industries.

Fuel Properties

The biodiesel recommended specifications indicated a pattern of fatty acid composition. This pattern indicates the biodiesel efficacy. The degree of unsaturation should not exceed four double bonds in the fatty acid molecules (Stansell et al., 2012), the percentage of oleic and linoleic should be high (Jang et al, 2005 and Dijkstra 2006) and percentage of linolenic acid should not exceed 12% (Chisti, 2007). The biodiesel Fatty Acid Methyl ester (FAME) pattern analysis of the algal oil to be determined by GC (Seppänen-Laakso et al., 2002).

The latest specification for B100 biodiesel fuel is ASTM D6751 (ASTM Biodiesel Specifications) with test method indicated are shown in table 10.4.

Table 10.4: ASTM D6751 Requirements for B100, 100% Biodiesel

Property	Test Method	Limits	Units
Calcium and magnesium combined	EN14538	5 max	ppm
Flash point	D93	93.0 min	°C
Water and sediment	D2709	0.050 max	Vol %
Kinematic viscosity, 40°C	D445	1.9-6.0	mm^2/s
Sulfated ash	D874	0.020 max	% mass
Sulfur	D5453	0.0015 max (S15) 0.05 max (S500)	% mass
Copper strip corrosion	D130	0.020 max	–
Cetane number	D613	47 min	–
Cloud point	D2500	Report to customer	°C
Carbon residue[a]	D4530	0.050 max	% mass
Acid number	D664	0.50 max	mg KOH/g
Free glycerin	D6584	0.020	% mass
Total glycerin	D6584	0.240	% mass

(Table Contd...)

Property	Test Method	Limits	Units
Phosphorus content	D4951	0.001 max	% mass
Distillation temperature, 90% recovered (T90)[b]	D1160	360 max	°C
Oxidation stability	EN14112	3 min	hours
Cold Soak filterability	Annex A1	360 max[c]	seconds
Alcohol control - One of the following must be met:			
(1) Methanol content	EN14110	0.2 max	Vol %
(2) Flash point	D93	130 min	°C

Biodiesel Specifications

The latest specification for B100 biodiesel fuel is ASTM D6751-07. ASTM is a standards group comprised of engine and fuel injection equipment manufacturers, fuel producers, and fuel users whose standards are recognized in the U.S. by governmental entities, including state agencies responsible for ensuring fuel quality. So called "biofuels" or "biodiesel fuels" that do not meet the ASTM standard outlined below are not legally biodiesel fuels and should not be used in diesel engines.

Engine Performance

The main target is to examine the possibility of utilization of biodiesel and different biodiesel and diesel blends in Compression Ignition (CI) engines and their influence on engine power, torque, fuel consumption and exhaust emission.

- All engine tests performed at full engine load at two different enginespeeds (1,600 and 2,688 min^{-1}) including the following engine and vehicle tests: (a) vehicle acceleration; (b) vehicle elasticity; (c) maximum speed; (d) fuel consumption and drivability check-out; and (e) behaviour of the vehicle on the road.

Economics of Algae Biodiesel Production

Photobioreactors require 10 times capital investment than open pond systems. The estimated algal production cost for open pond systems ($10/kg) and photobioreactors ($30-$70/kg) is two order magnitudes higher than conventional agricultural biomass respectively. Assuming that biomass contains 30% oil by weight and carbon dioxide available at no cost, estimated production cost for photobioreactors and ponds would be $1.40 and $1.81 per liter of oil respectively. However, for microalgal biodiesel to be competitive with petrodiesel, algal oil price should be less than $0.48/L. It has been estimated that 0.53 billion m^3 of biodiesel would be needed to replace current US transportation consumption of all petroleum fuels. The per unit area yield of oil from algae is estimated to be from 18,927 to 75,708 l per acre, per year; this is 7-31 times greater than the next best crop, palm oil (Demirbas and Demirbas, 2011). To produce this quantity (0.53 billion) of biodiesel, palm oil would need to be grown over an area about 111 million (M) hectares.

This is nearly 61% of all agricultural cropping land in the United States. Growing palm oil at this scale would be unrealistic because insufficient land would be left for producing food and other crops (Chisti, 2007). Therefore, the production of biodiesel from algae is more interested to overcome the problem of agricultural cropping land in the United States and in all other the worlds. The numerous benefits of biofuel generation from microalgae are motivation for further analysis and development: biomass yields of up to 100 to 150 tons dry matter per ha and year with lipid contents of around 40%, biodiesel yields of 40 to 50 tons per ha and year by far exceed the most promising yields from land crops.

Because of the high amount of polyunsaturated fatty acids, microalgal biofuel shows good flow properties under low temperatures reducing the risk of cold filter plugging and making it even suitable for aviation fuel. Special is the ability to influence the oil composition by the selection of the strain cultivated and the cultivation conditions themselves.

REFERENCES

Abdo, S.M., Hetta, M.H., Samhan, F.A., El Din, R.A.S. and Ali, G.H. (2012): Phytochemical and Antibacterial Study of Five Freshwater Algal Species. *Asian Journal of Plant Sciences*, 11(3): 109-116.

Abdo, S.M., Hetta, M.H., El-Senousy, W.M., El-Din, R.A.S., and Ali, G.H. (2012a): Antiviral Activity of Dreshwater Algae. *Journal of Applied Pharmaceutical Science*, 2 (2): 21-25.

Afify, A.M.M.,Shanab, S.M. and Shalaby, E.A. (2010): Enhancement of Biodiesel Production from Different Species of Algae. *Grasasy Aceites*, 61 (4): 416-422.

Alonso, D.L., Belarbi, E.-H., Fernández-Sevilla, J.M., Rodríguez-Ruiz, J. and Grima, E.M. (2000): Acyllipid Composition Variation Related to Culture Age and Nitrogen Concentration in Continuous Culture of the Microalga *Phaeodactylumtricornutum. Phytochemistry*, 54: 461-471.

Alonso, D.L., Belarbi, E.-H., Rodríguez-Ruiz, J., Segura, C.I. and Giménez, A. (1998): Acyl Lipids of Three Microalgae. *Phytochemistry*, 47: 1473-1481.

Ana, P.C., Luis, A.M. and Malcata, F.X. (2006): Microalgal Reactors: A Review of Enclosed System Designs and Performances. Biotechnology Progress, 22: 1490-1506.

ASTM Biodiesel Specifications. <http://www.afdc.energy.gov/fuels/biodiesel_specifications.html>.

Camacho, R.F., Acién Fernández, F.G., Camacho, F.G., Sánchez Pérez, J.A. and Molina, G.E. (1992): Prediction of Dissolved Oxygen and Carbon Dioxide Concentration Profiles in Tubular Photobioreactors for Microalgal Culture. Biotechnology and Bioengineering, 62: 71-86.

Carlsson, A., Beilen Van, J., Möller, R., Clayton, D. and Bowles, D.E. (2007): Microand Macroalgae - Utility for Industrial Applications. Bioproducts, E.R.t.E. P.o. S.R.-. and Crops, f.N.-f., CNAP, University of York: 86.

Chen, M., Tang, H., Ma, H., Holland, T.C., Ng, K.Y.S. and Salley, S.O. (2011): Effect of Nutrients on Growth and Lipid Accumulation in the Green Algae *Dunaliellatertiolecta. Bioresource Technology*, 102: 1649-1655.

Chisti, Y. (2007): Biodiesel from Microalgae. *Biotechnology Advances*, 25: 294-306.

Converti, A.,Casazza, A.A., Ortiz, E.Y.,Perego, P. and Del Borghi, M. (2009): Effect of Temperature and Nitrogen Concentration on the Growth and Lipid Content of *Nannochloropsisoculata* and *Chlorellavulgaris* for Biodiesel Production. *Chemical Engineering and Processing*, 48: 1146-1151.

Damiani, M.C., Popovich, C.A., Constenla, D. and Leonardi, P.I. (2010): Lipid Analysis in *Haematococcuspluvialis* to Assess its Potential Use as Biodiesel Feedstock. *Bioresource Technology*, 101: 3801-3807.

Demirbas, A. and Demirbas, M.F.(2011): Importance of Algae Oil as a Source of Biodiesel. *Energy Conversion and Management*, 52: 163-170.

Dijkstra, A.J. (2006): Revisiting the Formation of Trans Isomers during Partial Hydrogenation Oftricylaytion Oils, *European Journal of Lipid Science and Technology*, 108 (3): 249-64.

El-Baz, F.K., Aly, H.F., El-Sayed, A.B. and Mohamed, A.A. (2013): Role of *Spirulina Platensis* in the Control of Glycemia in DM2 Rats. *International Journal of Scientific & Engineering Research*, 4 (12): 1731-1740.

El-Baz, F.K., Abd el-Baky, H.H., El-Baroty, G.S. and Shalaby, E. (2004): Over-production of Rich in Y-Lininolenicacid by Blue Green Alga *Spirulinamaxima* and its Inhibitory Effect on Carcinoma Cells. In: Second Conference of Role of Biochemistry in Environment and Agriculture, 143-157. Faculty of Agriculture, Cairo University, Egypt.

El-Baz, F.K., Abuol-Enein, M.A., El-Baroty, S.G., Youssef, A.M. and Abd El-Baky, H.H. (2002): Anticarcinogenic Activity of Algal Extract. *Journal of Medical Sciences*, 2(5-6): 243-251.

El-Fouly, M.M., Youssef, A.M., El–Baz, F.K., Abdalla, F.E. and Abdel Hafeez, M.M. (1985): Studies on Fat Accumulation in *Chlorella* and *scenedesmus. Arch. Hydrobiol. Algological Studies*, 40: 439-457.

El-Kinawy, O.S., Zaher, F.A. and Abdallah, R.(2009): Effect of Different Extraction Techniques on Jatrophaoil Quality and its Evaluation as a Biodiesel Fuel.TESCE, 35(2): 36-46.

El-Kinawy, O.S. and Zaher, F.A. (2012): Studies on Esterification Kinetics of Short Chain Alcohols with Fatty Acids to Produce Biodiesel Fuel. Energy Sources, Part A, 34: 662-670.

Guschina, I.A. and Harwood, J.L. (2006): Lipids and Lipid Metabolism in Eukaryotic Algae. *Progress in Lipid Research*, 45: 160-86.

Hawash, S., Kamal, N., Zaher, F., El-Kinawy, O.S.and El Diwani, G.(2009): Biodiesel Fuel from Jatrophaoil via Non-catalytic Supercritical Methanol Transesterification. *Fuel*, 28: 539-43.

Illman, A.M., Scragg, A.H. and Shales, S.W. (2000): Increase in Chlorella Strains Calorific Values when Grown in Low Nitrogen Medium. *Enzyme and Microbial Technology*, 27: 631-635.

Jang, E.S., Jung, M.Y. and Min, D.B. (2005): Hydrogenation for Low Trans and High Conjugation Fatty Acids. *Comprehensive Reviews in Food Science and Food Safety*, 4: 22-30.

Jonker, J. (2010): Energy Production from Algae. Utrecht: Utrecht University.

Johnson M.B. and Wen Z., (2009). Production of Biodiesel Fuel from the Microalga Schizochytriumlimacinum by Direct Transesterification of Algal Biomass, Energy & Fuels, Vol. 23, pp. 5179C5183,

Knothe, G. (2005): The History of Vegetable Oil-based Diesel Fuels, in: Knothe, G., Van Gerpen, J., Krahl, J. (Eds.), The Biodiesel Handbook. Urbana: AOCS Press. pp. 4-16.

Kulkarni, M.G., and Dalai, A.K. (2006): Waste Cooking Oil-an Economical Source for Biodiesel: A Review. *Industrial & Engineering Chemistry Research*, 45: 2901-13.

Li, Y., Horsman, M., Wang, B., Wu, N. andLan, C. (2008): Effects of Nitrogen Sources on Cell Growth and Lipid Accumulation of Green Alga *Neochlorisoleoabundans. Applied Microbiology and Biotechnology*, 81: 629-636.

Mallick, N., Mandal, S., Singh, A.K., Bishai, M. and Dash, A. (2012): Green Microalga *Chlorella vulgaris* as a Potential Feedstock for Biodiesel. *Journal of Chemical Technology and Biotechnology*, 87: 137-145.

Miao, X. and Wu, Q. (2006): Biodiesel Production from Heterotrophic Micro Algal Oil. *Bioresource Technology*, 97: 841-846.

Molina-Grima, E., Belarbi, E. H., AciénFernández, F. G., Robles Medina A. and Chisti, Y.(2003): Recovery of Microalgal Biomass and Metabolites: Process Options and Economics. *Biotechnology Advances*, 20 (7-8): 491-515.

Mercer, P. and Armenta, R.E. (2011): Development in Oil Extraction from Microalgae. *European Journal of Lipid Science and Technology*, 113: 539-547.

National Energy Technology Laboratory (2005): Peaking of World Oil Production, Impacts, Mitigation and Risk Management.

Oswald, W.J. (1969): Current Status of Algae from Wastes. *Chemical Engineering Progress Symposium Series*, 65: 87-92.

Prabakaran, P. and Ravindran, A.D. (2012): Scenedesmus as a Potential Source of Biodiesel Among Selected Microalgae. *Current Science*, 102(4): 616-620.

Praveen Kumar, R., Shameera, K., Mahalakshmi, G., Akbarsha, M.A. and Thajuddin, N.(2012): Influence of Nutrient Deprivations on Lipid Accumulation in a Dominant Indigenous Microalga *Chlorella sp.*, Bum11008: Evaluation for Biodiesel Production. *Biomass and Bioenergy*, 37: 60-66.

Rasoul-Amini, S., Montazeri-Najafabady, N., Mobasher, M.A., Hoseini-Alhashemi, S. and Ghasemi, Y. (2011): *Chlorella sp.*: A New Strain with Highly Saturated Fatty Acids for Biodiesel Production in Bubble-column Photobioreactor. *Applied Energy*, 88(10): 3354-3356.

Reitan, K.I., Rainuzzo, J.R. and Olsen, Y. (1994): Effect of Nutrient Limitation on Fatty Acid and Lipid Content of Marine Microalgae. *Journal of Phycology*, 30: 972-979.

Rodolfi, L., Zittelli, G.C., Bassi, N., Padovani, G., Biondi, N., Bonini, G. and Tredici, M.R. (2009): Microalgae for Oil: Strain Selection, Induction of Lipid Synthesis and Outdoor Mass Cultivation in a Low-cost Photobioreactor. *Biotechnology and Bioengineering*, 102(1): 100-112.

Roessler, P.G. (1988): Effects of Silicon Deficiency on Lipid Composition and Metabolism in the Diatom *Cyclotellacryptica*. *Journal of Phycology*, 24: 394-400.

Rosenberg, J., Oyler, G., Wilkinson, L. and Betenbaugh, M. (2008): A Green Light for Engineered Algae: Redirecting Metabolism to Fuel a Biotechnology Revolution. *Biotechnology*, 19: 430-436.

Ryckebosch, E., Muylaert, K. and Foubert, I. (2012): Optimization of an Analytical Procedure for Extraction from Microalgae. *Journal of the American Oil Chemists' Society*, 89(2): 189-198.

Sato, N., Hagio, M., Wada, H. and Tsuzuki, A.M. (2000): Environmental Effects on Acidic Lipids of Thylakoid Membranes. *Biochemical Society Transactions*, 28: 912-914.

Seppänen-Laakso, T., Laakso, I. and Hiltunen, R. (2002): Analysis of Fatty Acids by Gas Chromatography, and its Relevance to Research on Health and Nutrition. *Analytica Chimica Acta*, 465(1-2): 39-62.

Soliman, H.M., El Kinawy, O.S. and Zaher, F.A. (2013): Production of Biodiesel Fuel from the Industrial Wastes of the Oil and Soap Industrial. *Journal of Applied Sciences Research,* 9(3): 2188-2195.

Spolaore, P., Joannis-Cassan, C., Duran, E. and Ismbert, A. (2006): Commercial Application of Microalgae. *Journal of Bioscience and Bioengineering*, 101: 87-96.

Stansell, G.R., Grey, V.M. and Sym, S.D. (2012): Microalgae Fatty Acid Composition: Implications for Biodiesel Quality. *Journal of Applied Phycology*, 24(4): 45-54.

Thompson, G.A. (1996): Lipids and Membrane Function in Green Algae. *Biochimicaet Biophysica Acta*, 1302: 17-45.

Widjaja, A., Chien, C.C. and Ju, Y.H. (2009): Study of Increasing Lipid Production from Fresh Water Microalgae *Chlorella vulgaris*. *Journal of the Taiwan Institute of Chemical Engineers*, 40: 13-20.

Xin, L., Hong-ying, H., Ke, G. and Ying-xue, S. (2010): Effects of Different Nitrogen and Phosphorus Concentrations on the Growth, Nutrient Uptake, and Lipid Accumulation of a Freshwater Microalga *Scenedesmus sp. Bioresource Technology*, 101: 5494-5500.

Zaher, F.A., Megahed, O.A. and El Kinawy, O.S. (2003): Esters of Sunflower Oil as an Alternative Fuel for Diesel Engine. *Energy Source*, 25: 1015-1022.

Zaher, F.A. and El-Kinawy, O.S. (2012): Favourable Conditions to Reduce Losses and Improve Quality of Biodiesel from Jatropha Oil. *Energy Sources, Part A,* 34: 793-798.

Pages: 159-168

AGRICULTURE DEVELOPMENT AND SUSTAINABLE ENVIRONMENT

Edited by: Jaswant Ray; Dr. Pawan Kumar 'Bharti'

ISBN: 978-93-5056-759-3

Edition: 2015

Published by: Discovery Publishing House Pvt. Ltd., New Delhi (India)

11

Water Pollution
Effects and Control Measures

Rupali Salunkhe and **Resham Bhalla**

INTRODUCTION

Water is a marvelous substance – flowing, rippling, swirling around obstacles in its path, seeping, drinking, trickling, constantly and moving from sea to land and back again. Water can be clear, crystalline, icy green in a mountain stream, or back and opaque in a cypress swamp. Rain falls in a gentle mist, refreshing plants and animals. A violent thunderstorm floods a meadow, washing away stream banks. Water is a most beautiful and precious resource. Water is also a great source of conflict. Some 2 billion people, a third of the world's population, live in countries with insufficient clean water. Some experts estimate this number could double in 25 years. Most of us today appreciate that water in most industrialized countries was once far more polluted and dangerous than it is now.

Factories and cities routinely dumped untreated chemicals, metals, oil, solvents and sewage into rivers and lakes. Toxic solvents and organic chemicals were commonly dumped or buried in the ground, poisoning

Lecturer Department of Zoology, LVH Arts, Science and Commerce College, Panchavati, Nasik - 422 003 (MS), (India).

groundwater that we are now paying billions to clean up. In 1972, President Nixon signed the Clean Water Act, which has been called the United States' most successful and popular environmental legislation. This act established a goal that all the nation's water should be "fishable and swimmable." In addition, water has an aesthetic appeal: the view of clean lake, river or seashore makes people happy and water provides for recreation, so many people feel their quality of life has improved as water quality has been restored. We still have a long way to go in improving water quality. Increasing industrialization in developing countries has led to widespread water pollution in improvised regions with little environmental regulation.

Any physical, biological, or chemical change in water quality that adversely affects living organisms or makes water unsuitable for desired uses can be considered pollution. Pollution–control standards regulations usually distinguish between point and nonpoint pollution sources. Factories, power plants, sewage treatment plants, underground coal mines, and oil wells are classified as point sources because they discharge pollution from specific locations, such as drain pipes, ditches or sewer outfalls. These sources are discrete and identifiable, so they are relatively easy to monitor and regulate. In contrasts, nonpoint sources of water pollution are scattered or diffuse, having no specific location where they discharge into a particular body of water. Nonpoint sources include runoff from farm fields and feedlots, golf courses, lawns and gardens, constructor sites, logging areas, roads, streets and parking lots. Whereas point source may be fairly uniform and predictable throughout the year, nonpoint sources are often highly episodic.

TYPES AND EFFECTS OF WATER POLLUTION

Although the types, sources and effects of water pollutants are often interrelated, it is convenient to divide them into major categories for discussion (Table 11.1) let's look more closely at some of the important sources and effects of each type of pollutant.

Infectious Agents

The most serious water pollutants in terms of human health worldwide are pathogenic organisms. Among the most important waterborne diseases are typhoid, cholera, bacterial and amoebic dysentery, enteritis, polio, infectious hepatitis, and schistosomiasis. Malaria, yellow fever, and filarisis are transmitted by insects that have aquatic larvae. Altogether, at least 2 million deaths each year are blamed on these water-related diseases. Nearly two-thirds of the mortalities of children under 5 years old are associated with waterborne disease. The main source of these pathogens is from untreated or improperly treated human wastes. Animal wastes from feedlots or fields near water ways and food processing factories with inadequate waste treatment facilities also are sources of disease-causing organisms.

Table 11.1: Major Categories of Water Pollutants

	Category	Examples	Sources
A.	**CAUSES HEALTH PROBLEMS**		
1.	Infectious agents	Bacteria, viruses, parasites.	Human and animal excreta.
2.	Organic chemicals	Pesticides, plastics, detergents, oil, and gasoline	Industrial, household, and farm use.
3.	Inorganic chemicals	Acids, caustics, salts, metal	Industrial effluents, household cleaners, surface runoff
4.	Radioactive materials production, natural sources.	Uranium, thorium, iodine, radon.	Mining and processing of Ores, Power Plants and Weapons.
B.	**CAUSES ECOSYSTEM DISTRIBUTION**		
1.	Sediments	Soil, Slit	Land erosion
2.	Plant nutrients	Nitrates, Phosphates, Ammonia.	Agricultural and urban fertilizers, sewage, manure
3.	Oxygen-demanding Wastes.	Animal manure and plant residues.	Sewage, agricultural runoff, paper mills, food processing.
4.	Thermal	Heat	Power plants, industrial cooling.

United Nations estimates that 90% of the people in developed countries have adequate (safe) sewage disposal, 95% have clean drinking water. The situation is quite different in less developed countries. The United Nations estimates that at least 2.5 billion people in these countries lack adequate sanitation and that about half these people also lack access to clean drinking water; especially bad in remote, rural areas where sewage treatment is usually primitive or nonexistent and purified water is either unavailable or too expensive to obtain. The World Health Organization estimates that about 80% of all sickness and disease in less – developed countries can be attributed to waterborne infectious agents and inadequate sanitation.

Oxygen –Demanding Wastes

The amount of oxygen dissolved in water is a good indicator of water quality and of the kind of life it will support. Water with less than 6 ppm will support game fish and other desirable forms of aquatic life. Water with less than 2 ppm oxygen will support mainly worms, bacteria, fungi, and other detritus feeders and decomposers. Oxygen is added to water by diffusion from the air and photosynthesis of green plants, algae and cyanobacteria. Oxygen is removed from water by respiration and chemical processes that consume oxygen.

The addition of certain organic materials, such as sewage, paper pulp, or food – processing wastes, to water stimulates oxygen consumption by decomposers. The impact of these materials on water quality can be expressed in terms of Biochemical oxygen demand (BOD): a standard test of the amount of dissolved oxygen consumed by aquatic microorganisms over a 5 days period. An alternative method, called the chemical oxygen demand(COD), uses a strong oxidizing agent (dichromate ion in 50% sulfuric acid) to completely break down all organic matter in a water sample. This method is faster than the BOD but gives much higher results because oxidizes compounds not ordinarily metabolized by bacteria. A third method of assaying pollution level is to measure dissolved oxygen (DO) content directly, using oxygen electrode. The DO content depends on factors other than pollution like temperature, aeration; but it is usually more directly related to whether aquatic organisms survive than is BOD.

The effects of oxygen-demanding wastes on rivers depend to a great extent on the volume, flow, and temperature of the river water. Aeration occurs readily in a turbulent, rapidly flowing river, depleting processes. Downstream from a point source, such as a municipal sewage plant discharge, characteristic decline and restoration of water quality can be detected either by measuring DO content or by observing the flora and fauna that live in successive sections of the river.

Plant Nutrients and Cultural Eutrophication

Water clarity (transparency) is affected by sediments, chemicals, and the abundance of plankton organisms, and is a useful measure of water quality and water pollution. River and lakes that have clear water and low biological productivity are said to be oligotrophic (oligo = little + trophic = nutrition). By contrast eutrophic (eu + trophic = truly nourished) waters are rich in organisms and organic materials. Eutrophication is an increase in nutrient levels and biological productivity. Some amount of eutrophication is a normal part of successional changes in most lakes. The rate of eutrophication and succession depends on water chemistry and depth, volume of inflow, mineral content of the surrounding watershed, and the biota of the lake itself.

Eutrophication has undesirable results. Elevated phosphorous and nitrogen levels stimulate "blooms" of algae or thick growth of aquatic plants. Bacterial populations also increase, fed by larger amounts of organic matter. The water often becomes cloudy or turbid and unpleasant tastes and odors. In extreme cases, plants and algae die and decomposers deplete oxygen in the water. Human activities can greatly accelerate eutrophication. An increase in biological productivity and ecosystem succession caused by human activities is called as cultural eutrophication; which is result from increased nutrient flows, higher temperatures, more sunlight reaching the water surface, or a number of other changes.

Inorganic Pollutants

Some toxic inorganic chemicals are related from rocks by weathering, are carried by runoff into lakes or rivers, or percolate into groundwater aquifers. Humans often accelerate the transfer rates in these cycles thousands of times above natural background levels through the mining, processing, using and discarding of minerals. In many areas, toxic, inorganic chemicals introduced into water as result of human activities have become more serious form of water pollution.

Among the chemicals of greatest concern are heavy metals, such as mercury, lead, tin and cadmium. Supertoxic elements, such as selenium and arsenic also have reached hazardous levels in some waters. Other inorganic materials, such as acids, salts, nitrates, and chlorine, that normally not toxic at low concentrations may become concentrated enough to lower water quality or adversely affect biological communities.

Metals

Many metals such as mercury, lead, cadmium and nickel are highly toxic. Levels in Parts per million ranges – so little that you cannot see or taste them – fatal. Because they are highly persistent, they accumulate in food chains and have cumulative effect in humans. Mercury pollution attracted the attention of the world in 1853 when more than 100 fisherman of Mina – mata area of Japan. Another mercury poisoning disaster appears to be in processes in South America. Since mid-1980s, a gold rush has been under way in Brazil, Ecuador, and Bolivia. Miners and their families suffer nerve damage from breathing the toxic fumes when they invaded jungles along with the Amazon River use mercury to trap gold and separate it from sediments.

A condition known as Itai-Itai (literally outch-outch) disease that developed in Japanese living near the Jintsu River was traced to cadmium poisoning from mining and smelting waste-water discharge.tin compounds used as antifouling agents on ship bottoms have been banned because of toxic their effects. Lead poisoning has been known since Roman times to be dangerous to human health. Lead pipes remain a source of drinking water pollution, especially in older homes or in areas where water is acidic and therefore leaches more lead from pipes. In 1990, the EPA (Environmental Protection Act) lowered the maximum limit for lead in public drinking water from 50 ppb to 20 ppb. Some public health officials argue that lead is neurotoxic at any level, and the limits should be less than 10 ppb. Mine drainage and leaching of mining wastes are serious sources of metal pollution in water.

Nonmetallic Salts

Desert soils often contain high concentrations of soluble salts, including toxic selenium and arsenic. Irrigation and drainage of desert soils mobilize these materials on a large scale and can result in serious pollution problems, as in Kesterson Marsh in California where selenium poisoning killed thousands of migratory birds in the 1980s.

Such salts as sodium chloride (table salt) that are nontoxic at low concentrations also can be mobilized by irrigation and concentrated by evaporation, reaching levels that for plants and animals. Salinity levels so high in recent years that millions of hectares of valuable croplands have had to be abandoned.

Acids and Bases

Acids are released as by-products of industrial processes, such as leather tanning, metal smelting and plating, petroleum distillation and organic chemical synthesis. Coal mining is an especially important source of acid water pollution. Thousands of kilometers of streams in USA have been acidified by acid mine drainage, some so severely that they are essentially lifeless. Coal and oil combustion also leads to formation of atmospheric sulfuric and nitric acids, which are disseminated by long-range transport processes and deposition via precipitation (acidic rain, snow, fog, or dry deposition) in surface water. Where the soils are rich in such alkaline material as limestone these atmospheric acids have little effect because they are neutralized.

In recent years, aquatic damage due to acid precipitation has been reported in about 200 lakes in Adirondack Mountains, of New York State and several thousand lakes in eastern Quebee, Canada. Game fish, amphibians, and sensitive aquatic insects are generally the first to be killed by increased acid levels in water. If acidification is severe enough, aquatic life is limited to a few resistant species of mosses and fungi. Increased acidity may result in leaching of toxic metals, especially aluminum, from soil and rocks, making water unfit for drinking or irrigation, as well.

Organic Chemicals

Thousands of different natural and synthetic organic chemicals are used in the chemical industry to make pesticides, plastics, pharmaceuticals, pigments and other products that we use in everyday life. Many of these chemicals are very toxic. Exposure to very low concentrations (even parts per quadrillion in cases of dioxins) can cause birth defects, genetic disorders and cancer. Some can persist in environment because they are resistant to degradation and toxic to organisms that ingest them. Contamination of surface water and groundwater by these chemicals is serious threat to human health.

The most important sources of toxic organic chemicals in water are improper disposal of industrial and household wastes and runoff of pesticides from farm fields, forests, roadsides, golf courses and places where they are used in large quantities. The bioaccumulation of DDT in aquatic ecosystem was one of the first of these pathways to be understood. Dioxins and chlorinated hydrocarbons (hydrocarbon molecules that contain chlorine atoms) have been accumulated to dangerous levels in the fat of salmon, fish eating birds and humans and cause health problems similar to those resulting from toxic metal compounds. In 2002, the USGS released the first-ever study of pharmaceuticals and hormones in streams. Scientists sampled 130 streams, looking for 95 contaminants, including antibiotics, natural and synthetic hormones, detergents, plasticizers, insecticides and fire retardants. All these substances were found, usually in low concentrations.

Sediments

Erosion and runoff from croplands contribute about 25 billion metric tons of soil, sediments and suspended solids to world surface water each year. Forests, grazing lands, urban construction sites and other sources of erosion and runoff add at least 50 billion additional tons. The sediments fills lakes and reservoirs, obstruct shipping channels, clog hydroelectric turbines and makes purification of drinking water more costly. Sediments smother gravel beds in which insects take refuse and fish lay their eggs. Sunlight is blocked so that plants cannot carry out photosynthesis and oxygen level decline. Murky, cloudy water also is less attractive for swimming, boating, fishing and recreational uses.

Thermal Pollution

Raising or lowering water temperatures from normal levels can adversely affected water quality and aquatic life. Raising water temperatures can devastating effects on sensitive organisms. Oxygen solubility in water decreases as temperature increases, so species requiring high oxygen levels are adversely affected by warming water.

Human cause thermal pollution by altering vegetation cover and runoff patterns, as well as by discharging heated water directly into rivers and lakes. The cheapest way to remove heat from an industrial facility is to draw cool water from oceans, river, lakes or aquifer, run it through heat exchanger to extract excess heat. A thermal plume of temperature can disrupt many processes of ecosystem and drive out sensitive organisms.

To minimize thermal pollution, power plants frequently are required to construct artificial cooling ponds or cooling towers in which heat is released into atmosphere and water is cooled before being released into natural water bodies.

WATER POLLUTION CONTROL

Appropriate land-use practices and careful disposal of industrial, domestic and agricultural wastes are essential for control of water pollution.

Source Reduction

The cheapest and most effective way to reduce pollution is usually to avoid producing it or releasing it to the environment in the first place.

- Elimination of lead in gasoline has resulted in a wide-spread and significant decrease in amount to lead in surface waters in United States. Careful handling of oil and petroleum products can greatly reduce the amount of water pollution caused by these materials.
- Although we still have problems with persistent chlorinated hydrocarbons spread widely in the environment, the banning of DDT and PCBs in 1970s has resulted in significant reductions in levels in wildlife.
- Modifying agricultural practices in headwater streams had positive and cost-effective impact on downstream water quality.
- Industry can reduce pollution by recycling or becalming materials that otherwise might be discarded in the waste stream. Both of these approaches usually have economic as well as environmental benefits.
- Variety of valuable metals can be recovered from industrial wastes and reused or sold for other purposes.
- The municipal sewage treatment plant benefits by not having deal with highly toxic materials mixed in with millions of gallons of other type of wastes.

Nonpoint Sources and Land Management

Among the greatest remaining challenges in water pollution control are diffuse, nonpoint pollution sources. Unlike point sources nonpoint sources have many origins and numerous routes by which contaminants enter ground and surface waters. It is difficult to identify – let alone monitor and control – all these sources and routes. Some main causes of nonpoint pollution are:

- **Agriculture:** The EPA estimates 60% of all impaired or threatened surface waters are affected by sediment from eroded fields and overgrazed pastures; fertilizer, from feedlots.
- **Urban runoff:** Pollution carried by runoff from streets, parking lots, and industrial sites contain salts, oily residues, rubber, metals, and many industrial toxins. Yards, golf courses, parklands, and urban grade ns often are treated with far more fertilizers and pesticides per unit area than farmlands. Excess chemicals are carried by storm runoff into waterways.
- **Construction sites:** New buildings and land development projects such as highway construction affect relatively small areas but produce vast amounts of sediments, typically 10 to 20 times as much per unit area as farming.
- **Land Disposal:** When done carefully, land disposal of certain kinds of industrial waste, sewage slues and biodegradable garbage can be a good way to dispose of unwanted materials. Some poorly run land disposal sites, abandoned dumps and leaking septic system, however, contaminate local waters.

Generally, soil conservation methods also help protect water quality. Applying precisely determined amount of fertilizers, irrigation water and pesticides saves money and reduces contaminants entering the water. Preserving wetlands that act as natural processing facilities for removing sediments and contaminants help protect surface and groundwater.

In urban areas, reducing materials carried away by storm runoff is helpful. Citizens should be encouraged to recycle waste oil and to minimize use of fertilizers and pesticides. Regular Street sweeping greatly reduces contaminants. Runoff can be divided away from streams and lakes. Many cities are separating storm and municipal sewage lined to avoid overflow during storms. A good example of watershed management is seen in Chesapeake Bay, The United States' largest estuary. Citizens' groups, local communities, state legislatures and federal government together established an innovative pollution-control programme that made the Bay the first estuary in America targeted for protection and restoration.

Sewage treatment is one of the most important steps in maintaining clean drinking water. Primary treatment removes strains and settles out solids. Secondary treatment, including aeration, digestion and chlorination removes pathogens and organic material. Tertiary treatment removes inorganic nutrients and oxidizes remaining organics. A variety of low-cost methods, such as constructed wetlands can be used to purify water.

Water legislation is credited with radically improved water quality. Legislation, including the Clean Water Act remains controversial; costs can be high and are largely borne by producers; it can be difficult to identify the best most affordable, or best practicable technology; and proponents of greater control object and stricter rules are needed and enforcement is too often lax.

REFERENCES

Albert, Robert W., et al.1993. Clean Water Act Twenty Years Later. Island Press.

Foster, D.L. 2000. Public Policies and Private Decisions: Their Impacts on Lake Erie Water Quality and Farm Economy. Journal of Soil and Water Conservation 309: 322-26.

Harvell, C.D., et al. 1999. Emerging Marine Diseases - Climate Links and Anthropogenic Factors. Science 285: 1505-10.

Nriagu, J.O. and Pacyna, J.M. 1988. Quantitative Assessment of Worldwide Contamination of Air, Water and Soils by Trace Metals. Nature (Lond.), 333: 134-139.

Paul, Michael., and Judy L. Meyer. 2001. Streams in the Urban Landscape. Annual Review of Ecological and Systematics. 32: 333-65.

Pickett, S.T., et al. 2001. Urban Ecological Systems: Linking Terrestrial, Ecological, Physical, and Socio-economic Components of Metropolitan Areas. Annual Review of Ecological and Systematics. 32: 127-57.

Shiva, Vandana. 2002. Water Wars: Privatization, Pollution and Profit. Southend Press.

Index

A

Acid medium, 61-72

Aeromonas, 34, 35

Agricultural Technical Committee (ATC), 21

Ahaetulla nasuta, 80

Ali, Sami I., 134

Alkali Manufactures Association of India, 119

Ariole, C.N., 32

Aspergillus, 34, 35, 38

- *equation*, 65
- *niger*, 109

B

Bacillus subtilis, 36

Bandicota bengalensis, 82

Bhalla, Resham, 159

Biodiesel production from microalgae, 134-158

- algae strains, 136-138
- biodiesel specifications, 155
- conversion of algal oil to biodiesel, 151
- cultivation of algae, 138-140
- drum-drier, 145
- economics of algae biodiesel production, 155-156
- engine performance, 155
- enhance lipids content in microalgae, 146-147
- extraction of algal oil, 145-146
- fatty acids composition in algal cells, 150-151
- fuel properties, 154-155
- harvesting and drying of algal biomass, 144
- introduction, 135-136
- nutrient starvation, 147-149
- photobioreactors: advantages of, 143
- photobioreactors: disadvantages of, 143-144
- running of photobioreactor (PBR), 142-143
- solar drying, 145
- transesterification of oil, 152-154
- types of photobioreactors, 140-142

Biodiesel Specifications (ASTM), 153

Biotechnological production of poly lactic acid (PLA) biopolymer and its applications, 105-116

- application of PLA in
  - biomedical fields, 113-114
  - packaging material, 114
  - in production of sports wear, 114
- applications of poly lactic acid, 112
- biological synthesis of lactic acid, 107
- blending effect on properties of PLA, 112
- chemical separation process for purification of lactic acid, 110
- chemical synthesis of lactic acid, 107
- introduction, 106
- isolation and purification strategies, 109
- mechanical properties, 112
- methods of production, 106-107
- microbial production of lactic acid, 107-108

molecular approach for PLA production, 108
properties of poly lactic acid, 111
recovery of lactic acid by electro dialysis, 110-111
rheulogical properties of PLA, 111-112
solubility of lactic acid based polymers, 112
thermoplastic properties, 111
use of recombinant for the production of lactic acids, 109
vectors used of production of lactic acid, 109

BOD, 162

C

C. vulgaris, 148
CED, 110
Chaetoceros, 148
Channa gachua, 95-104
Channa punctatus, 96
Chlorella, 148
Cirrhinus mrigala, 99
Clean Water Act, 160, 168
Clindamycin, 61-72
COD, 162
Copenhagen Climate Change Conference, 10
CSD, 4
Cynopterus sphinx, 82

D

Dave, Deeksha, 1
DDT, 165, 166
Diversity of vertebrates, 73-94
amphibians and reptiles, 80
birds, 80-82
introduction, 74
mammals, 82-83
materials and methods, 78
methodology for
amphibians and reptiles documentation and quantification, 78
birds documentation and quantification, 78
mammals documentation and quantification, 78-79
methodology, 78
observation, 75-77
recommendation for further conservation, 83-84
results and discussion, 79-80
study area, 74

DO, 162
Duttaphrynus melanostictus, 80

E

Effects of pesticides on aquatic and aerial oxygen consumption in an air breathing murrel fish, 95-104
discussion, 99-103
introduction, 96
materials and methods, 96-98
results, 98-99

Effects of social capital in agricultural productivity of selected food crops, 40-60
agro production indicators, 47-53
conceptual framework, 42-43
data source, 43
introduction, 41-42
methodology, 43
model specification, 43-45
results and discussion, 45-47
social capital indicators, 53-56
socio-economic characteristics, 45-47
study area, 43

El-Baz, Farouk K., 134
EPA, 164
Ezeah, O.I., 32

F

Federal Government of Nigeria, 21
Frogs and Toads, 78
Fusarium, 37

G

GDP, 21
Good photograph of birds, 78
Grace, Odeleye Taiwo, 19
Gram Sabhas, 13
Green plus Growth, 3
Green Technologies, 10
Green vine snake, 80

H

Heteropneustes fossilis, 99

I

Imran Khan, Y.D., 73
Inhibition effect of clindamycin on the corrosion of zinc in tetraoxosulphate (vi) acid medium, 61-72
  effect of concentration of clindamycin/ H_2SO_4 on zinc corrosion, 63-65
  effect of temperature, 65-67
  experimental details, 62
  gravimetric method, 63
  introduction, 61-62
  materials, 62-63
  results and discussion, 63
  thermodynamic/adsorption consideration, 68-71
ISEC, 74
ISED, 111

J

Johannesburg Declaration, 4
Juliet, Okafor Akudo, 40

K

Kesterson Marsh in California, 164
Kisku, G.C., 117
Klebsiella oxytoca, 36
Kumar, Amit, 105

L

Lactobacillus coryiformis, 107
Lactobacillus shamnosus, 108
Light emitting diodes (LED), 140
Luconostoc citereum, 109

M

MAE, 146
Mahalakshimi, B.R., 73
Malaria, 160
Marine alga (*Cladophora* sp.), 33
Marine aspergillus strain, 32-39
  effect of
    pH on growth and antimicrobial metabolite production by *aspergillus* sp., 34
    salinity on growth and antimicrobial metabolite production by *aspergillus* sp., 34-35
    temperature on growth and antimicrobial metabolite production by *apsergillus* sp., 34
  estimation of growth and antimicrobial activity assay, 34
  introduction, 33-34
  materials and methods, 34
  results and discussion, 35-37
Microalgae, 134-158
Mohamed, Amal A., 134
Montreal Protocol, 10
Mus musculus, 82
Mystus vittus, 96

N

Natural resources, 8
Nautiyal, Sunil, 73
NGOs, 4
Nigeria agriculture and environment, 19-31
  agriculture and its environmental in Nigeria, 22-23
  agriculture as sources of pollution, 23-24

air, 23
burning, 25-26
fertilizers, 25
heavy metals, 27
historical analysis of agricultural development in Nigeria, 20-22
housing and improper sewage disposal, 23
introduction, 20
major forms of pollution, 23
overgrazing, 26
solution/recommendation, 27-29
water pollution, 23

NSSO Survey report, 15

O

Ogoko, E.C., 61
Ogunsipe, A.O., 61
Okafor, Jeribe Chigoziru Ugochi, 40
Oreochronis mossambicus, 99
Osu Charles, I., 61

P

Pavlovalutheri, 148
Peafowl (*Pavo cristatus*), 80
PET, 114
PHA, 106
Photobioreactors, 143
PLA, 106
Poly lactic acid (PLA) biopolymer, 105-116
Pteropus giganteus, 82
PUFAs, 146, 150

Q

Qinghai-Tibet Plateau, 8

R

Rahman, Qaisur, 95
Rio Declaration, 3

S

Sadhu, D.N., 95
Safe use of chlorine, 117-133
basic mechanism of chlorine toxicity, 128
case study of chlorine exposure in Taiwan, 130-131
chemical properties, 118
fire and explosion hazards of chlorine gas, 126
fire extinguishing, 129-130
first aid in case of chlorine exposure, 128-129
handling of chlorine, 125
hazardous potentials, 118-119
introduction, 117-118
leakes of chlorine, 125-126
manufacturing process, 119-122
diaphragm process, 120-122
membrane cell process, 120
mercury cell process, 119-120
measurement of chlorine in ambient air, 122
method suggested for waste disposal, 132
personal protecting method, 130
physical examinations, 129
physical properties, 118
poisoning symptoms, 126-128
qualitative and semi-qualitative methods, 123-124
quantitative methods for chlorine, 124
safe drinking water act and SMCL, 119
sampling methods of chlorine, 122-123
storage of chlorine, 124
use of chlorine, 119

Salunkhe, Rupali, 159
Sarotheroden mossambicus, 99
Scenedesmus, 148
Second World War, 20
Secondary Maximum Contaminant Levels, 119
Self Help Groups, 13
Steve, Chukwukere, 40
STPD, 97
Sustainable development and environmental protection, 1-18

environment conservation and sustainable development, 9-10

forthcoming challenges, 14-16

gender equality and sustainable development, 13-14

green philosophy on sustainable development, 6-10

introduction, 1-3

meaning and concept of sustainable development, 3-6

scarcity of natural resources, 8-9

top of form, 10-14

towards equity and equality, 16-17

urbanization/migration, 12-13

T

TAG, 146, 147

U

UAE, 146

UN General Assembly, 3

UN Millennium Development Goals Report 2014, 11

UNCED, 3

UNDP Human Development Report 2011, 4

United States National Research Council, 22

USGS, 165

W

Water pollution, 159-168

acids and bases, 164-165

infectious agents, 160-162

inorganic pollutants, 163

introduction, 159-160

metals, 163-164

nonmetallic salts, 164

nonpoint sources and land management, 167-168

agriculture, 167

construction sites, 167

land disposal, 167

urban runoff, 167

organic chemicals, 165

oxygen-demanding wastes, 162

plant nutrients and cultural eutrophication, 163

sediments, 165

source reduction, 166

thermal pollution, 166

types and effects of water pollution, 160

water pollution control, 166

Wildlife Protection Act (1972), 78

World Health Organization, 162

WSSD, 3

Z

Zinc corrosion, 63-65

Zinc in tetraoxosulphate, 61-72

❋ ❋ ❋ ❋ ❋ ❋